A History of MONROE TOWNSHIP
Cumberland County, Pennsylvania

MONROE TOWNSHIP HISTORIANS

an imprint of Sunbury Press, Inc.
Mechanicsburg, PA USA

an imprint of Sunbury Press, Inc.
Mechanicsburg, PA USA

Copyright © 1993, 2000, 2007, 2025 by Monroe Township Historians.
Cover Copyright © 2025 by Sunbury Press, Inc.

Sunbury Press supports copyright. Copyright fuels creativity, encourages diverse voices, promotes free speech, and creates a vibrant culture. Thank you for buying an authorized edition of this book and for complying with copyright laws. Except for the quotation of short passages for the purpose of criticism and review, no part of this publication may be reproduced, scanned, or distributed in any form without permission. You are supporting writers and allowing Sunbury Press to continue to publish books for every reader. For information contact Sunbury Press, Inc., Subsidiary Rights Dept., PO Box 548, Boiling Springs, PA 17007 USA or legal@sunburypress.com.

For information about special discounts for bulk purchases, please contact Sunbury Press Orders Dept. at (855) 338-8359 or orders@sunburypress.com.

To request one of our authors for speaking engagements or book signings, please contact Sunbury Press Publicity Dept. at publicity@sunburypress.com.

FIRST LOCAL HISTORY PRESS EDITION: May 2025

Set in Adobe Garamond Pro | Interior design by Crystal Devine | Cover by Lawrence Knorr | Edited by Lawrence Knorr and the Monroe Township Historians.

Publisher's Cataloging-in-Publication Data
Names: Monroe Township Historians, author.
Title: A history of Monroe Township, Cumberland County, Pennsylvania / Monroe Township Historians.
Description: First trade paperback edition. | Mechanicsburg, PA : Local History Press, 2025.
Summary: The history of Monroe Township, Cumberland County, Pennsylvania, is recounted from its formation during the Colonial Era through the early 20th century, including details of many of the homes of Churchtown (aka Allen).
Identifiers: ISBN : 979-8-88819-277-1 (paperback).
Subjects: HISTORY / US History / Mid-Atlantic.

Designed in the USA
0 1 1 2 3 5 8 13 21 34 55

For the Love of Books!

Front cover image: From the *News From Home* insurance company magazine, August 1945.
Back cover image: F. W. Beers / Atlas of Cumberland County, 1872.

Table of Contents

Foreword by Lawrence Knorr — v

Chapter 1. The Formation of Monroe Township — 1

Chapter 2. The Geological History of Monroe Township — 8

Chapter 3. An Archaeological History of Monroe Township and Surrounds — 11

Chapter 4. The Yellow Breeches Creek: A Precious Natural Resource — 16

Chapter 5. The Early Settlers — 25

Chapter 6. Hands Willing to Serve: A History of the Fire Companies in Monroe Township — 38

Chapter 7. Monroe Township Churches and Cemeteries — 44

Chapter 8. The Houses of Churchtown — 48

Chapter 9. Colonel Henry Zinn and the 130th Pennsylvania Infantry — 178

Appendix A. Alphabetical Index to Early Settler's Names — 188

Appendix B. Patent Tract Information for Early Settlers — 192

Appendix C. The Old Graveyard at Mount Zion — 217

Foreword

Many years ago, while researching the Knorr family history, I came across a note about a brother of my immigrant ancestor, Hans Peter Knorr. This brother, Johannes Knorr (also spelled Knauer or phonetically as Kenower), had settled in Heidelberg Township, in what is now Berks County, with his wife, Eva Anna. The Knorrs were Wertheimers who all sailed together on the *Duke of Bedford*, arriving in Philadelphia on September 14, 1751. I was never certain why brother Johannes split away from Hans Peter and their other brother, Johannes Melchior Knorr. The latter two collaborated quite a bit in the Philadelphia area and then Berks County. The only additional detail I knew about Johannes was that he "later went to Allen Township, Cumberland County." Of course, as you will see in this history of Monroe Township, it was once part of the larger Allen Township, which also included Upper and Lower Allen Townships.

From the family history research, I learned that Johannes Kenower/Knorr settled in Allen and had a son named Jacob, who married Mary Magdalena Strock, and three daughters: Barbara, who married D. Kishler; Catherine; and Anna Margaretha, born September 22, 1766, at Heidelberg. That same year, Allen Township was formed in Cumberland County, coinciding with Johannes's move.

For many years, that was all I knew about "Great Uncle" Johannes until my wife, Tammi, and I started looking for a house. We had been living in the Camp Hill area, and when the kids said they wanted a swimming pool, we brought in a pool salesman to provide an estimate. After a sleepless night following the sticker shock, I told Tammi we would be better off moving to a place with an existing pool. She said to me, "If you are going to make me move, I want to live in my dream house." She then produced a sheet describing the old farmstead at 1602 West Lisburn Road in Monroe Township, Cumberland County.

"But it doesn't have a pool," I said.

"Yes, but it's my dream house," she said, "and we can always have a pool installed later."

So, after negotiating with the owner via the real estate agent, I was able to provide Tammi with her dream house, and the children never got the pool!

Not long after moving in during the Spring of 2012, I met Sharon Nelson, thanks to Glen and Lois Sarvis, who provided the local history. As someone who has always been interested in history, I was thrilled to have some resources about the immediate area. As I looked closely at Sharon's work on the various land records, I was stunned to see the name Jacob Kenower associated with the very house I was living in. What were the odds? It was almost impossible that I could accidentally, serendipitously, move into a home on the land of my immigrant uncle.

Then, Glen Sarvis shared old photos of the brick repairs on the road-side (SW) of the house. Beneath was an earlier log structure! Encased within the larger brick home was a smaller two-story log house, not unlike Mechanicsburg's Frankenberger Tavern. I now suspected this was the likely home of Jacob Kenower and perhaps his father, Johannes.

We have since been unable to place the grave of Johannes Kenower, who died sometime after 1766. Son Jacob and his wife died in the early 1800s and are buried in the Old Cemetery at Mount Zion, in Churchtown. Thus, Johannes likely died before the church at Mount Zion was built. Perhaps Johannes was buried on the old family farm sometime before 1795. If so, I need to look around a little more and be careful about digging that pool!

After Jacob Kenower moved to the Boiling Springs area, the Baker family moved onto the farm and owned it for over a century. Christian Baker was the primary owner for the longest duration, so Tammi and I have referred to the property as the Christian Baker/Jacob Kenower Farm. It also doubles as the headquarters of our family business, the book publisher Sunbury Press, Inc.

Thus, without realizing it, perhaps through Providence, I have been guided to the pioneer homestead of my family and now live here happily, enjoying our wonderful township. I am also honored to contribute this book, a compilation of improved resources about the history of our township, as well as some new additions. You will find a lot more information about our local hero, Colonel Henry Zinn, thanks to Suzanne Sunday. You will also find more details about the early settlers. Of course, Kevin Vanderlodge's and Sharon Nelson's collaboration about the homes of Churchtown is priceless, as is Sharon's research about the various properties of the township.

So, enjoy the history of our beloved township, which is now 200 years old as of this writing. While a lot has changed over the centuries, the area retains a priceless pioneer charm.

Lawrence Knorr, Ph.D.
May 2025

CHAPTER 1

The Formation of Monroe Township

by Daniel J. Heisey

One of the lessons of history—though some deny she has them—is that when mankind wants something, he tends to get it. Desire does not guarantee success, of course, and, in the course of human events, as in physics, an equal or opposite force may thwart even the most determined will. Such contests, whether upon the far-flung fields of battle or within the refined machinations of custom—even that custom called law—give history her fire, vigor, and zest. Across the ages, we share tragic loss, exult in victory, hail the villain's demise, and bask in the glory of virtue triumphant. Human nature is constant, and we never tire of its all too-familiar conflicts and passions.

In 1822, a group of men in the southeastern corner of Cumberland County, Pennsylvania, felt crowded. They lived in Allen Township, so named in 1766 for Chief Justice William Allen (1704–1780), an area ranging from the Susquehanna River to near Boiling Springs, from the Trindle Road to the Yellow Breeches Creek and South Mountain. According to the United States Census of 1820, Allen Township comprised 2,995 people; ten years before it had 1,837. In 1800, there had been 1,724. By 1820, the county itself had forty to fifty people per square mile, making it one of the more populous in the Commonwealth.

The place drew farmers and industrialists: The first document, a mortgage recorded in Cumberland County on 9th September 1750, is for a grist mill and "plantation" of a hundred acres along the Yellow Breeches.[1] While the valley's watery nature was captured in place names—Trindle Springs and Boiling Springs—the commerce of the day left its mark on the landscape as well. Whiskey Spring and Furnace Hollow Road indicate the occupations (or pre-occupations) of early settlers.

In 1823, "divers inhabitants" of Allen Township petitioned the January Session of the Cumberland County Court of Quarter Sessions to divide the township. The petitioners claimed to "labour under great inconvenience and many difficulties on account of the great extant [sic] in boundary of the present township of Allen, which renders it difficult for the township officers to perform the duties imposed on them by Law with facility." By law the "township officers" had to maintain the road in the township, keeping them open and the statutory thirty-three feet (two rods) wide.

It was the age of the great canals and their mules plodding along the towpaths before railroad tracks and telegraph wires laced

---

1. Mortgage of Roger Cook and wife to Richard Peters, Esq., May 5, 1750, Cumberland County Deed Book I, page 1. According to the descriptive information in the mortgage, the tract in question was located in what is now Upper Allen Township, directly adjacent to patent tracts no. 5 and no. 9, shown on the map in the center of this book.

together the countryside. The countryside of Allen Township was full of rolling fields and thick woods, spring-fed streams and limestone farmhouses. Limestone abounded, and the red clay just beneath the rich brown soil made excellent bricks. In August 1820, in the region we now know as Monroe Township, David Krysher announced he had found a vein of marble on his land and called on "any person of good character, experienced in working Marble" to apply.[2]

Although there had been a financial panic in 1820, the Court of Quarter Sessions was busy with petitions for new roads, often leading to mills either on the Conodoguinet or Yellow Breeches creeks. New roads meant easier access for the farmer to the mills grinding his corn or wheat into meal or flour, but they also meant greater responsibility for the road supervisors who were elected to clear and repair the roads and their drainage ditches. It is worth remembering that those supervisors did the work themselves by hand and that roads were not paved.

The petitioners further requested (as the law required) that the Court appoint "three impartial men to enquire into the propriety of dividing" Allen Township. They were to report to the next session of the Court "with a Plot or a draft of the division line." By law, one of these men had to be a surveyor. The judges—John Reed, James Armstrong, and Isaiah Graham—named John McClure, William Line, and Colonel John Wise, "or any two of them," to study the matter and report to the Court their findings.

Of these three viewers, Colonel Wise is the most obscure. "John Wise" is a fairly common name; identifying him in the militia rolls in the published *Pennsylvania Archives* seems impossible. If he served in the ranks in 1793, in 1823 he would have been around fifty. Wishful thinking guesses at kinship with Jacob Wise, reputed to be the builder around 1804 of what is now regarded as the oldest house in Churchtown.

John McClure married into the prominent Presbyterian Blair family of Carlisle and lived at Willow Grove. In 1812, he, his brother-in-law Joseph Knox, and William Barber built the first paper mill on a mountain stream south of Carlisle.[3] In 1815, with Barber and Archibald Loudon, publisher and postmaster of Carlisle, McClure laid out plans for Papertown, now Mount Holly Springs.

Joining, and no doubt leading, the colonel and the entrepreneur was a politician. William Line was born in 1785 in Manheim, Lancaster County, and around 1810, he moved to what is now Churchtown, Cumberland County. There, he taught school and ingratiated himself with the local gentry; in 1812, he married Rebecca Wise, daughter of Jacob Wise, of oldest house fame. Line was a Jeffersonian Democrat; Governor Simon Snyder appointed him in 1813 justice of the peace for Allen Township.[4]

Line used his skills as a teacher to moonlight as a surveyor and a "scrivener," apparently displaying some proficiency in both trades. In 1814, he was appointed deputy surveyor for Cumberland County,[5] and in 1818, three years after he had moved to Carlisle, he was appointed by Governor William Findley to the then combined office of Register of Wills and Recorder of Deeds, a job requiring

---

2. "Marble Quarry," *The American Volunteer* (August 31, 1820) 1. This notice was repeated on 7 and 14 September 1820.

3. For McClure's mountain land, see Cumberland County Deed Book 1TT, page 247.

4. Cumberland County Commission Book 1V, page 265.

5. Cumberland County Commission Book lAA, page 27.

perfect penmanship.[6] Line capped his career much as he had begun it; in 1828, he became an associate county judge and returned to Churchtown, where Jacob Plank built him a log house.

The viewers took their time. They reported to the next session of the Court that they had not reached a conclusion, and the matter was continued. In August 1824, they appeared again before the Court, and again, the Court granted a continuance. Each time, the Court acted "on the motion of Mr. Ramsey." Clearly, he represented the petitioners.

It was not necessary in early nineteenth-century America for men practicing law to be trained lawyers. There were few law schools, and formal study of the law was done under an established attorney. This period of apprenticeship was known as "reading law." Abraham Lincoln was not a rarity in being self-taught. The legal profession was disdained as an elite inimical to democracy, and rural counties with rolled-up sleeves were strongly Democratic.

So, a possible candidate for "Mr. Ramsey" is Searight Ramsey. He died, *The American Volunteer* rather unhelpfully noted, in September 1839 "at an advanced age." Census returns suggest he was born around 1770. In 1822, Governor Joseph Hiester—"Old Sauerkraut"—appointed him coroner for Cumberland County. Searight Ramsey was a prosperous, educated gentleman; the inventory of his vast estate near the mountain in South Middleton Township lists numerous household and farm implements, as well as a case full of books. His association with Monroe Township is indicated in that inventory, for his administrator was Jacob Ritner of Churchtown, who oversaw cash paid to one Jesse Beltzhoover.[7]

A better possibility is William Ramsey. He was an ambitious man, developing real estate—he built the first hotel in Carlisle Springs—and seeking county office. In 1809, he ran as the Democratic candidate for sheriff, but the job went to his Federalist opponent. Governor Snyder appointed Ramsey prothonotary, and Ramsey became an influential Democrat in the county.

After he left office in 1817, Ramsey was admitted to the Bar and soon developed a thriving practice in Carlisle. An old-fashioned man, he was known with some affection as "Billy Ramsey with his queue," for even into the 1830s, he wore his hair long and bound in a tail in the fashion of the latter eighteenth century. It seems more likely that the prime movers behind dividing Allen Township would have sought out the stolid and powerful William Ramsey of Carlisle to advance their cause rather than Searight Ramsey, well-read but obscurely ensconced on his farm in the shadow of the South Mountain.

On Monday, November 8, 1824, William Line and John McClure appeared before the judges in Carlisle with their draft and report. The viewers had completed their work on 25 October, having taken almost two years to survey and study the situation. They agreed with the petitioners that Allen Township should be divided "owing to the great extend [*sic*] of Territory which renders the duties of the different Township officers extremely difficult." They then set forth "the most equal division that could well be in point of inhabited Territory and population." The judges approved the division, pending appeal,

---

6. Cumberland County Commission Book 1CC, page 516.

7. See Cumberland County Will Book D, page 261; see also Cumberland County Deed Book 1V, page 679.

13 November—Saturday, a reminder that our ancestors worked a six-day week. After an interval for appeal, on January 15, 1825, the division was "confirmed, and ordered to be entered of Record."

News surely spread by word of mouth, for the local newspaper made no mention for four months. Then, the announcement came as an afterthought in a notice of the formation from "the upper part of East Pennsborough" of Silver Spring Township. "Our readers, generally, know," the paper began its second of two sentences, "that some months ago, Allen township was divided, and the upper end of it formed into a township, which is called MONROE."[8]

The Court, in its order, noted that "the Estern [sic] end" of the township was to be called Allen, "the other end by the name of Monroe." That is, by the name of James Monroe, the fifth president of the United States. Monroe Township would thus be the only municipality in Cumberland County named for a federal figure. All others, when named for people, are named for colonial worthies—William Penn, Edward Shippen, James Silver, William Allen—or for politicians of the Revolution—John Dickinson and Thomas Mifflin. There are counties in Pennsylvania named for Revolutionary heroes—Franklin, Fayette, McKean—and for Revolutionaries who became federal officials—Washington, Adams, Jefferson. In 1836, five years after James Monroe died, a county m Pennsylvania was named for him.

Such a memorial is understandable, but one must pause to consider why men in Cumberland County would have wanted to name a township for Monroe during his presidency. Henry Adams observed that "The value of Pennsylvania to the Union lay not so much in the democratic spirit of society as in the rapidity with which it turned to national objects."[9] While most of the nation's first historians, poets, and philosophers centered around Boston—"long . . . the intellectual capital of America"[10]—Pennsylvanians have always been deeply aware of their commonwealth's vital place in national affairs. They quickly recall Valley Forge, Independence Hall, and Gettysburg.

In December 1823 President Monroe announced a political and diplomatic view of the Western Hemisphere that would be known as the Monroe Doctrine. The General Assembly of Pennsylvania lost no time resolving to endorse the Doctrine, saying Monroe expressed "the sentiments of millions of freemen." Governor John Schulze then sent the resolution to Monroe.[11]

James Monroe was the last of the Founding Fathers to be president. He is, in American history, a transitional figure, from the giants at the forefront of forming the Republic to the younger men who were office clerks or foot soldiers during the Revolution. Fresh from William and Mary College, Monroe fought in the War for Independence—he stands behind Washington in Emmanuel Leutze's famous painting, "Washington Crossing the Delaware"—and then read law under Thomas Jefferson. Monroe served in the Virginia House of Delegates and the Continental Congress, and

---

8. "New Townships," *The American Volunteer* (April 28, 1825) 3. By "upper," was meant "upstream."

9. Henry Adams, *History of the United States of America during the First Administration of Thomas Jefferson*, vol. I (New York: Charles Scribner's Sons, 1909) 115.

10. Winston S. Churchill, *A History of the English-Speaking Peoples*, vol. II (New York: Dodd, Mead & Co., 1956) 171.

11. Frederic A. Godcharles, *Daily Stories of Pennsylvania* (Milton, PA: Self-published, 1924) 837.

in 1790, he was elected one of the first United States senators. He served twice as governor of Virginia and was minister to France both under Washington and Jefferson, for whom, in 1803 he purchased Louisiana. He was James Madison's secretary of state, and, as tended to happen in the early Republic, from that post, he succeeded to the presidency.

For some twenty-five years, the young nation had been split by vicious attacks between Federalists and Democratic-Republicans. Monroe, a southern Democrat, toured the country and seemed to charm the people with his dignity and grace. Like his mentor, Jefferson, he admired and imported elements of French culture; his homes and his wardrobe were resplendent with elegance from the Napoleonic Era. The conservative Philip Hone, one-time mayor of New York, had high regard for Monroe and visited the ex-president during Monroe's retirement in Manhattan.[12] While president, Monroe had settled the long-festering border dispute with Canada, removed the forts along the frontier with that British colony, and in 1819, Monroe acquired Florida from Spain.

A Federalist newspaper dubbed the peace and prosperity of Monroe's America "The Era of Good Feelings."[13] Monroe, suave and wily, saw his charmed career in public life as promoting national unity. He chose as his secretary of state the Federalist John Quincy Adams, an act of bipartisanship characteristic of Monroe's nationalism. Adams, the son of a president, was from Massachusetts, and Monroe's choice of him also shows a good political sense of geography.

In 1820, Monroe was re-elected with all but one vote in the Electoral College. Only Washington himself had been so anointed. After Washington, presidential elections had become rancorous, riotous events, where whiskey, bloodshed, and cash combined to give voting in America a certain Latin flavor. Monroe's sweep to a second term bespoke national confidence and tranquility. The stoic John Quincy Adams hailed in later years that era as "the golden age" of the Republic.[14]

It was not to last. Upon Monroe's decision in 1824 not to seek a third term, the old electoral chaos returned. That November, electors were split amongst four candidates— Andrew Jackson, John C. Calhoun, Henry Clay, and John Quincy Adams. The election, according to the Constitution, was cast into the House of Representatives, where Clay, as Speaker, engineered Adams' election. America then entered 1825 with surly bitterness. Many smelled a deal, the odor of which clouded over Adams' one contentious term despite his able secretary of state, Henry Clay.

The formation of Monroe Township had less to do with the "great extent" of Allen Township—its size had been the same since 1766—than with a growth in population symptomatic of economic abundance and political stability. The community was traditional, Protestant, predominantly of German or Scots extraction, tending to vote Democratic, but clearly grateful for the sort of nationalism espoused by Monroe, a nationalism as federalist as that of the officially non-partisan George Washington, long and justly revered. The naming of the new township "Monroe" echoes through the valley and across the years as a witness to a brief era of national harmony.

---

12. See: Allan Nevins, ed., *The Diary of Philip Hone, 1828–1851* (New York: Dodd, Mead, & Co., 1936) 32, 44.

13. See: Henry Ammon, *James Monroe: The Quest for National Identity* (New York: McGraw-Hill Book Co., 1971) 366; cf George Morgan, *The Life of James Monroe* (Boston: Small, Maynard, & Co., 1921) 354.

---

14. Allan Nevins, ed., *The Diary of John Quincy Adams, 1794–1845* (New York: Longmans, Green, & Co., 1928) 307.

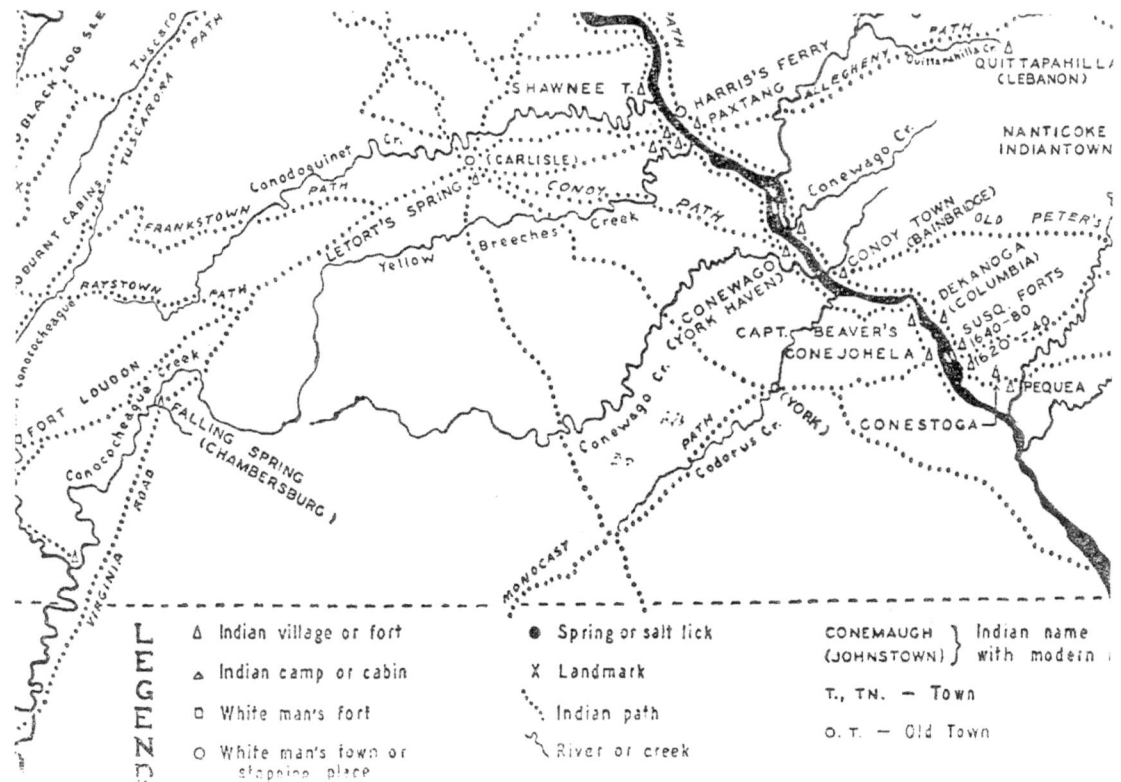

Indian trails and villages in Cumberland County prior to settlement. (From Wallace, Indian Paths of Pennsylvania*).*

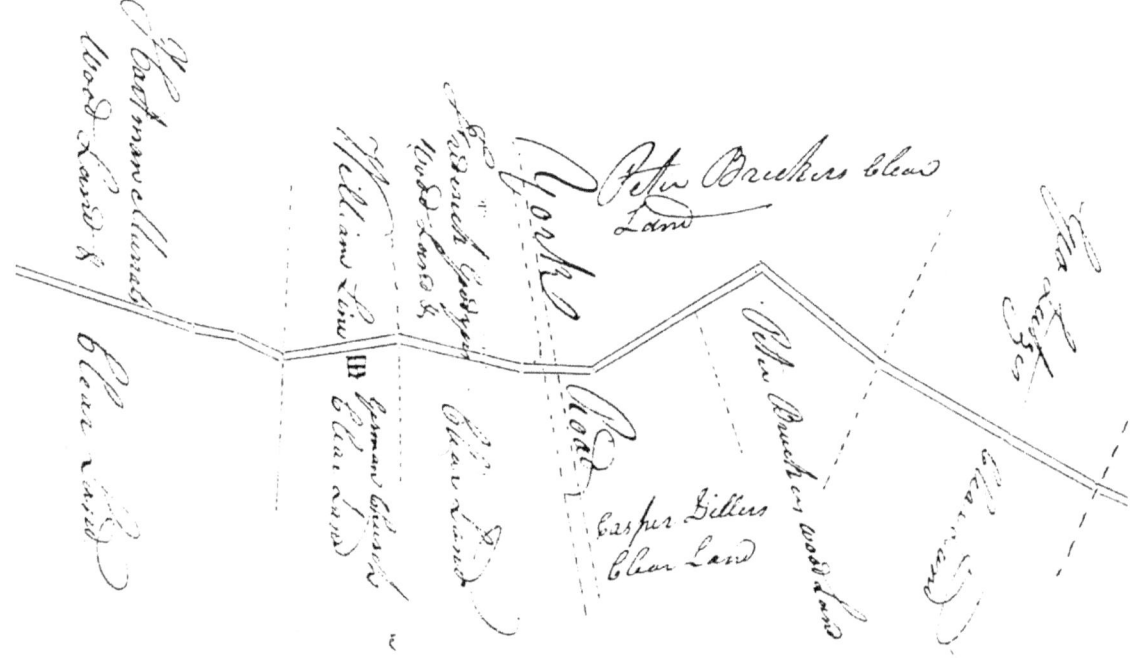

Portion of a map on a Road Docket paper laying out Boiling Springs Rd. through Monroe Township, 1813. (Cumberland County Historical Society)

The Formation of Monroe Township 7

Text and map from Act Dividing Monroe Township off from Allen Township, January 1825 session of Court of Quarter Sessions. (Cumberland County Road Docket, vol. 1, p. 419.)

CHAPTER 2

The Geological History of Monroe Township

by Glen A. Sarvis

The oldest geological features found in our area are in the volcanic roots of the South Mountain region. Basaltic and rhyolitic lava flows formed in a rift active during the late Precambrian and early Cambrian periods, 597–570 million years ago. Ba alt is a dark-gray or black igneous rock, dense and fine-grained. Rhyolite is the lava form of granite. Sandy sediments then poured into a continental shelf area, forming the layer that today is the quartzite conglomerate of the White Rocks area.

During the Cambrian and Early Ordovician periods, 560–500 million years ago, the sediments that make up the limestones and dolomites of the Cumberland Valley region were deposited in a shallow sea known as the Proto-Atlantic Ocean. Dolomite is a type of limestone or marble rich in magnesium carbonate.

During the remainder of the Ordovician up until the Permian periods, 445–220 million years ago, mountain building to the east and north provided sediments that form the present-day rock strata found west and north of us. Locally, these layers have eroded and are no longer found in our area. During this time, the collision of Europe and Africa with North America caused extensive uplifting, folding, reverse faulting and thrusting responsible for the rise of the Appalachian Mountains and Plateaus. Extensive metamorphism altered the rocks during this period of compression and mountain building.

Today the rocks of South Mountain are, therefore, metarhyolites, metabasalts, and quartzite. There are some deposits of marbleized limestone as well. Also, the rock strata in the valley area are highly folded and fractured. In many places, the strata are completely overturned. The rock strata of the South Mountain were overthrust atop younger layers to the west. The Reading Banks thrust fault runs roughly parallel to Boiling Springs Road through the township.

During the Triassic through Early Jurassic periods, 250-190 million years ago, the modern Atlantic Ocean formed. Rifting caused a basin to form to the East of South Mountain. Stretching of the crustal rocks allowed volcanism to return. Magma moving upward through an elongated crack in the older rocks formed the diabase dike through the Cumberland Valley that we call Ironstone Ridge, along which the Appalachian Trail currently runs. Diabase is an altered basalt with very small, light-colored crystals enclosed in a later-formed matrix of darker material. The dark-colored, loosely piled stone walls that line the trail and the roads in some places along this ridge are made out of diabase.

During the time from the Mid Jurassic to the present, the Atlantic Ocean has continued to widen, and the only major change in the Monroe Township area has been due to erosion. Harder rocks underlie the hilly areas, and softer, more soluble lime tone underlies our flat places. Boulders, gravel and sand are found near the base of South Mountain as they continue to wash down the slopes. Finer gravel, sands, silts and clay are found in the flatter areas of the valley. Sinkholes and springs are common in the valley area due to the porous nature of the soluble lime tone. Along the Yellow Breeches Creek, there are a variety of erosional and depositional features that are continually changing as periods of drought and flood alter the local terrain.

Over the past 6 million years there have been many changes in the geological structure of the earth as a whole, as well as this area in particular. Clues to these changes remain all around us—in the lay of the land, the exposed outcroppings of rock, and the stones used to build early dwellings—revealing their part of the story to all who take the time to look.

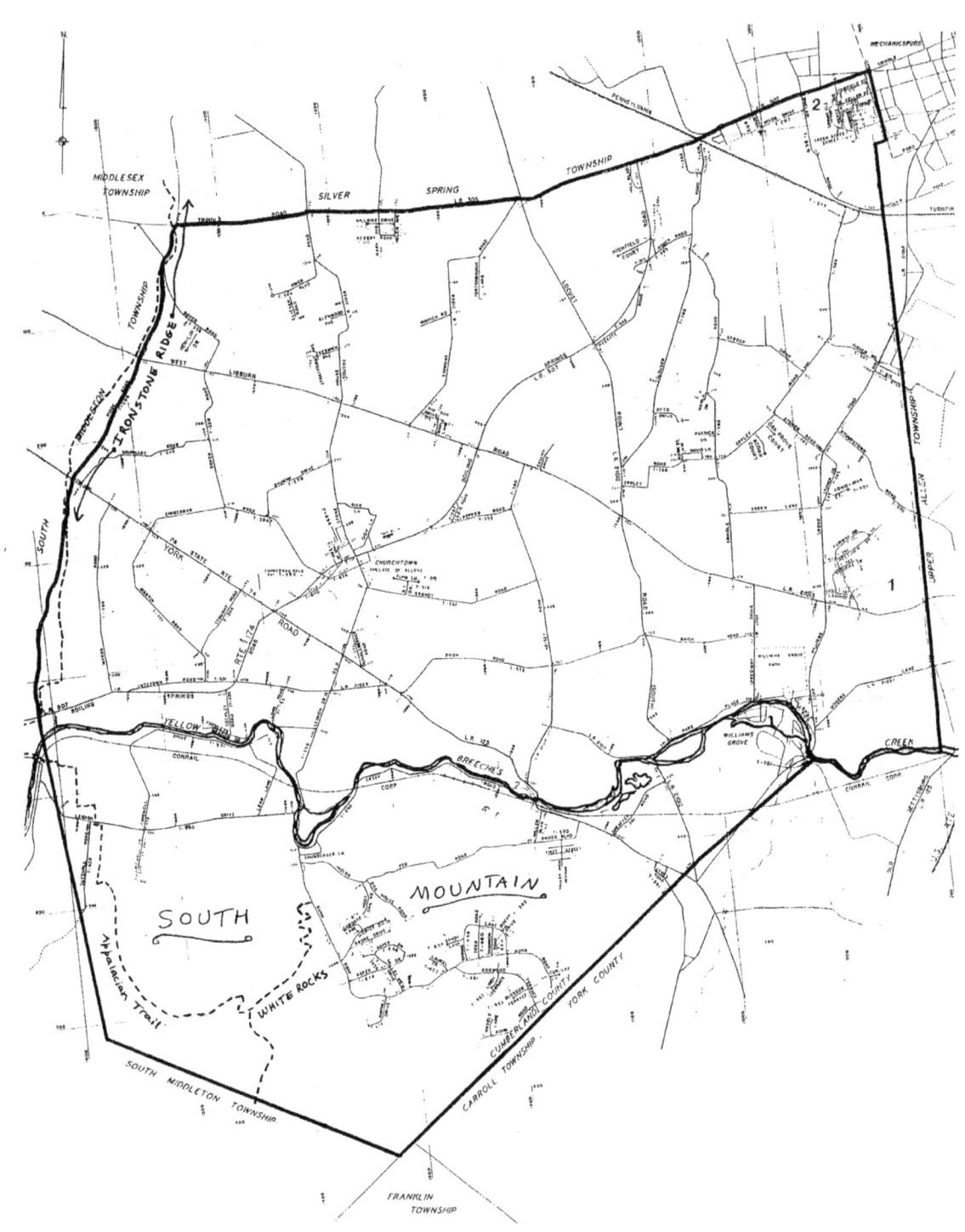

Modern map of Monroe Township, showing some geological features.
(Adapted from Monroe Township Official Map with Numbering System, 1980, revised 1991.)

CHAPTER 3

An Archaeological History of Monroe Township and Surrounds

Based on a presentation by Joe Baker

There are several key factors in any area that influence where and how the original Native American population lived. One is the local geology.

The lay of the land closely defines the Pre-European history of this area—in this case, the Yellow Breeches watershed. Watersheds are convenient categories to use in sorting through pre-history. Included in this watershed are the Yellow Breeches Creek itself and Mountain Creek, which stem from profoundly different geographical locations. Mountain Creek flows down from Pine Grove, where the bedrock is quite different from that found in the Cumberland Valley below.

It is known as Catoctin formation or rhyolite and is a coarse stone, forming the core of the South Mountain above Mt. Holly Springs. One might not expect that such rock would be suitable for the manufacture of stone tools, but the early Native Americans obviously used it for such. On the mountain, their quarrying pits still exist, some 6 to 8 feet in depth. Quarrying pits found among quartzite rock tend to be the result of more recent prospecting, but pits among rhyolite are usually pre-historic. There were natives up on South Mountain quarrying rhyolite at least seven millennia ago.

No other rock looks like South Mountain rhyolite, so the discovery of prehistoric rhyolite tools in other locations can reveal much about the trade and travel patterns of the local native population. Rhyolite tools have been found all over the northeastern United States and as far away as Maine.

There are two primary water sources for the Yellow Breeches—South Mountain runoff and limestone springs. The Cumberland Valley is a prime limestone country with the characteristic fertile, very productive soil. There are many springs, but they are found in very restricted and predictable locations due to the fact that limestone absorbs water. This leaves most of the soil very dry, so early Native American settlements in this area had to be close to creeks and springs. Therefore, anywhere a spring is found today, typically, there would have been at least a small Stone-Age settlement there at some point in the past.

A second factor that would have influenced the local native population is climate. In the Ice Age, this area was not covered by glaciers, but just 100 miles to the north lay the Laurentide Ice Sheet. This feature was 1,500 miles across, one mile thick, and held such a volume of frozen water that the ocean level dropped 150 feet. It dominated northern North America for 100,000 to 150,000 years.

Archaeological history is divided into periods as follows:

- The Paleo-Indian Period, 12000?–6000 B.C.
- The Archaic Period, 6000–1500 B.C.
- The Transitional Period, 1500–1000 B.C.
- The Woodland Period, 1000 B.C.–1550 A.D.
- The Historic Period, 1550 A.D. to the present

Archaeologists have no idea when humans first migrated into Pennsylvania, but likely, it was sometime during the Ice Age in the Paleo-Indian Period. Discoveries in North and South America continue to change the accepted theories regarding migration and settlement timeframe. Actual artifactual evidence found in Pennsylvania thus far only dates after the Ice Age.

During the Ice Age, this area was taiga and tundra, and over time, it changed into the landscape and vegetation we know today. So when the Native Americans first arrived here, they faced a very different climate and terrain than that which now exists. It was only about 8,000 years ago that our current climate began to exist.

Before the imported blight wiped them out, chestnut trees were one of the most common types of nut-bearing vegetation and were used by the natives as a food source. In pre-historic periods, they also hunted elk, bison and mammoths. Bison and mammoths died out here, but elk persisted into the nineteenth century. About ten or eleven thousand years ago, more familiar game, such as white-tailed deer, began to appear in this area.

The Pennsylvania Historical and Museum Commission maintains an electronic database of all pre-historic archaeological sites known thus far to exist in the Commonwealth. Most of the local sites documented by this database are known to the PHMC because residents have reported them and filled out forms to have the sites registered. In all, Cumberland County currently has 174 sites registered, with a dozen or so added each year. The details recorded about each site vary. Some are very complete, while other data simply documents that a particular person found some arrowheads in a particular location.

Many of the sites in Monroe, South Middleton, and Dickinson townships are near the Yellow Breeches or natural springs and were recorded by Tex Stoerzinger, a local sheriff who had an extensive collection of artifacts and kept detailed records.

The oldest artifacts that have been found here are common all over the continent: large fluted spear points dating from about twelve thousand years ago. The local rhyolite was not commonly used for these items, but at least one example has been documented. Twelve thousand years ago, the natives were big game hunters who lived in tiny family bands. Their diet must have been similar to that of the Eskimos or Northern Cree, as there were not many edible plants growing on the taiga. Sites from this period are rarely found and contain scant evidence. However, we know that these groups of people must have traveled over great distances since their tools were made of rock that sometimes came from very far away. Jasper from Lehigh and Onondaga stone from New York are examples of foreign stones found in local sites.

The fluted point evolved into many different stone heads, as shown in the illustration on the next page. From about 8000 B.C. to A.D. 1000, darts and spears were used.

Spears were made more powerful and effective by hurling them with a sling-like device called an "atlatl."

The natives here developed a way of life in Pennsylvania that lasted thousands of years—longer than anything we have done. For example, excavations on City Island in the Susquehanna have documented the repeated seasonal use of the same campsite there for over 4,000 years. Their small, spread-out, interrelated bands eventually established "home turfs" during the Archaic Period.

Spear points and pottery of old are a lot like cars and hairstyles today. You can date them according to how they look. The earliest artifactual evidence found thus far in Monroe Township dates to the Archaic Period. Documented to date are one site from the early Archaic Period, one from the mid-Archaic, and six from the late Archaic, all scattered along the Yellow Breeches Creek.

Some of the earliest pottery in the world is classified as "Vinette" pottery, fashioned from clay mixed crudely with crushed rock, fired very unevenly, and sometimes decorated. The pottery probably did not last very long for its users, but the vessels could be quite large—about the circumference of a beach ball. They were not objects that a nomadic band would have carried around. Thus, the discovery of Vinette pottery at a site is a sign that the people were beginning to settle down. This was the beginning of the Woodland Period, around 1000 B.C.

During this period, the Native Americans here lived in little villages in round post and pole houses, or sometimes in elongated ones—forerunners of the Iroquois longhouses. They had become farmers, cultivating "the three sisters"—corn, beans, squash—and even plants we know today as "weeds." By the end of the twelfth century A.D., these villages were being surrounded by log palisades, which tells us that the communities were not getting along very well with their neighbors. By this time, the population may have grown to the point that the communities were competing for game and other resources.

In Monroe Township, three sites have been dated to the Transitional Period and three dating from the Late Woodland Period. Basically, the whole period sequence is represented here, except for the Paleo-Indian Period, which is represented by nearby sites in neighboring townships.

It was the Late Woodland Indians who first made contact with the Europeans. To our knowledge, no Susquehannock Indians were living in Cumberland County, although they may have hunted here. John Smith encountered the Susquehannock in the Upper Chesapeake at the beginning of European / Native American relations. Until the 1750s, Cumberland County was the frontier, and few literate people were here or took the time to record who and what they encountered in this area. We do know that Washington Boro, aero the Susquehanna near Columbia, was home to a large community of Susquehannock, numbering 3,500 individuals or more.

There may have been Shawnee at the mouth of the Yellow Breeches, but no one is exactly sure where the Shawnee range was. Shawnee place names are spread out all over the Eastern United States. Archaeologists are unable to determine what tribe is represented by a certain site. The Native Americans did not leave us a written record. In reality, we have little or no idea who they were, what they called themselves, and what language they spoke.

By A.D. 1600 we start to find Western artifacts from the fur trade with the Europeans at local sites. Most of the area natives who died violently during this period died at the hands of other natives, vying with each other in a vicious competition for trade. Many others, sometimes entire villages, died from diseases such as smallpox, influenza, measles, and even alcoholism, all introduced by the European traders and settlers. Pennsylvania is one of only three states today in the United States that has no Indian Reservations, as the native population here was almost completely wiped out. Many of the Indians who died during the time of the fur trade never even laid eyes on a white man. It is very sad. In a regrettable end to this sad story, in 1756, the last seven Susquehannocks were routed out of Conestoga Town during Pontiac's War and placed in the Lancaster jail for their protection. Later, in a drunken rage, a group of men known as the Paxton Creek Boys invaded the jail, dragged the Susquehannocks out and lynched them.

Archaeological artifacts left behind by these people are now our only source of information about the history of this area prior to the arrival of the Europeans. Despite the scattered documented sites, we still know very little about the archaeology of the Yellow Breeches watershed. There have been no formally sponsored excavations here. We only have cataloged artifacts from surface sites. However, this is not necessarily unfortunate. Digs can be destructive, especially if they are not well planned or executed. Leaving a site undisturbed can sometimes be a form of preservation, too.

Stone Age archaeological sites are non-renewable resources. When one is destroyed, the information that it might have yielded is gone forever. What can you do if you discover artifacts or a site? Contact the Pennsylvania Historical and Museum Commission's Bureau of Historic Preservation and request a returnable form on which to record information about your discovery. Experience in archeological fieldwork at various organized digs around the Commonwealth is also available each year to interested volunteers.

We have a responsibility to manage and protect these non-renewable resources. The biggest threat to them, as well as many other types of resources, is urban sprawl. While the housing needs of the current population must be met, we also have a responsibility to plan well, and to factor in the effect our actions will have on our heritage. The future of our past is in all of our hands.

An Archaeological History of Monroe Township and Surrounds

CULTURAL PERIODS	DATES	PROJECTILE POINTS
COLONIAL (Susquehannocks and other Historically recorded tribes)	1760 A.D. 1550 A.D.	GUNS / BRASS ARROWHEADS
LATE WOODLAND (Mississippian)	1550 A.D. 1000 A.D.	
MIDDLE WOODLAND (Hopewell)	1000 A.D. 500 B.C.	
EARLY WOODLAND (Adena)	300 B.C. 1000 B.C.	
TRANSITIONAL	800 B.C. 1800 B.C.	
ARCHAIC	1000 B.C. 8000 B.C.	
PALEO-INDIAN	8000 B.C. 10,000 B.C.	

Cultural Periods and Point Types

Native American Artifacts.
(Pennsylvania Historical and Museum Commission,
Historical Pennsylvania Leaflet No. 31,
Pennsylvania Archaeology: An Introduction.)

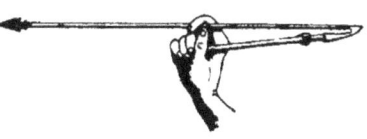

Spear Thrower, Archaic Period

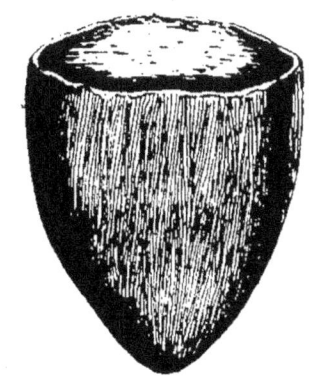

Clay Pot, Early Woodland Period

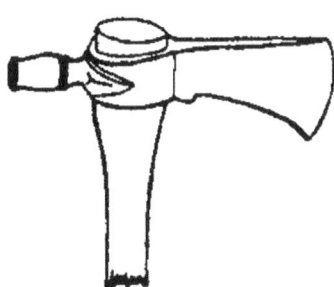

Pipe Tomahawk, Historic Period

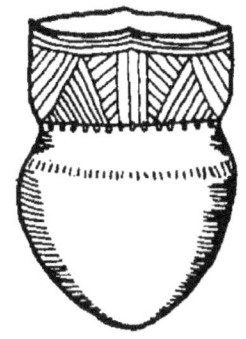

Incised Pot, Late Woodland Period

CHAPTER 4

The Yellow Breeches Creek: A Precious Natural Resource

by Wendy Plowman

What did the Yellow Breeches look like before settlers arrived?

If we could look back in time, before Europeans settled along the banks of the Yellow Breeches Creek, we would see a much different landscape than we see today. Picture a land cape with no mills, houses, barns, cows, dams, sewer plants, or bridges—a landscape with primeval hardwood forests interspersed with pristine wetlands and grassy meadows flourishing with native plants and wildflowers. Lenni-Lenape, Delaware, and Shawnee natives (known in the 1700s as Shawanese) camped here and there along the stream, particularly where natural springs surfaced along its tributaries. Native American artifacts have been found in several significant sites in Monroe Township.

In *A History of Cumberland County*, written in 1879 by Rev. Conway P. Wing, D.D., the creek was referred to as Callapasscink (spelled Callapatscink in a 1909 Report), interpreted as "where the waters turn back again" because of all the twists and turns along its path. Long before that, the creek was referred to as Shaawna in a letter written in 1731 to Peter Chartier by "the Commissioners and the Governor's order." Could it be because of the "Shawanese" that lived along its banks?

Pure water from subterranean limestone springs supported a healthy population of native brook trout. According to Charles Lose, Ph.D., in his 1928 book, *The Vanishing Trout*, "Trout were mostly of the primitive native variety, black with silver sides, the fish that were once held in the hand of the Great Spirit." In this same book, Lose relates a story told by Jesse Logan, a Native American of the Cornplanter Indian Reservation in Warren County, the last of the race of Shikellamy. The story told how Manito (a good spirit, deified in the religion of the Algonquian people) visited the land of the Iroquois to lead his lost children back to the happy hunting ground in the far east. He grew weak with hunger and cold on his long quest. At nightfall, he stopped beside a pool in the Seneca country, which was overshadowed by large white pines and hemlocks. Noticing that it was full of handsome trout, as black as ebony, he reached in his hand and easily caught the largest of the superb game fish. Looking at it, he was struck by its beauty and agile grace and decided to control his hunger and let it live. He dropped it back into the deep pool. The trout went its way, but instantly, its sides took on a silvery hue where the fingers of the Great Spirit had held it. All of its kind became marked with the same silvery sheen as a token of their having been handled by the kindly Manito. For that reason, the Seneca Indians and others of the Six Nations would not eat trout. Trout were sacred to the highest instincts of their race. Most likely, the Shaawna or Callapasscink supported a healthy number and size of native brook trout that no doubt the first European settlers were pleased to catch and eat.

Who were the first settlers along its banks?

In the early 1700s, among these lush and pristine surroundings, Scots-Irish settlers began moving into the area along the stream bank. Up until the treaty of the French and Indian Wars in 1763, the natives had been steadily pushed west to Ohio and never returned. A steady flow of new Scots-Irish pioneers continued to settle here, followed a few years later by those of German ancestry.

How did Yellow Breeches Creek get its name?

There are many stories about how the stream became known as the Yellow Breeches Creek. One story claims that an early settler washed his buckskin breeches in the creek and yellowed the water. A similar story involves an incident in which Indians stole doeskin breeches from a wash line, and when they dipped them into the creek, they turned yellow. Still, another story tells of a great number of "yellow beech" trees that once grew upon its banks, the name becoming a distortion of yellow beeches. However, this story is difficult to believe unless the storyteller was referring to the native American beech *Fagus grandifolia* which in present time doesn't normally grow along the Yellow Breeches. There is also a tree called yellow birch, *Betula Alleghaniensis*; however, this deciduous tree, even though native to Pennsylvania, isn't commonly found in Cumberland County. As early as 1764, on a survey map by surveyor John Armstrong, the creek was identified as Yellow Breeches Creek. A favorite legend among residents is the story of soldiers who stained their white "britches" yellow while fording the stream. Each legend has potential because no one knows for sure just how the creek really got its name.

What are some interesting details about the stream?

The stream meanders in an easterly direction 55.9 miles, or 33 miles as the crow flies, from the Michaux State Forest to the Susquehanna River. It changes from a freestone stream in its headwaters to a limestone stream in the Cumberland Valley. The majority of the creek flows over gentle slopes from an elevation of 735 feet near Walnut Bottom to 290 feet at the Susquehanna River in New Cumberland. The Yellow Breeches has a constant flow of fertile subsurface water and maintains a year round temperature from about 50 to 60 degrees Fahrenheit. According to a report in the *Pennsylvania Scenic River Study*, as the Yellow Breeches flows into the limestone bedrock of the valley, the carbonate rocks dissolve to form carbonic acid, releasing carbon dioxide and water. Such nutrient-laden water is good for building viable natural communities accommodating increased plant photosynthesis and growth of micro-plankton, which enhances the food chain and provides for higher-level biotic communities.

The limestone faults bisecting the main channel here have allowed the stream to flourish not only because of its carbonate and carbon dioxide-producing capabilities but also its neutralizing capabilities which protect the water from increased acidity. Being alkaline, it is a very good buffer of acidity and the source of the stream's natural fertility.

How did the creek change after the settlers arrived?

By 1825, when Monroe Township was formed, the landscape had changed drastically. Mills, farms, and settlements appeared all along the waterway. The settlers cleared the forest land, drained the wetlands, dammed the stream, and built roads that ran through the creek so they could easily traverse from place to place. Even though they valued the stream for their sustenance, without understanding the significance of their activity, the new residents caused great damage to it. The dams, which were necessary for water power to run the mills, also raised the temperature of the water, which, along with the depletion of the forest cover and pollution from human activity, eventually led to the brook trout's demise in the main stem of the creek.

In the nineteenth century, crossing the creek could be troublesome when the water was higher than normal, particularly during the spring rainy season. Eventually, bridges were built. The first bridge on the entire length of the creek was built of wood at New Cumberland in 1792. During the 19th century, twenty-seven additional bridges appeared, four of them in Monroe Township.

During the nineteenth century, streams became magnets for development and industrial activity. According to John R. Miller's report for the Cumberland County Historical Society in 1909, George Hopple, a miller who bought land in 1823 from Samuel Goodyear, who was also a miller from Allen Township, operated a mill along what today is known as Spring Road. In 1839, Hopple sold the mill to Michael G. Beltzhoover, who rebuilt it and also ran a distillery a short distance down the creek. Remnants of the original dam exist today.

The report further states that Leidigh's Mill operated to the east a mile or so further down the creek at Leidigh's Station, along the Philadelphia, Harrisburg & Pittsburgh Railroad line. A distillery ran in connection with this mill. The area was also known as Junction Mills from the original name of the adjacent 350-acre plantation. Leidigh's Mill bridge, built in 1885 of iron at a cost of $1,484, has since been replaced by a concrete and steel structure.

According to release papers filed in 1872 at Cumberland County Courthouse for a deed dated April 1, 1839, Joseph Brandt purchased land about a half mile east of Leidigh's Mill and built a clover, saw and chopping mill. According to the deed, the mill was 300 rods, nearly one mile upstream from Brandtsville. A map of Cumberland County, dated 1858, shows that a road once connected Creek Road with York Road (Route 74) on the other side of the creek (See page 58). Because the creek is shallow at this location, wagons forded through the stream. A handsome stone home of early vintage, once owned by Judge Thomas Neely of Harrisburg, overlooks the creek at this site today. Remnants of the old road exist in front of the home, climbing a hillside and extending along a portion of the present driveway. The road then divides and runs along a tree line. Further on, the old road converges with York Road near the crest of a hill, opposite where an early schoolhouse had once been located.

Twenty-three-year-old Martin Brandt settled in Monroe Township in 1773 when he began purchasing land. He eventually bought up to 1,000 acres. Mr. Brandt built a small stone house but replaced it with a large brick house and barn, which all stand today as the Deckman farm on the banks of the Yellow Breeches Creek. Brandt married and supported a large family.

The Hoover gristmill, which was located on the north side of the Yellow Breeches at the village of Brandtsville, was built by Martin Brandt in the early 1800s, sold to P. A. and D. V. Ahl, and then sold back to Martin Brandt, Jr.'s sons, George and Samuel Brandt, in 1856. George Brandt operated a distillery nearby. About 1900, the grist mill was turned into an ice manufacturing plant for residents as well as the railroad to meet the growing needs of long-distance transportation of perishables. In the 1930s, Greenawalt's laundry replaced the ice business. According to local gossip, the business failed because one too many sheets ended up torn!

On the south side of the creek, across from the gristmill, and possibly built by Martin Brandt about 1825, operated Evan's sawmill and clover mill. Wood was lumbered from the adjacent South Mountain. Much later, the railroad purchased the existing buildings and, for many years, used the main house for a railroad workmen's dormitory, eventually renting it out and finally selling it to Earl and Sylvia Yeingst in 1964. Steam engines replenished their water supply from a large wooden holding tank located adjacent to the railroad and a mill race. The house for both the grist mill and clover mill exist today, as do remnants of the mill dam. In the mid-1800s, the Brandt family also mined red and yellow ochre, a paint pigment, and iron ore on South Mountain and operated several large farms in the immediate area.

The first covered wooden bridge in Monroe Township was built in 1840 directly downstream for a mere $1,450. The bridge washed out in the early 1930s and was replaced by a metal truss bridge. In 1972, that bridge washed away in high water caused by Hurricane Agnes and was replaced with a steel and concrete structure.

Located about three-quarters of a mile downstream from Brandtsville was Brandt's mill, probably a sawmill. It was presumably built by Martin Brandt, Jr, or one of his descendants. (Martin Brandt, Jr. met an accidental death in 1815 at age 37 by a runaway team of horses.) Remnants of a broken dam exist today. A road went through the creek here from York Road to the Martin Brandt farm on the north side of the creek. The road was closed off when the railroad was built.

Givler's mill, also known as John Clark's grist mill, located about a mile further east, was originally built by John Clark in 1774. The mill was owned and operated by the Clark family until 1848, when it was sold to Benjamin Givler. In 1867, an iron bridge was built near the mill for $3,765 but apparently washed out in high water at some point because it was replaced in 1911 by a single-lane, reinforced concrete structure that continues to serve the township today as part of Locust Point Road.

The last two mills on the creek were located further east at Williams Grove. John Clark also built both of these mills in 1785, passing them down through the family until they were sold to James Williams in 1848. The mill at Williams Grove burned down around

1900. The second mill was located a short distance away from where Dogwood Run empties into the Yellow Breeches. It is here that the creek forms the dividing line between York and Cumberland counties. A wooden bridge was built at William's Grove in 1866 at a cost of $2,900.

When did the creek begin making an ecological turnaround?

During the first half of the twentieth century, the Yellow Breeches Creek further deteriorated because of erosion, pollution from sewage, and general neglect. There were no state or federal laws in place to help protect Pennsylvania's streams. The red flags waved, and Pennsylvanians became aware of the need to legislate waterway protection. With the development of The Clean Water Act of the 1970s, resource management tools and guidelines were put in place that helped turn things around. Historical documentation and continued monitoring are excellent ways to help ensure that the future holds hope for this precious natural resource.

What significance does the Pennsylvania Scenic River Study and designation serve?

In 1975, Pennsylvania listed prioritized river candidates nominated for consideration as components of the Pennsylvania Scenic Rivers System. In 1975, the Yellow Breeches Creek was listed as a priority lB river candidate. A listing of lA is required before becoming eligible for the study to be initiated. In 1985, a local support group interested in having the creek studied for possible designation as a Scenic River petitioned the state to have the status of the Yellow Breeches Creek changed from priority status lB to lA, which was the first necessary step in convincing the Department of Environmental Resources task force to begin the Scenic River Study. This citizens' group eventually formed the Yellow Breeches Creek Alliance, whose main purpose was to have the stream designated a Pennsylvania Scenic River.

Four years later, DER Secretary Arthur Davis concurred with the recommendation of the Task Force to change the priority status from lB to lA. In May 1989, DER (currently the Department of Conservation and Natural Resources) held informational public meetings in York and Cumberland Counties, officially initiating the study to determine the creek's eligibility for Scenic River designation.

After four years of intensive study, legislation was finally passed to have the creek designated as a Pennsylvania Scenic River. The study included a historical summary and a study of land resources such as physiography, topography, geology, soil characteristics and slopes. The aquatic and terrestrial environments, including amphibians, birds, mammals, reptiles and fish, were studied, as were land use and transportation characteristics. Population trends and socio-economic characteristics were included. Landowner surveys were completed and taken into consideration. Management guidelines were developed, and finally, legislation was written and passed in August 1992. The process was arduous but well worth the effort. This was the first time in history that so much information was gathered and documented about Yellow Breeches Creek.

An evaluation of the data gathered for the study and proposed designation indicated that it satisfied the eligibility criteria for outstandingly remarkable geological, historical, recreational, fishery/wildlife and vegetation value. Of the five possible classification types that characterize a Scenic River—Wild, Scenic, Pastoral, Recreational and Modified Recreational—recommendations included 5.1 miles of a Scenic tributary (upper reaches) and 45.3 miles of Pastoral (mid-section) and 5.5 miles of Recreational (lower reaches).

The historical portion of the study traced the development over some 295 years, which extended from the arrival of the early settlers in 1730 to the present. The corridor includes an extensive variety of historical structures and offers a brief glimpse of early life, its economy and contributions to the development of Pennsylvania and the United States.

Three nationally significant historical sites were included in the study. The presence of nearly 300 historical structures that had been surveyed for the study along the Yellow Breeches also adds to its documented historical value.

The benefits of the designation itself are somewhat tenuous. However, the designation draws attention to the waterway as a resource of statewide significance and is an aid in the protection of its outstanding aesthetic, ecological, pastoral, cultural and recreational values. It also:

- Acts as a catalyst to increase awareness of the creek's value, encouraging local initiatives in developing ideas and guidelines for protecting the waterway.
- Provides the availability of technical assistance on local management issues such as littering and trespass problems. Also stream bank restoration techniques and vegetative planting technical assistance are available.
- Ensures that all state agencies support the intent of Scenic River designation in their actions within the corridor.
- Prohibits additional construction of flow impoundments in the Scenic designated area.
- Elevates the waterway's standing in competing for state funding of resource conservation projects within the designated corridor.

Today, the Yellow Breeches Creek is at a crossroads. Further development in Monroe Township is underway at a rather brisk pace. The biggest threat is the increased population and the resultant human activity. It's not known how much more pressure this valuable natural resource can endure before there is further decline. Hopefully, those empowered to make decisions that affect Yellow Breeches Creek will recognize the importance of their decisions and do what is right for those who live in Monroe Township today, as well as for future generations to come. It seems that today, we are more aware of what we stand to lose if we don't pay attention to what history has told us. Proper management and environmental planning are key to maintaining Yellow Breeches Creek's current water quality and aquatic resources. We recognize the problems we've caused, and now it's time to become part of the solution.

Swimming by the Bradtsville bridge, ca. 1920. Pictured from right to left are Sophia Greenawalt, Mary E. Hoover, unidentified, Miriam L. Hoover (smallest child), Anna Hoover, unidentified and John B. Hoover.

Williams Mill bridge, which stood from 1806 until 1941, ca. 1920s.

The "ol' swimmin' hole" along Creek Rd. at Brandtsville, ca. 1920s.

Williams Mill bridge, ca. 1920s.

Flooding Yellow Breeches, Brandtsville, 1936.

Dam at Brandtsville, 1936.

(Photographs courtesy of Miriam L. Hoover)

Dam at Brandtsville, 1936.

John Blair ("Bud") Hoover and dog "Ching" by the dam at Brandtsville.

The store at Brandtsville, ca. 1930s.

From left to right, Mae W., Anna and Mary Hoover with dog "Tossie" at the ruins of the old mill at Brandtsville, ca. late 1920s.

(Photographs courtesy of Miriam L. Hoover)

Brandtsville bridge, built in 1840 at a cost of $1,450. Torn down after 92 years in 1932. A new span was built in 1933, and another replaced it in 1982. Photo ca. 1920s. (Photograph courtesy of Miriam L. Hoover)

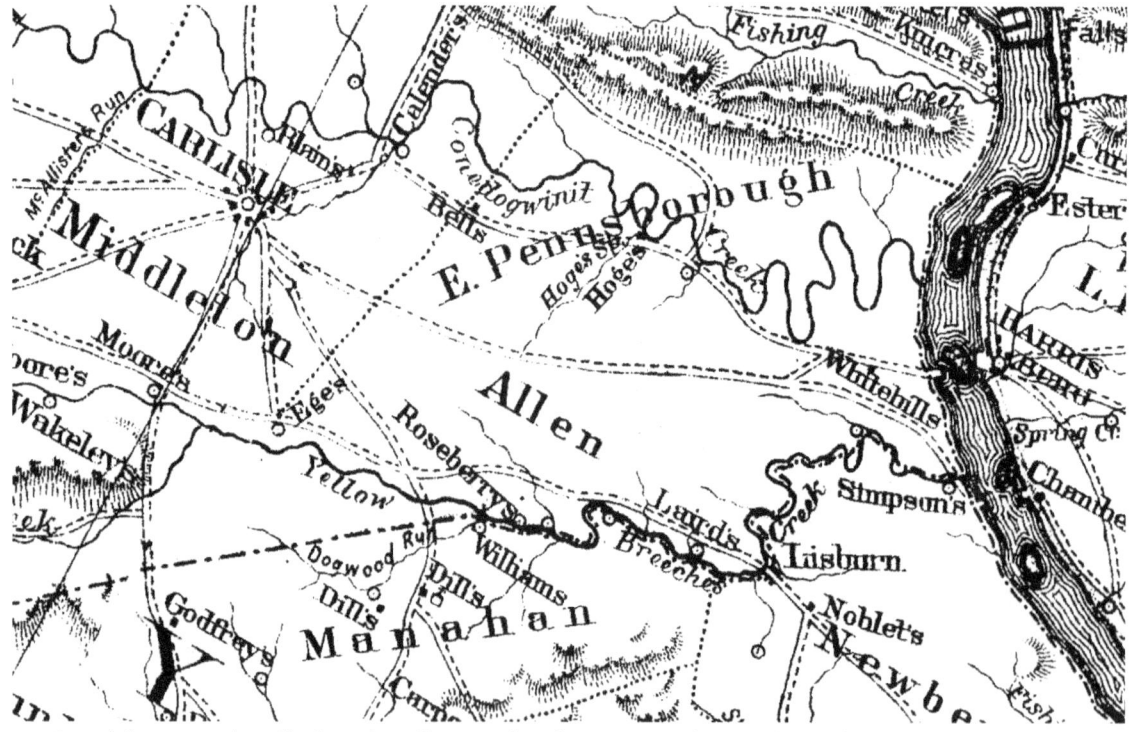

Detail showing early mills along the Yellow Breeches, from A Map of Pennsylvania *by Reading Howell, 1792. (Pennsylvania State Archives, Manuscript Group 11, map no. 2.)*

CHAPTER 5

The Early Settlers

by Sharon R. Nelson

As the centuries pass, our collective memory of the people and events that colored them dims. History becomes a skeleton of highlights, turning points and the actions of famous people, while the names and lives of more ordinary folks, who persevered through (and often despite) the more well-known occurrences, fade away. Many of us live today in Monroe Township not knowing who first cleared and cultivated the land we farm, not knowing who first built the houses we see and live in or when, and not knowing who laid out the roads we drive on or why. Before Monroe Township was founded in 1825, before its predecessor Allen Township was founded in 1766, and even a decade or two before the County of Cumberland was formed in 1750, the settlement of the land in our area by the Europeans had already begun.

The Paper Trail

Some curious souls have braved the tedious and often frustrating world of deed tracing, as well as researching other records such as wills, tax assessments and censuses, attempting to track down local ancestors or prior owners of their properties. Dead ends have sometimes stymied those attempting to work backward through the paper trail into the 1700s—missing documents that were never officially recorded. There is, however, a helpful resource for early community history that is often overlooked and underutilized. The records of the Commonwealth Land Office, held by the Pennsylvania Historical and Museum Commission at the Pennsylvania State Archives, can be a rich source of information on the early settlers in any Pennsylvania locale.

The Land Office was established in 1682 under the Proprietary Government of William Penn and continued its functions under the Commonwealth of Pennsylvania. Agents of the Land Office were responsible for surveying claims, receiving purchase money and issuing grants of land. After the outbreak of the Revolutionary War in 1775, the Land Office functions were suspended, and ownership of most of the Penn family's lands was transferred in 1779 to the Commonwealth of Pennsylvania by an act of the General Assembly. In 1781, the Land Office operation was recreated by the Revolutionary Government as the State Land Office and was assigned both the records and continuing responsibilities of its Proprietary predecessor.

The Patenting Process

For the most part, every parcel of land in the Commonwealth can be traced back to an original land grant from the Proprietary or

State Land Office. The primary documents associated with the transfer process of each parcel from government ownership to private hands were as follows:

- A **Warrant** was a certificate authorizing the survey of a tract of land or accepting a survey that had already been done. The warrant initiated the title of a property and provided the basis for legal settlement but did not convey all rights to the property. Usually, a warrant was initiated when a claimant submitted a Warrant Application. Occasionally, other types of documents such as Blunston Licenses, West Side Applications, or Orders to Survey were used instead of or in addition to Warrants and Warrant Applications, serving a similar purpose. These additional types of documents usually came into play in cases when the land was in dispute between two parties or when the land was settled and claimed before the Proprietary government had actually purchased it from the Indians.

- A **Survey** was a sketch to scale of the boundaries of the tract of land with an exact determination of acreage. Sometimes, resurveys were done for a new claimant, to correct an error, or to replace an original survey that had never been recorded. If a tract was subdivided before the patent was obtained, new surveys were normally done for all the "pieces" that were divided off, and separate patents were issued for each smaller tract.

- A **Patent** was the final, official deed from the Penn family or the Commonwealth which conveyed clear title and all rights to the owner. Before a county could record any deeds for a property, a patent was to be secured (although that did not always happen). Between 1766 and 1812, the Land Office required patentees to give names to their patent tracts to facilitate record keeping. Names for patents ranged from the obvious (No. 53, Andrew Holmes' "Holmes's Tract" and No. 84, Jacob Bricker's "Bricker's Hall") to the descriptive (No. 31, "Dalebrook" and No. 41, "Rural Grove"). Some paid homage to remote lands (such as No. 40, "Denmark" and No. 60, "Andalusia"), while others seemed to be plays on the patentees' names (No. 18, John Kitch's "Kitchen Garden," No. 2, William Abernathy's "Aberdeen" and No. 20b, George Guyer's "St. George's").

Here are some examples of how the patenting process worked for several different Monroe tracts. The numbers correspond to tract numbers on the Patent Tract Overlay Map at the end of this chapter.

70.) ed. 2/14/1769
58 acres, 74 perches
Weiss, John: warrant, 3/11/1776 (Cumb. W297)
Weiss, John: survey, 4/20/1802 (A-14-87)
Weiss, Jacob: patent, 2/12/1814 (H-10-288)

3.) ed. 11/1/1732
"Claremont," 300 acres
Heald, Thomas: Blunston license, 4/30/1735 (p.14)
Heald, Thomas: warrant, 11/1/1735 (Lanc. H66)
Heald, Thomas: survey, 11/11/1735 (C-84-63)
Clark, John: patent, 6/14/1785 (P-3-399)

53.) ed. 5/24/1766
"Holmes's Tract," 111 acres, 31 perches
Wallace, Ruth: west side application, 5/8/1767 (#3629)

Holmes, Andrew: warrant to accept older survey, 4/13/1772 (Cumb. H236)
Wallace, Ruth: survey, 8/21/1767 (A-18-271)
Holmes, Andrew: patent, 4/15/1772 (AA-13-88)

82.) ed. 2/21/1785
"Junction," 348 acres, 140 perches
Wolf, Leonard: warrant, 2/21/1785 (Cumb. W343)
Wolf, Leonard: surveys, 12/27/1785 (C-233-64 & 65)
Wolf, Leonard: patent, 6/19/1786 (P-6-353)

The earliest warrants for Monroe Township land were granted in 1735, while the latest were received by the early 1800s. However, as the examples illustrate, the number of years between the granting of the warrant and the granting of the patent varied widely. In some cases, all of the steps in the process occurred within a year or two, while in other instances, the procedure may have dragged on for decades through several generations or changes of ownership. Often, the process may have been purposefully drawn out by the occupants of the land, who were not anxious to pay the survey and the patent fees. Some delays may have been due to the fact that the state did not have enough surveyors to get around to all the tracts in a timely manner. In 1835, the state actually passed legislation to get its revenue from land tracts that had never been patented. Appraisers were sent around to appraise and categorize (i.e., "graduate") the unpatented properties and to demand that the present owners pay up a certain percentage of that value and complete the process.[15] Although the patenting of tracts in Monroe Township began as early as 1742 (tract no. 6), even before the official purchase of this area from the Indians, many of the tracts in Monroe Township were not patented until the first several decades of the 1800s. The latest patent found thus far (for tract no. 35) dates from 1930, while several others were granted as late as the 1840s and 1850s.

Additional Information

For each parcel of patented land, there is more information to be gleaned from the Land Office records than just the names and dates associated with the warranting, surveying and patenting of that tract. Note in the copied survey below that the tract is surrounded by the names of its neighbors.

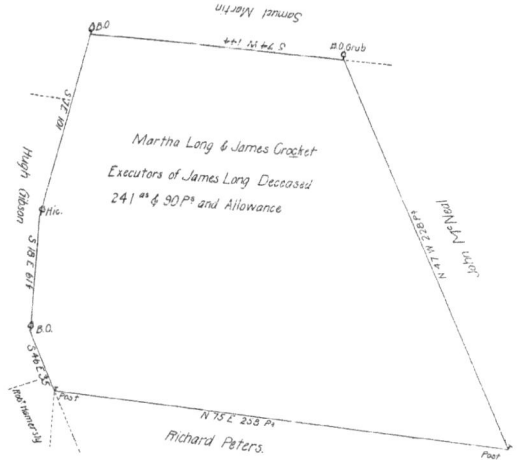

This tract of land, patented as "Union," is where the Monroe Township Municipal Building and the Monroe Elementary School currently stand.

Similarly, the surveys for each of "Union's" neighboring tracts will show a neighbor name associated with "Union," which will, of course, date from whenever the neighboring survey was done. Here is a summary of this data for "Union":

---

15. Pennsylvania State Archives, Record Group 17, XV. Graduated Land Certificates, Commissioners' Certificates, [ca.1835], microfilm LO 27.1-12.

<u>additional names:</u>

Muchmore, Shadrach, formerly James Long: between 9/27/1750 and 6/16/1764 (from tract no. 27, B-2-74)

Strike/Stroke/Strock, Joseph: 2/14/1769 to 4/20/1802 (from tract no. 71, C-55-290; tract no. 40, M-254(?); tract no. 78, C-166-90; tract no. 70, A-14-87)

Kenower, Jacob: 12/20/1803 (from tract no. 20, A-14-1, 2, 3 & 4)

Note how these names and date spans fill in gaps and expand beyond the information provided by "Union's" warrant, survey and patent data shown below.

49.) ed. 5/4/1765
"Union," 241 acres, 90 perches

Long, Martha & James Croket, executors of James Long, deceased, in trust for his heirs: warrant, 5/4/1765 (Cumb. L90)

Long, Martha & James Crocket: survey, 5/19/1785 (C-115-39)

Knawer, Jacob, et al.: patent, 8/10/1793 (P-20-129)

Since most parcels of patent land had at least three or four distinct neighboring tracts, the surveys for those neighboring tracts will provide at least three or four dated names for the original parcel in question.

Putting Together the Pieces of the Puzzle

Of course, this method can only work if one is able to identify and locate the surveys of a property and its neighbors. Fortunately, the records of the Land Office include a number of helpful resources that enable this sort of research to be done. Names of tract owners and neighbors can be looked up in alphabetical indexes to warrantees and patentees, as well as in indexes to more specialized documents such as West Side Applications. Also, starting in 1833, Land Office draftsmen began to neatly copy the old original surveys, many of which were damaged and difficult to read, into new bound volumes called Copied Survey Books. Over the years, the survey numbers for adjacent tracts were often penciled into these books as they were discovered. Using a combination of these resources, it is usually possible to locate all the "pieces of the puzzle," as it were, and put together a fairly complete map of the interconnected patent tracts for a particular municipality. In fact, in 1907, the legislature authorized the Land Office to construct such maps, known as "Warrantee Township Maps," for the entire state.

Unfortunately, this task proved to be so difficult and time-consuming that fewer than half the counties in the state were actually completed, and the project was recently abandoned altogether as a state function. It is now up to private researchers to complete the job for their respective areas if they wish. Monroe Township, and indeed most of Cumberland County, were among the areas that Land Office draftsmen never completed. Over the last few years, this author has attempted to pull together the information needed to create a complete Warrantee Township Map, or Patent Tract Map as it is called in this book, for Monroe. The overlay map and the simplified map at the end of this chapter are the result of that work, as are the accompanying name and date lists in Appendices A and B.

Then and Now

One problem that the Land Office draftsmen always encountered was determining where the current township boundaries, or indeed any current features, lay in relation to the connected survey tracts. At the time the surveys were drawn, most current township boundaries, and indeed most current townships, did not exist. The Land Office employees took their best guess, relying on official township metes and bounds to establish shape and size, and using bodies of water and other geographic features, as well as sporadic references on the surveys themselves, as reference points. However, unless a specific property lies along a distinctive portion of a creek or run or an old political boundary, it is often difficult to use these maps to determine which of hundreds of patented tracts coincide with a parcel of land that exists today.

With some tracts, it is easy. No. 82, named "Junction," is obviously located on an unmistakably shaped portion of the Yellow Breeches, which would stand out to anyone familiar with the area.

"Bricker's Hall"

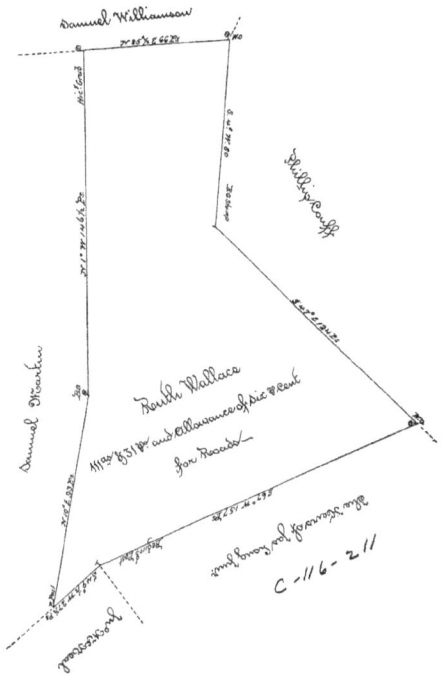

"Holmes's Tract"

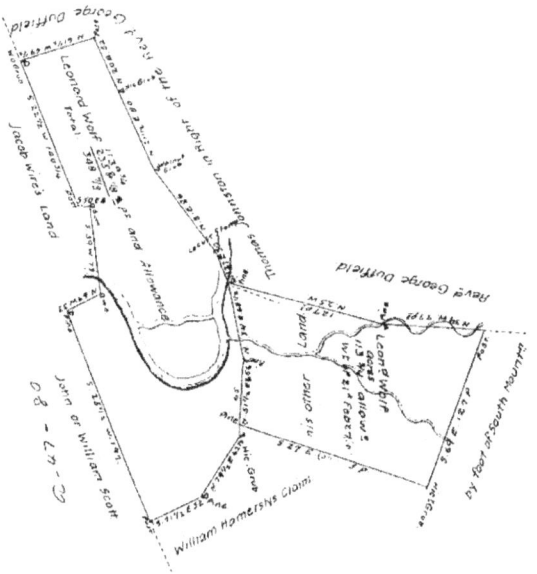

No. 84, "Bricker's Hall," on the other hand, could be anywhere, as could no. 53, "Holmes's Tract."

Local historian Kevin Vanderlodge, while working on his publication *A Walking Tour of Churchtown*, once lamented to me that he knew what patent tracts were located in the Churchtown Area, but he couldn't figure out where their respective boundaries had been in relation to a current map. As I looked over his drafts of the surveys, all connected, I thought I recognized familiar shapes—a distinctive pattern that I had seen somewhere before. I pulled out a road map, studied it, looked at

Kevin's connected drafts again, and embarked on a creative sizing exercise with a photocopying machine. With a similarly sized copy of both the map and the drafts in hand, I went over to a window and held them both up, one on top of the other.

Voila! Many of the survey boundaries seemed to match up exactly to portions of the roads, and more particularly, bends and intersections in the roads.

Kevin was delighted. I was intrigued. If this was true for the Churchtown area, why not for the rest of the township? For that matter, why not for any area? I thought of that oddly bent portion of Simmons Road and the private Fertenbaugh Lane between Trindle Road and Lisburn Road, for example. Surely that must have followed an old property boundary, I thought. It is hardly the best way to get from point A to point B. Certainly, no one would have laid out roads in that convoluted configuration without a good reason! Sure enough, see how the shape of tract no. 53, "Holmes's Tract," fits right in there along those roads.

Further experimentation revealed that fewer road correlations exist in other areas of the township. However, in this rural landscape, many current property lines and field hedgerows still seem to retain the shape of old patent boundaries as well. Although most of the original patent tracts have since been subdivided,

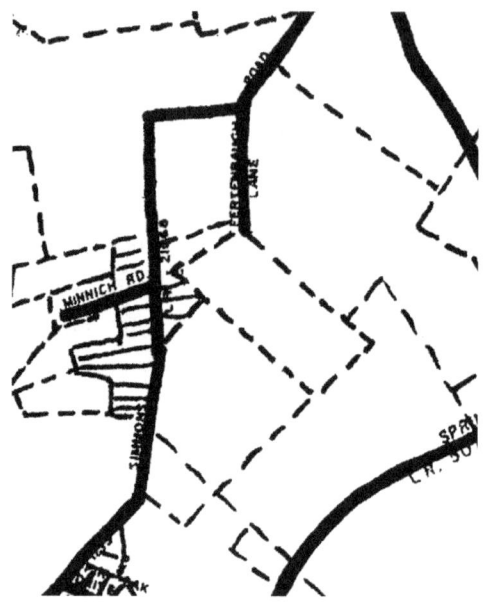

the divisions and reconfigurations have often been within the original boundaries rather than across them. For example, note the shape of tract no. 84, "Bricker's Hall." Now, look at the depiction of current township property lines along Indian Peg Road. Notice any similarities?

As you can see, over 200 years later, many of the original property division lines still appear to be intact and easily recognizable.

By putting all the adjoining surveys together in a connected draft and then correlating such features as bodies of water and tract shapes with modern documents such as the township zoning map and the county's aerial photograph tax parcel maps, it is fairly easy to see where the boundaries of many of the old survey tracts currently lie. This is how the Patent Tract Overlay Map for Monroe Township was constructed.

Keyed to this map, for convenience, is a list (see Appendix B) of all the names and dates associated with each tract that have been found so far in the primary Land Office documents (warrants, surveys, patents, and their respective indices). When all of this information is viewed together, you have, if not a complete picture, at least the beginnings of a picture of who all lived here during the 1700s and early 1800s.

A Grain of Salt

Be aware, though, that this name and date information provided by Commonwealth Land Records for each patent tract is not a complete record of property ownership and occupation. In some cases, it may be misleading or even incorrect.

Discrepancies may exist among the information provided by the various types of records for a particular property. The names of the official warrantee, surveyee and patentee are generally assumed to be correct, albeit with minor spelling variations, but the names ascribed to a tract by neighboring surveys sometimes conflict. For instance, one tract may name as its current neighbor a person whom other neighboring surveys claim had been, by that time, dead for decades. A person who was "squatting" on or renting an adjacent tract may be named in a neighboring survey, but the records for the tract in question reveal that a different person actually held the warrant or patent. Also, the tracts were patented and subdivided at different times, so neighbor names shown on later surveys may only apply to the portion of the neighboring patent tract that was closest rather than to the tract as a whole.

In addition to inaccuracies in the information provided about the names of neighbors, there are other issues to be aware of as well. Just because a person's name was associated with a tract of land does not necessarily mean that he or she ever lived there. If you look at the alphabetical list of landowners in Appendix A, you will notice that some names are associated with multiple tracts. Michael Ege, for example, founder of the Iron Works in Boiling Springs, laid claim to most of South Mountain and many tracts were warranted, surveyed and/or patented in his name. Richard Peters, who became Proprietary Secretary for William Penn's heirs in 1737 and lived in Philadelphia, not Monroe Township, seems to have taken advantage of his position by having many large, prime tracts of land warranted, surveyed or patented in his name, including the land on which Boiling Springs is presently situated, and an enormous 797-acre tract stretching through the heart of present-day Monroe Township from Churchtown all the way to Williams Grove. Peters might have been acting as an agent for his employers, the Penn family. However, by 1792, the problem of land speculation in Pennsylvania had grown so controversial that the Commonwealth passed a law requiring that all subsequent land claims had to be both occupied and improved within 10 years, and the total amount of land any one person could claim was limited to 400 acres.[16]

---

16. Donna Bingham Munger, *Pennsylvania Land Records: A History and Guide for Research* (Wilmington: Scholarly Resources, Inc., 1991) 143.

For these reasons, the information from neighboring surveys should always be taken with a grain of salt. Nevertheless, even a list of possible names and dates associated with each tract, often spanning half a century or more, is a helpful place to start in researching the history of a parcel of land.

Further Research

Much additional information about these properties and the people associated with them is available in other historical documents at the county, state and federal levels. Digitized images of the official Warrants, Surveys, Patents and other related documents can be viewed at the Pennsylvania State Archives in Harrisburg, or on its website. In particular, the Patent Books themselves, containing official copies of the patents granted, can provide evidence of intermediate owners of a tract between the warrantee and the patentee. They read like deeds tracing a chain of title, and there was no time to examine more than a handful of them in detail for this project. The four County Copied Survey Books kept in the Cumberland County Recorder of Deeds Office are also of interest. Their surveys are not quite the same as the Land Office surveys, providing additional information from different years and sometimes about later subdivisions of patent tracts. County Road Dockets and Road Docket Papers, available at the Cumberland County Historical Society, can also reveal information about later divisions and ownership of the land. The names of individuals can be looked up in State and Federal Censuses, the 1798 Federal Direct Tax, state military service records, and county tax records, as well as name indexes to deeds, wills and court proceedings. To any who decide to use this research as a stepping stone for further investigation, I wish you good hunting.

The Results

Without further ado, may I present some of the early settlers in our township as documented by the Land Office Records at the Pennsylvania State Archives. The Patent Tract Overlay Map, which attempts to show both tract boundaries and current property lines, is located on the next two pages. It is followed by a simpler, easier-to-read version provided for reference, showing only the patent tracts and their numbers. Appendix B, at the end of this book, contains detailed information about each tract and the people associated with it. Appendix A is an alphabetical index designed especially for genealogists, showing all the personal and company names found, with references as to the tract number(s) that each name is associated with. Just to make it interesting, since any attempt at a consecutive numbering system would be thwarted by the non-linear configuration of the tracts, the tract numbers have been assigned chronologically according to the earliest date documented by the Land Records cited for each tract. While not a foolproof system by any means, this still gives some reflection of the settlement pattern and how it progressed through the decades.

Note: Most of the statements in this chapter regarding the records and history of the Commonwealth Land Office are standard working knowledge of the archivists at the Pennsylvania State Archives, of which this author is one. Statements made about the history of Monroe Township are based on an analysis of the data in Appendix B.

Patchwork fields form familiar shapes in this aerial photograph of Churchtown and surrounds, ca. 1937–1942. Tract nos. 49, 20, 70, and 24 can be seen especially clearly. (Pennsylvania State Archives, RG-31, Aerial Survey of Pennsylvania)

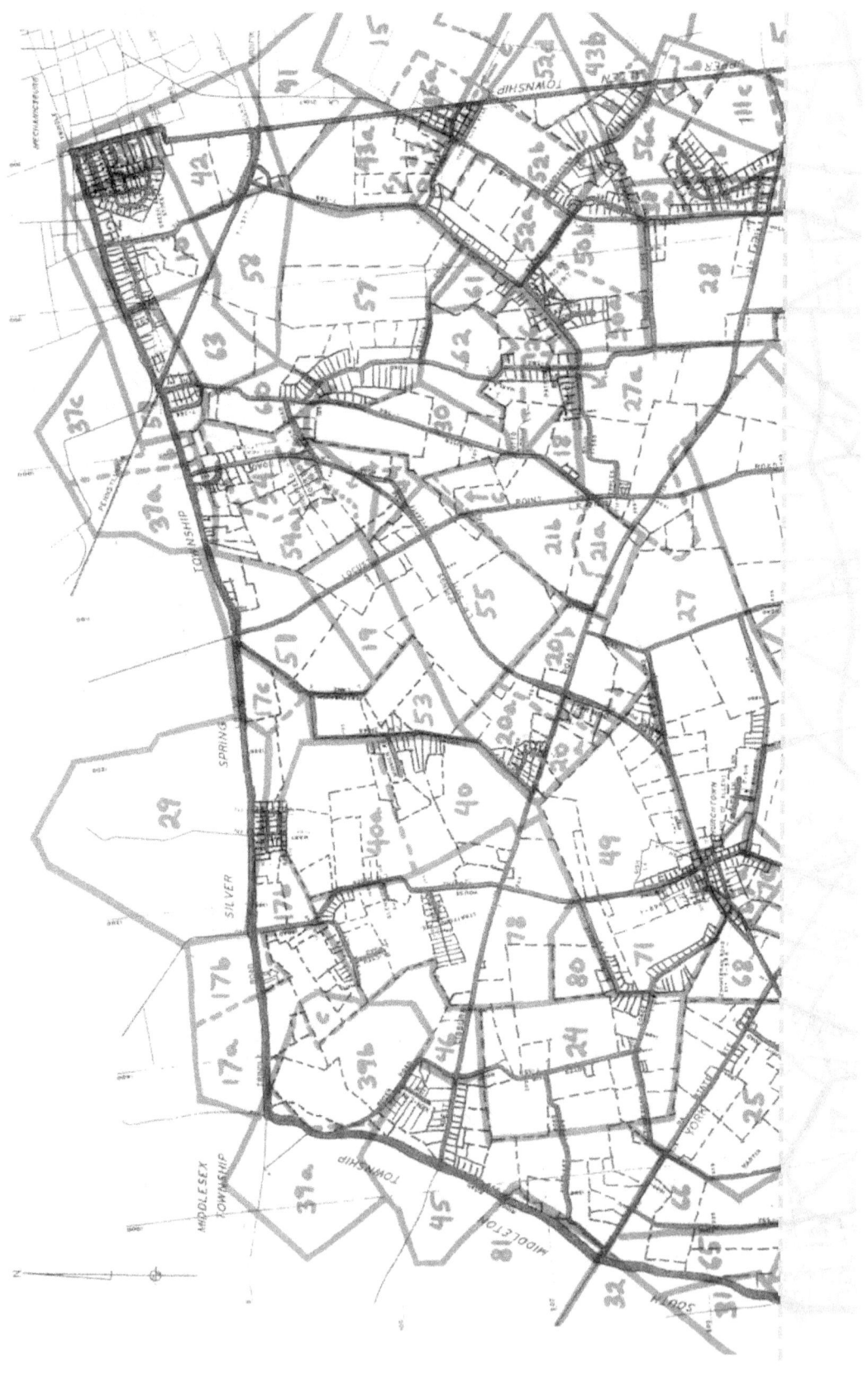

The Early Settlers 35

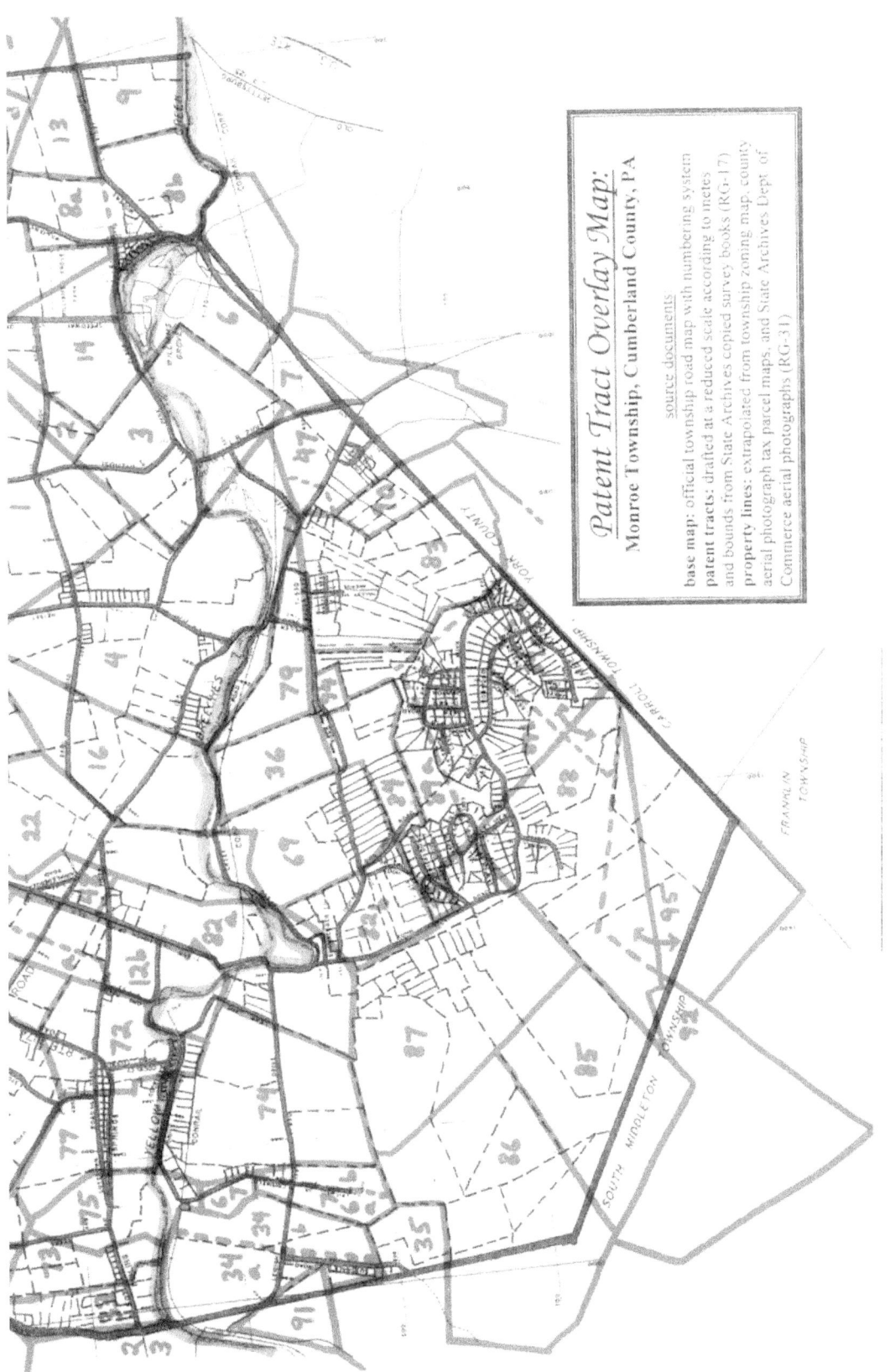

Simplified Patent Tract Map showing tract boundaries and numbers only.

Monroe Township, 1858, from the Map of Cumberland County, Pennsylvania, from actual surveys by Henry F. Bridgens. (Pennsylvania State Archives, Manuscript Group 11, map no. 75 [computer enhanced] photostat.) Note that few of the family names of original patentees, from only 50-100 years earlier, appear on this map.

CHAPTER 6

Hands Willing to Serve: A History of the Fire Companies in Monroe Township

by Jacob L. Heisey

PREFACE

For one to better understand this essay, geography, topography and population must be addressed. During the latter part of the eighteenth century, what is now Monroe Township was, for the most part, an undeveloped, wooded area. Politically, the area was a part of Allen Township. The earliest structures were probably log cabins built by the first settlers. A church was built about 1795 to serve the Lutheran and Reformed congregations. The first house of record in Churchtown is reputed to have been built by Jacob Weiss in 1804. In 1829, Peter Livinger laid out a plan of lots (indexed in the first Plot Plan Book of sub-divisions recorded in the Cumberland County Recorder of Deeds office). This plan called for 14 lots in an area bounded by Church Street on the north, Main Street on the west, High Street on the south, and Green Street on the east. The lots in these blocks were auctioned off in 1830. At this time there were approximately 200 property owners in present Monroe Township. Monroe was created in 1825 by court decree. The village of Churchtown had perhaps fifty structures, notably dwellings and stables.

There was no indoor plumbing. Outdoor privies were a necessity. Wells were dug by hand and were few. The main source of water was from cisterns which collected the run-off from the house roofs. The population in 1830 for all of Monroe was 1,562. By 1860, it had grown to 1,832. Churchtown accounted for possibly one-fourth of the population. The Public School Law as a local option. By 1860, Monroe Township had adopted the Public School Law and had several schoolhouses in the township. Churchtown had two schoolhouses on one lot located in front of the Lutheran/Reform church.

It should also be noted that what roads and streets did exist were dirt or mud. They were poorly maintained by today's standards. Transportation was limited to walking, horseback riding, or horse-drawn buggies and wagons. *The American Volunteer*, published in Carlisle, was the dominant newspaper. Electricity, telephones, automobiles, and other conveniences now taken for granted had not yet been invented. Also of interest are the names that were applied to the streets of Churchtown. Church Street is now (for the most part) Boiling Springs Road; Main Street is now Old Stone House Road. High and Green Streets remain unchanged. (For a late nineteenth-century map of Churchtown, see page 51.)

The nearest fire company was the Union in Carlisle, a distance of six to seven miles away.

Needless to say, the all-wooden structures of the day would have been destroyed by the time a hand-pulled engine would arrive. Possibly as a result of several bad experiences, the townspeople were motivated to form their own fire company. This was accomplished and became an important part of the village of Churchtown for the next fifty years or more.

THE FIRST FIFTY YEARS

"Agreeable to notice the Citizens of Churchtown met at No. 1 School House, on Thursday evening, November 15th, 1860, for the purpose of making arrangements to purchase a Fire Engine". Following this initial entry in the minute book, the Union Fire Company of Churchtown became more than the dream of a few of the local leaders. The first step, of course, was to appoint a committee to raise funds. Forty-eight citizens pledged a total of $294.50. The next step was to "see after engine." It would appear that a decision had been made to purchase a used engine from the Union Fire Company of Carlisle. While the minutes refer to the hearing of others and a letter received from Baltimore, nothing was done regarding any other equipment. The engine purchased from Carlisle was a "Bull Eye," which had been purchased new by Carlisle Union after the courthouse fire of 1845. By December 11, 1860, the purchase had been completed, and for a sum of $300, the engine, together with all apparatus, two axes and fifty feet of hose, had found a new home. A guarantee was furnished by the seller, and payment was to be made within 60 days. The next effort was to collect the pledges.

On December 28, 1860, a committee was appointed to draft a constitution and by-laws. On January 11, 1861, ground to build an engine house was acquired (the lot was 16' x 25') and cost $20. The site was located on High Street near an alley that ran between High and Church Streets. The constitution provided for members from the age of 18 and upward with the following officers to be elected on the first Monday of February: President, Vice President, Secretary, Treasurer, three Directors, three Trustees, one Engineer, and one Assistant Engineer. Appointed officers included two axemen, three laddermen, and one janitor.

Operating procedures were clearly spelled out in the by-laws. "Engineer shall take charge of the pipe and apply water according to first director. Engineer shall have sole charge of engine. Member arriving first at the engine house, at an alarm of fire, shall be entitled to the trumpet, which he shall retain until the arrival of a Director when he shall resign it into his hands." The dues were 25 cents per year. Fines were imposed for, among other things, pitting on the floor of the meeting room. The fine for this infraction was ten cents, with half going to the member reporting the incident. The membership of the company was all male, but the ladies did receive recognition on February 10, 1863: ". . . a vote of thanks was tendered to the ladies of Churchtown for their great exertions and services rendered in supplying water for the engine at the late fire."

In March of 1863, the Hall was completed. In May 1863 it was agreed to rent the Hall to the International Order of Odd Fellows. On May 23, 1863, a special meeting was held for the purpose of escorting the returning Civil War volunteers into town. There is no further reference to the matter. In June of 1863, Confederate troops had occupied Carlisle and Mechanicsburg and were also scattered over the valley.

In September of 1865, the company held a "fare" at "church." Also noted was the following act: ". . . exonerated of 50 cents conerfiet [sic] money in treasury." [sic] A bell was purchased for the engine house, and a hose carriage was purchased for $49.50. The church was perhaps not agreeable to having another fair held on their grounds, for the 1866 fair was held on James C. Baker's farm. Thereafter, reference was made to selling the small engine house and, in May 1868, to extending the bell rope to the "lower store." It should be noted that two squares were referred to, the upper of which was the intersection of Main and High Streets, and the lower of which was at Church and Main.

A reference in the 1873 minutes authorized the Treasurer to loan $750 at six percent interest, a high rate for the time. No reference is made to using a bank. Money was loaned to members, with some difficulty in collecting payments, and indications are that some were never collected.

In October 1874, the hall was rented to the Grangers. No further reference is made, so it is not known whether a Grange operated in Churchtown or if this was a one-time rental. Likewise, in February 1875, an agreement was made to rent to the fraternal group Patriotic Order Sons of America for $15.

In June 1876, arrangements were made to participate in the Centennial Parade in Carlisle. Ellen Goodyear made a flag for $4.50 plus $7.35 for the cost of bunting. At the same meeting, ground rules were set forth for those participating in the parade: ". . . any member becoming intoxicated on the 4th of July before the parade, at the parade or after the parade before the company returns home shall be fined $5 and be expelled from the company."

For whatever reason, 1879 was apparently not a productive year for the company. On February 3 (election night), the minutes read as follows: "After ransacking the stores, hotel and Post Office, 13 members of CUF Company met in their hall at 7 1/2 P.M." (!) Taxes were paid for 1879 as follows: 38 cents road tax and 95 cents state and county tax.

The minutes for June 4, 1883, note that it was time to "get wheels for ladder," while those for March 1885 relate to "looking for new engine." A new or newer Rumsey engine was acquired to replace the Bull Eye. It is not clear when this was accomplished; however, there was a reference made in May 1887 to "put bells on new engine." Later, a bill from A.W. Plank for $2 to put bells on was rejected as being an "excessive charge."

An interesting method for breaking a tie vote for director was used in 1886: ". . . meet at A. G. Burtner's store on Saturday afternoon at 2 o'clock Feb. 6, 1886, and the one who can pump the highest shall be first director". At this meeting also, loan-holder Filler was informed his note was being turned over to "Lawyer Leidigh" for collection and that he, "after not acting altogether as is required, was discharged from his office of Janitorship."

Talk was held in 1889 to repair the old engine known as "The Bull Eye." Another interesting matter occurred concerning building a bridge over the gutter in front of the engine house. Samuel Darr, Supervisor for the "upper end," agreed to furnish some old planks, but the members would have to build the bridge.

In 1897, the first mention of a bank was made. The treasurer was directed to write the First National Bank in Mechanicsburg to see if members who issued drafts had the money on deposit to cover said drafts. Apparently they did, as the next mention of banking was making a deposit in "The Bank of Carlisle" (probably the Carlisle Deposit Bank).

In March 1890, there appeared to be more interest in parading. "When we have 20 members, we get uniforms." Mention is also made of a "banquet at public house." In June 1900, $25 was given to the band. In November it was agreed to loan the band $30. However, the band was apparently shortlived as in July 1902; several members were directed to pick up instruments from members or offer to sell them to the members for ten dollars. Apparently, the band did buy caps if no other part of a uniform. At about the same time, the fire company also bought hats. The firemen must have had parade uniforms, as mention is made of care and keep of same. In 1902, overalls and leggings were purchased.

In 1908, the minute book became filled, and no further record is known of what occurred in the years that followed. There is an indication from scraps of notes found that some interest was shown in buying a motorized engine. This never happened. Considering all the verbiage used in recording the minutes, there is no specific mention of ever fighting a fire. There are, however, two references to billing people for "hire of engine." One of these persons refused to pay the $15 charge.

The most notable Churchtown fire, of which a record can be found, occurred in 1937 when two dwellings situated on Main Street near the corner of Main & High were destroyed. Fire protection service at this time was furnished by the Union of Carlisle and Washington of Mechanicsburg.

The last chapter on the Union Fire Company of Churchtown was written in the 1950s when several residents of Churchtown agreed with the Union of Carlisle to house the now antique equipment until Monroe/Churchtown had a suitable place to keep the old engine and apparatus safely. In the mid-l970s, the Monroe Fire Company attempted to regain possession of this equipment, but the Union Company did not want to return it. The Common Pleas Court Judge ruled in favor of Monroe, and the equipment is now permanently at home in the Monroe firehouse.

THE NEXT FORTY YEARS

In 1937, the owners of Williams Grove Park, Roy Richwine and Sons, along with some of Mr. Richwine's associates, formed the Williams Grove Fire Company. This company was based in the park. The engine house was a small weatherboard building that was barely large enough to house the homemade engine. The need for a fire service was necessitated not only by the park operation but also by the large number of summer cottages situated at the upper end of the grove. During the forties and fifties, with Clay Hall as Fire Chief, the company served the Williams Grove area. After the racetrack was built in 1939, it also served the track with a water truck. Water was drawn from the creek at the bridge entrance to the park. An old gasoline tanker was converted and equipped with spray arms. Water was distributed on the track to settle the ever-present dust.

In the sixties, new members revitalized the company, and it became more viable. A new firehouse was built on the racetrack side of the grounds. Initially, it housed one truck. Later, a kitchen and another bay were added. In 1977, the name of the company was changed to Monroe Fire Company. At that time, an ambulance service was added. The location of the company had two drawbacks. One was the fact that it was not centrally located within the township. The other, and sometimes a bigger problem, was flooding. In the Agnes Flood of 1972, most of the company's records were destroyed.

MONROE FIRE COMPANY TODAY

In 1985, the Township of Monroe built a new combination firehouse and multipurpose room. All equipment has been replaced since moving to the new facility located at 1225 Peffer Road just east of the village of Churchtown. The current equipment roster consists of a 1981 E-One Spartan engine, a 1997 E-One tanker, a 1992 E-One Ford minipumper, a 1995 Suburban utility van, a 1991 Chevrolet pick-up truck, a 1974 brush truck, a 16 ft. water rescue boat and a 12.5 ft. inflatable boat. Also on board are two AEDs (electronic defibrillators) for use in medical assistance calls. The Fire Company invites interested persons to stop by and see the facility and the equipment.

The Monroe Fire Company building is a designated shelter to be used in the event of disaster or other emergencies. Evacuees from the Williams Grove Trailer Court were housed here during a recent flood. During the severe snowstorm of March 1993, stranded motorists were rescued and housed until the roads were cleared.

In 1999, the Monroe Township Fire Company began running medical assistance on cardiac emergencies, became part of a multi-department wildfire strike team, and received a Life Safety Achievement Award for its fire safety and prevention programs at Monroe Elementary School and various daycare facilities.

Hands Willing to Serve: A History of the Fire Companies in Monroe Township 43

*Then and Now: Fire-Fighting Equipment of Monroe Township.
(Photographs by permission of Monroe Township Fire Company)*

CHAPTER 7

Monroe Township Churches and Cemeteries

by Jan Reynolds
based on information compiled by Jan Reynolds, Dottie Carew,
Macyle Candela, Esther Givler, Arthur Loscher, Daniel J. Heisey,
Andrew Sheely and Kevin Vanderlodge

We are fortunate to have five churches within Monroe Township, which is still mainly a rural area. The oldest church was built in 1795 and the newest congregation just started in 1988. All are of different Protestant faiths, with ministers through the decades bearing mostly German, English and Celtic surnames. This, of course, coincides with the early settlement patterns in our area.

Mt. Zion Evangelical Lutheran Church
325 Old Stone House Rd.

The oldest church is Mt. Zion Evangelical Lutheran Church, located in the center of the village of Churchtown at the intersection of Boiling Springs and Old Stone House roads. In 1790, the Lutheran and German Reformed denominations united in building a church. The adjoining cemetery lot, on one corner of the village square, was granted to the church in 1795. The earliest extant record in the church's collection is the deed dated April 18th, 1795, from Jacob and Anna Wise to "the German Lutheran and Calvin Reformed Church." The land is described as being located in "Allen Township," as Monroe Township was not yet formed. Actually, even before the first church building was erected, burials were occurring at the crossroads. The first known burial there was in 1788 and the last was in 1870, according to the monument now standing on the site. The earliest recorded church act was the baptism of Rebecca Weber on October 24th, 1795. A Communion Service is recorded as being held on July 24th, 1796, by the Reverend F. D. Shaeffer for nineteen communicants. No further records were found until 1802 when the same pastor baptized seventeen infants. Communion records show that the number of regular communicants increased steadily over the decades from 39 in 1803 to 128 in 1833. In 1849, trustees M. G. Beltzhoover, Joseph Brandt, and Enoch Young paid $150 to Jacob and Elizabeth Strock for the parcel of land on which the present church building is now located.

This brick church was built in 1849, and the Reverend A. Babb, D.D. preached the sermon at the laying of the cornerstone. The original log church building was torn down. In 1853, the two congregations (Lutheran and German Reformed) became one and changed the name of the church from "Christ's Church" to "Mt. Zion Church of Churchtown." In 1932, the Reformed congregation disbanded and withdrew its members and support. The Lutherans carried on under the name Mt. Zion Lutheran Church. A new wing was added in 1964 with facilities for fellowship and education.

Pastors who served the church have included: Rev. Benjamin Keller, 1825–1828; Rev. Charles Heyer, 1828; Rev. C. F. Sheaffer, 1831–1835; Rev. John Ulrich, 1835–1842; Rev. J. Kempfer, 1843–1847; Rev. J. N. Hoffman, 1848–1849; Rev. John Ulrich, 1849–1851; Rev. Samuel Henry, 1851–1853; Rev. John Ulrich, 1853–1854; Rev. Nitterauer 1854–1858; Rev. William Kipp, 1858–1864; Rev. Barnitz, 1864; Rev. H. R. Fleck, 1865–1871; Rev. G. F. Sheaffer, 1871–1873; Rev. D. Sell, 1873–1875; Rev. D. Beckner, 1875–1877; Rev. G. H. Slaybaugh, 1877–1881; Rev. H. R. Fleck, 1881–1889; Rev. H. D. Shimer 1899–1905; Rev. J. W. Weeter, 1905–1907; Rev. J.E. Grubb, 1908–1912; Rev. J. K. Robb, 1912–1916; Rev. P. Y. Livingston, 1916–1917; Rev. D. B. Treibley, 1918–1930; Rev. E. G. Brame, 1930–1950; Rev. Charles R. Stevens, 1950–1953. Rev. John E. Wilson, 1961–1965; Rev. William C. Jacobs, 1961–1965; Rev. Paul L. Foulk, 1965; Mr. Darwin Gearhart, 1966; Mr. Theodore A. Wachhaus, 1966–1967; Rev. Glenn T. Hafer, 1967–1971; Rev. Jered L. Hock, 1972–1977; Rev. Sarah A. Heintzelman, 1978–1991; C. Arthur Neal, Jr., 1991; William Butt, 1992; Rev. Robert Yankovitz, 1992–1998; and Rev. Kathleen G. Coleman, from 1999.

Although the original cemetery was next to the church, the present larger one is located half a mile to the west at the intersection of York and Boiling Springs roads.

Churchtown Church of God
351 Old Stone House Rd.
The Churchtown Church of God was formed in 1832 at the intersection of York Road and Old Stone House Road. It was known as Bethel Church. The present church building on Old Stone House Road, Churchtown, was built in 1849. Around 1889, the two-story building was remodeled into a one-story sanctuary. A parsonage was acquired in 1932, just north of the church, and renovations to the church were made in 1939 and 1957. Carillon bells were added in 1960 and are heard each evening at 7:15 and on Sunday mornings. 1973 saw the acquisition of seven-and-a-half acres of land to the rear of the church for future use. In 1992, a pavilion, complete with water, electricity and picnic tables, was built. In addition, a children's playground and playfield are currently in use.

Some of the more recent pastors have been Supply Pastor Clarence Miller, 1933–1958; Pastor James Snade, 1959–1964; Pastor Preston Lucas, 1964–1969; Pastor Thomas Smith, 1969–1975; Pastor Frank Demmy, 1976–1980; Pastor Yoline Conely, 1980–1984; Pa tors Mark and Patricia Rothermel, 1984–1989; Pastor Kenneth Woomer, 1990–1996; Pastor Lee Card, 1996–1998; and Pastor John Good, from 1998.

A small cemetery, Bethel Cemetery, is still located at the corner of Old Stone House Road and York Road near the site of the original church building. There are 26 headstones remaining, all but three of which are for infants or children.

Churchtown Mennonite Church
1341 Church St.
The Churchtown Mennonite Church was organized about 1830 with the earliest record stating that Henry Martin preached around 1830 in the Maple Grove schoolhouse. This schoolhouse, now converted to a residence, is still standing at the corner of Park Place and

Heisey Road. The first meeting house was erected circa 1835 on John Erb's property on Lisburn Road in South Middleton Township, with the congregation being formed out of the Slate Hill congregation. The present church building was built in 1885 on Church Street in Churchtown.

Ministers have been: John Erb, 1834–1844; Christian Herr, 1834–1865; David F. Brubaker, 1848–1851; Henry Weber, 1865–1920; Jacob M. Herr, 1871–1907; Reuben Cockley, 1907–1924; Paul Huddle, 1927–1936; Mervin J. Baer, 1951–1960; Paul M. Weaver, 1956–1975; Daniel N. Kraybill, 1967–1991; Noah D. Rudolph, 1977–1981; and John G. Brubaker, from 1981.

A cemetery is located just west of the meeting house on the congregation's lot in Churchtown.

Cumberland Valley Brethren in Christ Church
1071 York Rd.
Cumberland Valley Brethren in Christ Church was formed in 1968 and met at the Chapel building in Williams Grove Park for quite a few years. The church was formed with thirteen people, and in 1974, officially became part of the Brethren in Christ denomination. The present church at 1071 York Road, Dillsburg, was erected in 1981 and enlarged in 1988.

Pastors have been Rev. Raymond Bert, 1968–1996; Rev. John Fries, 1996–1997; and Rev. Fred Miller, from 1997.

No cemetery is connected with this church at present.

Crossroads Bible Church
1022 York Rd.
A Sunday morning teaching and preaching time by Pastor Gregory L. Sheffer at his home on Rhoda Boulevard in early 1988 was the beginning of Crossroads Bible Church. At the first meeting, there were eleven people present, including the Pastor, his wife, three children and his parents. During the autumn of 1988 the small congregation approached the members of the Knights of Pythias Lodge at 1285 High Street in Churchtown to inquire about the rental of the first-floor meeting hall for the church. An agreement was reached, and starting in October of 1988, the church met on Sunday mornings and then added Wednesday and Sunday evening meetings as the year progressed.

The church grew, and in early 1993 it was decided to purchase land in the general vicinity. The members of the church voted on purchasing approximately seven-and-a-half acres of ground at Route 74 and Locust Point Road near the York County line in October of the same year. As the church continued to grow, the decision was made to break ground and build it starting in September 1995. The congregation, along with help from many good neighbors and contractors, built a log church to fit into the rural setting. The dedication for the new facility was held in May of 1997.

Crossroads Bible Church is an independent, non-denominational Bible preaching church. The founding Pastor, Rev. Gregory L. Sheffer, is the current Pastor as the church enters the new millennium.

No cemetery is connected with this church at present.

United Brethren Church
The United Brethren Church once had a church and cemetery in Churchtown, and the cemetery still exists on Brandt Road. The

cemetery has fifty-six persons buried there, but only twenty-three headstones survive.

The church building formerly stood near the corner of Brandt and Old Stone House Roads. It was a large, rectangular brick building similar in size to the other two brick churches on Old Stone House Road and stood close to the street. Both the church and cemetery are shown in the 1858 Bridgens Cumberland County Map. The church is believed to have been torn down in October 1893 by the Reverend Hauck and a crew of local workmen for reasons not known.

SOME FAMILY CEMETERIES

Baker Cemetery is located on Lisburn Road near the corner of Old Stone House Road. It was originally associated with the Church of the Brethren of Boiling Spring. In the *Beers Cumberland County Atlas* of 1872, this lot is shown as "Dunkard Ch. Cemetery" and is also shown on the 1858 Bridgens map.

Brandt Cemetery, off of Park Place, is a family cemetery that dates back at least to 1858.

Lutztown Cemetery is another known family cemetery that exists near the historic stone house known as "Twin Springs" in Lutztown. During the nineteenth and early twentieth centuries, the cemetery was not only used for burials by the Bricker family but also by other local people, such as the Crocketts.

A cemetery survey conducted by the Cumberland County Commissioners in 1921 located the graves of Peter Bricker and H. J. Kelley on the Twin Springs property and declared them to be Revolutionary War veterans. According to the *Biographical Annals*, Peter Bricker was born in 1735 in Lancaster County and married Mary Barr. Bricker's father, also Peter Bricker, came to Lancaster County from Switzerland ca. 1711. The published *Pennsylvania Archives*, Series V, reveals that Peter Bricker served in the third Battalion of the Cumberland County Militia, eighth Company, in March and April of 1781. Kelley was listed in the Cumberland County Militia, fifth Company, fifth Battalion.

Toward the middle of the twentieth century, the cemetery became neglected, and the headstones were removed.

CHAPTER 8

The Houses of Churchtown

by Kevin Vanderlodge and Sharon Nelson

Many of the architectural descriptions of houses and outbuildings found in this book were written based on external observations only from the 1990s, coupled with data from county tax records about how the buildings were classified in the early years of their existence.

Unfortunately, early tax assessors were not always clear in the way they described buildings. Log houses, which have, in actuality, been standing strong for nearly two hundred years now, were at first categorized in the tax lists as "log" but later as "frame," presumably because they'd been sided over and because "frame" was perhaps considered a less primitive designation by a socially conscious, technologically evolving populace—especially when true frame houses came into vogue.

Even the term "log" was used indiscriminately in the county records. In some cases, it referred to houses that were truly made of hand-hewn, square-cut logs, notched together in the popular vee-notch method or fitted into corner posts. In others, it was used—probably for lack of a more specific category—to describe half-timbered houses. Half-timbered buildings are constructed of square-cut wooden beams held together by wooden pegs in a mortise-and-tenon fashion. Most of the beams in the outer walls form tall rectangular compartments, sometimes braced diagonally by shorter beams. The spaces in between are, at least in this locality, stuffed with unmortared bricks, which are not weight-bearing but serve as filler and insulation. The wooden beams are a bit more slender than true logs, resulting in external walls that may be noticeably thicker than those of frame houses but not quite so substantial as those found in many log homes.

Unfortunately, without indiscriminately tearing walls apart, this raises questions about the construction of old Churchtown houses that were taxed as "frame" and "log." Are they really log, or are they half-timbered? Are they truly framed, having completely replaced earlier non-frame structures? Or are they just-sided-over, added-onto versions of log or half-timbered buildings that remain "hidden" underneath?

Kevin Vanderlodge did the best he could to address these issues in the time that he had available. But if you live (or have lived) in a Churchtown house and notice a discrepancy between the verbiage in this book and what you've personally observed inside the building, *please consider letting us know*. We'd love to discover more "hidden" log and half-timbered homes in the village, and we would also like to keep future editions of this book correct in terms of the way that houses are described and the way that historical data is interpreted.

Contact the Monroe Township Municipal Office to see who's currently involved in documenting the history and architecture of the township.

The Houses of Churchtown

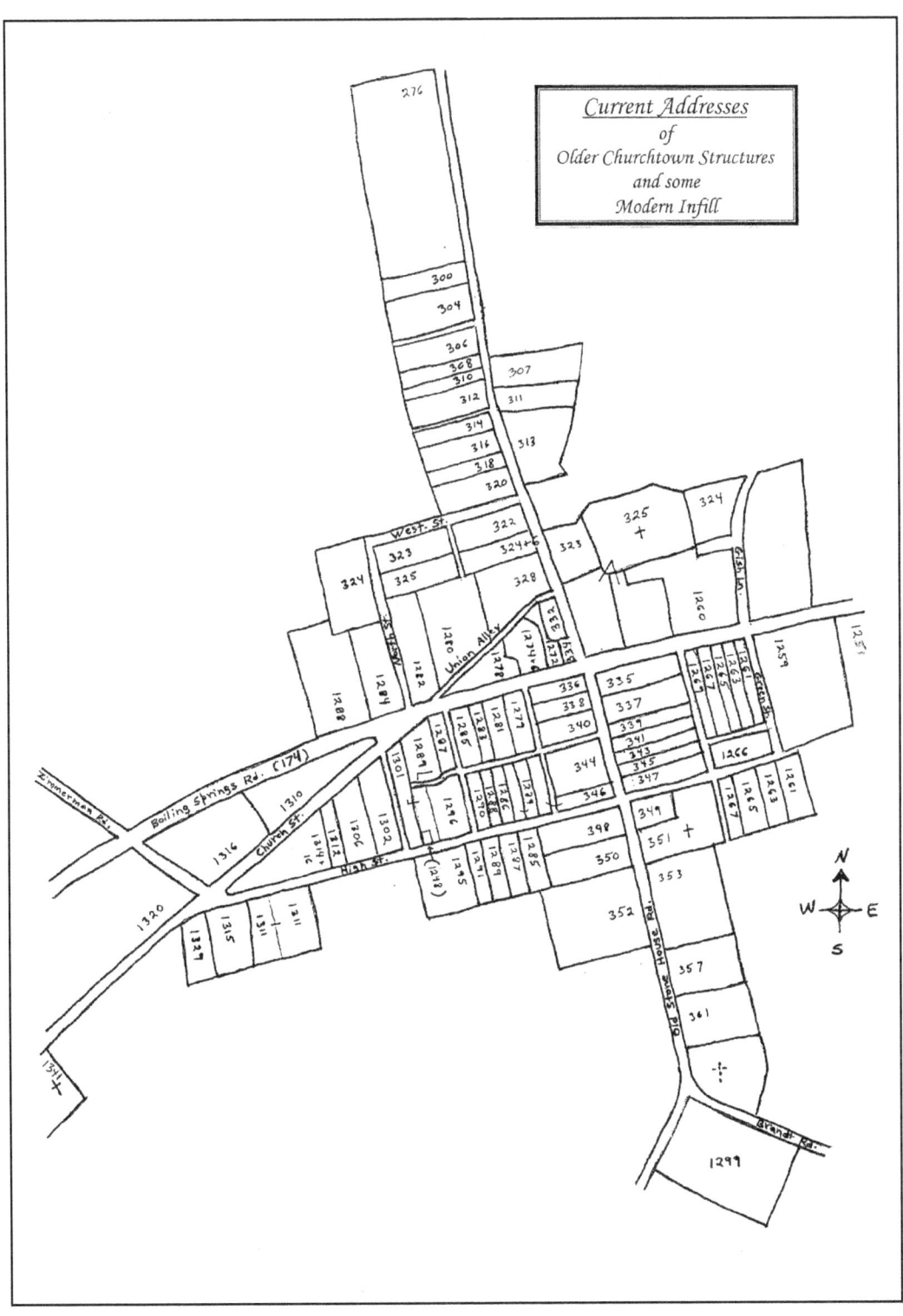

Current Addresses of Older Churchtown Structures and some Modern Infill

50   A HISTORY OF MONROE TOWNSHIP

Churchtown Business Notices

Brindle George...Resident, cor Main and High sts
Brindle Willis H...Farmer and Stock Grower, Church st
Bowman Henry...Insurance Agent for Allen and E. Pennsborough Co., cor of Church and Greene sts
Burtnett James...Mail Contractor, High st
Cook J. W...Agent for Cobbin's Domestic Bible
Diller P. A...Iron, Stove and Hardware Merchant. Also, manufr of Tin Ware, Church st
Drager Conrad...Tailor, cor Main and North sts
Dill John O...Farmer and Stock Grower, Main st
Enck Levi...Butcher and Dealer in Meat, cor Church and Green sts
Farnbaugh Joseph...Farmer and Stock Grower, Church st
Gates Levi...Manufr of Saddles and all kinds of Harnesses, Church st
Goodyear Frederick...Dealer in Stock and Butcher, Church st
Herman G. T. B...Dealer in Dry Goods, Groceries, Queensware, Hats, Caps, Boots, Shoes and Coal Mdse, cor Main and Church sts
Hoffman C. L...Cooper, High st
Kean Thomas...Laborer, Main st
Lenher L. H...Physician and Surgeon, Main st
Landis H. W...Dealer in Fruit and Ornamental Trees, Main st
Lahman Samuel...Inspector of Election, cor of North and West sts
Menear F. C...Dealer in Lime, Main st
Meashey John...Carpenter, Joiner and Undertaker, Main st
Plank Samuel...Dealer in Grain, cor Main and High sts
Plank John...Dealer in Dry Goods, Groceries, Queensware, Hats, Caps, Boots, Shoes, Patent Medicines, and General Merchandise, cor Main and Church sts
Plank A. W...Manufr of and Dealer in Tin Ware and Grain, Church st
Paul John...Resident Farmer, cor Main and High sts
Rinehart Jesse...Blacksmith, Horse Shoer, Wagon Ironer. All kinds of Repairing at short notice, High st
Shroad S. J...Resident Farmer, Main st
Wonders Daniel...Dealer in Stock and Butcher, Main st

Churchtown, 1872, from the Atlas of Cumberland County, Pennsylvania.
From actual surveys by and under the direction of F.W. Beers,
(Monroe Township Historical Society collection, poster adaptation, 1994)

GENERAL HISTORY OF CHURCHTOWN

In the early half of the 1700s, Monroe Township was still Indian land. The Shawnee held tenuous claim to it with a group of sixty families who had come up from Florida in about 1689. They settled just to the north of the township with seasonal encampments along the Yellow Breeches. Several tracts traversed the forests that surround the township—the Allegheny to the north and another to the south—but there are no known trails within the township.

A vacuum was created by the departure of the Shawnee to Ohio in 1727. A few braves had raided a neighboring tribe that was under the protection of the powerful Six Nations, and so most of the Shawnees fled. Three years later the Scots-Irish began their invasion (nature abhors a vacuum) into Cumberland County. A survey was made through Monroe Township in 1732 with a north-south line established just to the east of the future village of Churchtown. East of that line was the Manor of Paxton. This was a 7,551-acre tract set aside for the use of the Shawnee, whom the Proprietary government was hoping to lure back from Ohio and French influence. But the Shawnee had no desire to return. In 1765 and 1767, this tract was resurveyed into 28 lots and sold off.

One of the first warrants west of the Manor was taken out by Adam Steel for 233 acres in 1746. It extended from a point south of the Yellow Breeches to an area just north of present Route 174. Adam Steel died intestate and the warrant passed to his sons William and Richard. They sold this land to William and Robert Hamersley in 1763. Robert sold his half-share to William in 1765. By this time, other warrants were being taken out surrounding this tract. This was a period of transition for Cumberland County. The early warrantees of Monroe Township bore Scots-Irish names like Duffield, Peters, Hamersley and Scott. But in the 1770s came an influx of Germans from the eastern counties who were reminded of their homeland. The Scots-Irish were true pioneers; the unexplored valley over the next mountain range continually called out to them. They blazed new trails, and when they felt hemmed in, they moved further into the interior. The Germans came behind them, improved the land and settled it. For many years, there was friction between the two groups; not until the 1820s and 1830s did the tensions finally subside. These are merely trends in Pennsylvania migration patterns. In Monroe Township (part of the larger Allen Township prior to 1825), many Scots-Irish stayed behind and married into the newly arrived German families. One found a spouse where one could.

Jacob Wise (also spelled Weiss, Wire) came in 1771. A 21-year-old tailor from Cumru Township, Berks County, he was the son of George Michael Wise (who later migrated here) and the brother of John and Felix, both of whom took out warrants for land in Monroe Township. What is confusing is that there were two Jacobs in the area at the same time, living almost side by side. Jacob, whose wife was Mary, is the man we are concerned with. In 1785 Jacob bought the Steel tract from William Hamersley, this land being contiguous to the warrant taken out by his brother John Weis for 50 acres in 1776.

In 1772, the road from York to Sterret's Gap was laid out through the northwest corner of the 58-acre patent. Along this road a church had been built in 1790 for the united congregation of the Lutheran and Calvinist members. This log church was on the present-day site of the Mt. Zion Lutheran Church, on the Churchtown square. In 1795, Jacob deeded half an acre from the Steel tract for a burying ground. Seven years later, now 52 years old, he began selling off some of his land. Seven acres of the 50-acre tract went to Peter Bricker, while Peter also bought 45 acres from the Steel warrant.

In 1804 (according to local tradition), Jacob built the first house within the boundary of today's village. The original structure at #344 Old Stone House Road is log (with a much later frame addition), and one of the outbuildings built was a blacksmith shop since Jacob, Jr. was a smithy.

In 1805, Jacob was one of four farmers who each donated half an acre for the school lot also on the square. The others were Hartman Morrett, Jacob Kenaur and Jost Strock. A new school was built that year to replace an earlier one built on the same site in 1779. This lot lies along Route 174, and a much later schoolhouse now occupies the same site.

The area around Jacob's new house was sparsely settled, with much of the land still in timber. Between 1804 and 1812, a second log house was built on the other side of Sterret's Gap road. Since Jacob had ten children, this may have been for one of them. In 1812, his daughter, Rebecca, married William Line, the village teacher, and they began construction of the third house also made of logs. The address is now #352 Old Stone House Road. The log house was raised in two days with a community "house raisin'." It took two days to build because most of the time was spent playing "long bullets," a popular game at the time. The object was to throw a three quarter pound bullet the longest distance. A lot of time was spent retrieving bullets instead of notching logs.

Churchtown developed very slowly. When Jacob Sr. died in 1817, most of his land had been sold off. In 1814, the tract around the house, 6 acres and 36 perches, was sold to Jacob, Jr., who immediately sold it to his brother-in-law William Line. In 1815, William sold this tract off in lots. Four acres, including the house, went to Rudolph and David Krysher, who deeded it the next year to Abraham Paul. One acre and 36 perches went to Ferdinand Edelblutes and a half acre each to Peter Livinger and Rudolph Krysher. In the 1817 tax assessment there were only four houses listed.

How Churchtown got its name has been lost over time. In the 1790s and for many years afterward, the only prominent features on Sterret's Gap road in this area were the church and school. In 1812, it was known as a village with no name. The first document found to date which lists Churchtown by name is a January 1822 license for a tavern. Sometime prior to 1850, the name was changed by the post office to Allen because of confusion with the Churchtown in Lancaster County.

Another possibility for the name of Churchtown lies with the origin of the Diller Family. Casper Diller bought 313 acres just to the west of Churchtown, much of the land straddling Route 74, the old York Road. This was the Culbertson warrant that Casper bought in 1785. His family lived in Churchtown for generations, his daughters marrying into most of the old township families. Casper came from Churchtown, Lancaster

County. There may have been others from there as well. He was a wealthy landowner and may have had something to do with naming the village.

There was considerable movement of people from the eastern counties through this area. By 1828, three stores had opened, all on Sterret's Gap Road (Route 174). Sam Hyer had a two-story brick house, a frame warehouse and a large summer kitchen on his lot south of Old Stone House Road. Adam Stonesberger, across the Gap Road, had a two-story log house, a blacksmith shop and a tanyard. To the east of Hyer, he also had a two-story brick store that he rented out to brothers Robert and David Sturgeon. The other merchant in the village was David Krysher. He was renting a store at the southeast intersection of the Gap Road and Old Stone House. This corner was a store of one sort or another until operations ceased about twenty-five years ago.

In 1822, Abraham Paul received his tavern license, though he may have run it as a tavern or tippling house even earlier. Two economic factors influenced his desire for a license, as well as his development of lots in Churchtown. One was the incredible number of 'movers' passing through. The lands in the eastern counties were losing their fertility and a number of younger sons were finding their inherited plots too small to eke out a living on. With the availability of cheap land west of the Susquehanna all the way through to Ohio and Indiana, literally thousands of people were heading west, and it was not infrequent for a farmer or gentleman to double as a landlord or tavern keeper.

Secondly, the American economy had plummeted after the War of 1812 and it was not until the mid-twenties that the levels of prosperity reached pre-war levels. It is not a coincidence that the growth of Churchtown mirrored the economic growth spurts of Cumberland County. When, in 1830, Peter Livinger put some of his land into lots, he found ready buyers. All fourteen lots offered were sold, and new houses were built immediately.

But Paul had to fight to get his tavern license. There has been a tradition that the log house he bought and ran as a tavern #344 Old Stone House Rd. had been a tavern for a number of years, run by Jacob Wise. Tavern keepers had to get a yearly license. These records have been checked from 1804 through 1822, and none issued to Wise has been found. Of course, he could have operated without a license. When Paul applied for a license, he stated that he "lives in Church Town, on the road leading from Middlesex to York (i.e. Old Stone House). There is no tavern in that town, and the road is very much traveled—no tavern in the neighborhood on that road—from its junction with the Harrisburg Road till Moore's tavern, upwards of 16 miles. Churchtown is the only town in the township—the meetings must be held there—there is a store in the town kept by Samuel Hyer—and a blacksmith shop (run by Adam Stonesberger)—but no tavern."

Paul was a weaver, but he claimed bad health prevented him from working his trade. He may not have told the whole truth on his application. The Lutheran and Calvin church also submitted a petition to try and stop Paul and another man from getting a license. They claimed that there were four taverns within one to two miles of Churchtown, and two more would have "serious and immoral consequences to the young men of

Churchtown." One of the four taverns has been identified. It was the "Sign of the Spread Eagle" and had been run by Martin Brandt on the York Road about a mile south of town. The petition got about a dozen signatures, the more noteworthy being Jacob Kenower, Sr. and Jr. (Jacob, Jr. was the son-in-law of Jacob Wise, Sr.), Mathias Young, George Belshoover, Michael Morrett and Jacob Wise, Jr. It was all to no avail, as Paul was granted a license that year and subsequent years.

Within the present boundaries of Monroe Township, there have not been many prominent persons who could claim some sort of connection with the village. Just southwest of the Steel warrant lived the Crockett family in the last decades of the 1700s. Here lived George, James, William and John. It was John who moved to Tennessee, where his famous son Davy Crockett was reared.

Jacob Ritner, the son of future Governor Joseph Ritner, bought one of the Livinger lots in 1830 and built a house before moving on. Lastly, there was Jacob Plank and his family. Jacob was the inventor of the Plank Plow, and his son Sam invented the Plank Shifting Beam Plow. Except for these few, Churchtown can claim no famous sons or daughters.

In 1833, Churchtown became the center of quite a religious stir. Dr. John Zollinger, from Carlisle, started a denomination with its roots in the village. Here, he preached his first sermon, and soon, he was traveling throughout the township and adjacent territory, spreading his message. That same year, a church was built along the road from Carlisle to York. His teaching resembled Quakerism. He preached that the Holy Spirit was directly approachable and could intervene in human affairs upon request. There was no church hierarchy, no ministers and no creed except the Bible. The sect got quite a lot of opposition from the more traditional denominations, but it flourished for quite a while until it finally became obscure.

Throughout the 1830s, Churchtown continued to attract new settlers. By 1838, there were about 25 houses within the village, and this stayed about the same until the mid-1840s when Churchtown experienced another spurt in growth and the importance of the village as an economic center seemed assured. There were over 65 families and a population of about 240. This was to double in the next twenty years.

When the war came in 1861 Henry Zinn, a schoolteacher living in the village, raised a company which became Company H, 7th Pennsylvania Reserves. They were mustered on May 28, and Zinn became their captain. Other Churchtown men in this company were Henry Filler, Henry Goodyear, and David Plank. Theirs was a three-month regiment, and they were shipped to Washington, D.C., via Baltimore. When they got to the Maryland state line, they were ordered from the trains and told to load their muskets. They marched through Baltimore; trouble was anticipated from the local inhabitants. The company mustered out in August, and those signing on to continue their service became the 36th Pennsylvania Regiment. Zinn resigned his captaincy in November 1861, but the regiment went on to fight at Gaines Mills, Bull Run, Antietam, Fredericksburg and The Wilderness, where most of the company was captured.

There were other regiments in which contingents of Churchtown men served, but most of these saw little real action, the 130th Pennsylvania Infantry being the exception.

These were Company F, 101st; Company F, 130th, led by Colonel Zinn until he died at Fredericksburg on December 13, 1862; Company A, 158th; Company I, 195th, and Companies A, B, & D, 20th Pennsylvania Cavalry. All together about 30 men living in Churchtown when the war broke out served.

Life in Churchtown has always typified that of any working-class village: full of neighborhood brawls, gossip, scandals and the minor dramas that fill one's life. Perhaps the most fun and excitement that the villagers ever had was in June 1863 when a few scouts from the Confederate army passed through the streets on their way to Mechanicsburg; it was their job to find any evidence of the Union army's advance. The approach of the rebels, which had been known some days in advance, caused quite a commotion among the residents, many of whom took considerable time and effort to move their livestock and hide their valuables. It was all over before anything had actually begun, and by the time the fainthearted had overcome their embarrassment, life returned to its everyday normalcy.

During the war there was initiated an income tax for those who earned over $600 per year. They were taxed at three percent on every dollar over that amount. This gives us a list of the wealthiest people in Churchtown at that time. They were George Brindle, $3,068; Moses Bricker, $2,136; Sam Diller, $2,100; Dr. Lenher, $1665; Henry Greybill, $1,400; Sam Plank, $1,350 and David Neisley, $1,340. All the other men earned less than $600.

Post-Civil War years produced another economic spurt in Cumberland County and the opening of additional lots to the north of town. But the death knell had already been sounded for Churchtown, though no one had heard it. The only railroad in the township, the Dillsburg and Mechanicsburg Railroad, ran well to the south of the village, ending any chance that new life would be infused into Churchtown as a railroad depot. The village slowly became a backwater, and between 1875 and 1900, most businesses either closed or moved to a more lucrative area. Churchtown was also affected by the explosion of the Machine Age in the waning years of the nineteenth century. Many of the small craftsmen became obsolete, and as their trades became extinct, these men became day laborers, forced to work for another man for their livelihood. As better roads and transport came to Churchtown, the men and women sought better-paying jobs in the bigger towns of Carlisle, Mechanicsburg and Harrisburg. They took the trolley, train or their new cars to their place of employment, returning each night to Churchtown. The village soon became a bedroom community for the Harrisburg metropolitan area and the West Shore, which it has remained to this day.

One business did find its way to Churchtown in 1902. A hosiery mill was built along an alley between Church and High Streets, and for eight years, it employed up to 30 women and girls. A trolley line had been built through Churchtown in 1901, which gave access for girls on outlying farms to come to the village to work. But the boom was short-lived, and nothing remains on the site.

Churchtown, about 1900, was quite a picturesque little village. Main Street (Old Stonehouse Road), running north-south through the village, rose to a slight hill. The whole way along the street, the homes were a mixture of frame and brick, all two stories high. The sidewalks ran all the way up to High

Street and were brick, not concrete like today. Each sidewalk was stepped to accommodate the slope, and at each step was a gaslight. Horse troughs lined both sides, and trees gracefully arched their branches over the road. In front of the village well and some homes were benches where the folks gathered during the day and evenings. All that is gone, and what remains is a caricature of a former sereneness. Now, cars and trucks noisily speed their way along Route 174 through the village and the only strangers who have recently stopped awhile to chat with the locals were the hikers along the Appalachian Trail, which followed Old Stone House through the village. Even that is now gone. The Machine Age has been hard for Churchtown.

THE INDIVIDUAL PROPERTIES

This tour starts at the intersection of Old Stone House Road and High Street, looking east. In 1830, the land in front of you was owned by Peter Livinger. That year Jacob Horting built the first log house along here at the eastern end of High Street, on the left, which was then just a wagon track. The land to your left, along Old Stone House, was developed into lots in 1830. The big brick house to your right was built in 1843 for Dr. John Ahl.

(Unless otherwise noted with a "(2007)", these photos were taken during the 1990s, around the same time as the first edition of this book was written.)

1266 High Street

Walk east along High Street until you get to Locust Alley. High Street (until very recently just called "the alley") from here to the eastern end was opened in 1843, the year after John Ahl bought a two-acre tract from Peter Livinger. Ahl's tract went from Old Stone House to the end of High Street, being all the lots on your right. In 1830, Peter Livinger sold the lot at the northeast corner of High and Locust to Jacob Horting. It was 160' by 42'. Probably that same year, he built a log house that once stood at the end of High Street facing Green Street. The Horting family was poor. In 1835, when the county assessors made a list of poor children in the township, his two children were the only ones listed for Churchtown. A daughter, Sarah, died here in 1831 at the age of six.

Most of the owners of this house no longer standing at the corner of High and Green Streets were tradesmen. About 1834, a shop was built on the lot; it was used by Ben Correll (1836–1839), Eli Smith (1829–1840), Michael Fissel (1840–1844, a coachmaker, and George Keesaman (1844–1850), a butcher. While living here, George Keesaman's first wife, Mary Morrett, died in 1848. He wasted no time getting remarried. The first child by his second wife, born here in December 1848, died exactly 2 years later. Keesaman also served as an inspector of elections in 1845 and as a school director in 1848. These were locally elected positions.

In 1850, Keesaman sold this lot to Daniel Stees, who then sold it to Ross Anderson. Anderson was a tailor who had been renting on Boiling Springs Road prior to moving here and was a brother to Richard, a village blacksmith. Ross was taxed for a one-story log house in 1856 and 1859; in 1862, it was described as being very small. As early as 1859, he was an invalid, and the 1865 tax records call him sickly. By 1874 he was crippled and mostly bedridden. After he died (1874–1876), his widow Margaret (1820–1891) continued to live here. One son, William, was a barber who lived just across the street at the Jonas Wagner house. William was a Civil War vet who served for much of the war. He enlisted as a musician in Company A, 20th Pennsylvania Cavalry, and during his first term, his horse fell on him and injured his spine. When his enlistment was up, he ignored the pain he was in because his parents were poor and needed the $300 bounty money. He seems to have been a dutiful son. When he returned home in the fall of 1865 he moved back in here with his parents and lived with them until his marriage in 1879. He tried to earn a living as a day laborer but could not do any hard work because of his injury. Dr. Lenher treated him until 1870, but without and knowledge of chiropractics, there was little that could be done. From 1867–1870 William did some carpentry, then gave that up and became a barber. He was 5'8" and about 160 pounds.

After Margaret Anderson's death, the log house along Green Street was rented out. One tenant was Simon Richwine, who will be mentioned later. Simon never married, and although he had family in the village, he was unable to live with them. The story goes that his sister Lizzie (who lived at #1269 Boiling Springs Rd.) was very neat and clean, but Simon couldn't live by her standards, so he lived alone. The house was torn down prior to 1898. In 1935, the land was sold for $5 to Bessie Shugart for back taxes from 1925 to 1934.

In 1851, Anderson sold part of his lot, measuring 72' by 42', to James Burnett. It is possible that the building now converted into a house—near the corner of High Street and Locust Alley—was the shop that had

1266 High St.

been built behind the old log house. Burnett, a teamster and later the village mail carrier (1870), had just sold his new house at #1282 High Street before buying this building. He lived here for many years. He was the township constable in 1848, 1853 and 1854. (In 1853, Burnett beat Dr. Ahl for the constable position. Ahl may have had the last laugh. Three years later, he was elected to the House of Representatives.) After Burnett's first wife died, he married Catherine Morrett, widow of Joseph Morrett. By 1870, he was renting the house; his tenant was Joseph Gilbert, a painter. In 1872, Burnett sold the house to Moses Bricker, who sold it back to Burnett in 1874 for $600. Burnett, now a widower, sold the house to Mary Goodyear, the wife of Peter A., for $300 in 1881. Mary died in 1903, and her heirs sold the house to Martha Baker for $260 in 1904. Martha lived here until she sold it to Bessie Shugart in 1928. Bessie later bought the adjoining lot to the right.

This building is a one-and-a-half-story brick-encased log structure with an exposed common bond brick façade on the first story. The three-bay building has a gabled roof, is covered with corrugated metal, and is mostly sided with aluminum. The first-story windows are 1/1 and crowned with lintels, while the eyebrow windows of the upper half story have modern sliding panes. The entrance has a small front stoop, and a one-story wing extends from the rear of the structure. Outbuildings include a wooden outhouse and garage.

As you walked down High Street, off to your right, you may have noticed a group of outbuildings, four in a row. The white one was, until the 1940s, here at the intersection of Locust Alley, on the lot behind the church. It was used as a creamery where local farmers brought their milk to be processed. John Hoerner operated it around 1900, though it seems to have been out of business in 1915. Hoerner lived in the brick house next to the church.

On your right are the six lots sold by Dr. Ahl between 1843 and 1846. They were all sold with the understanding that the fence, which ran along the back of the lots and fronted an alley, would be maintained. This alley formed the boundary between the village and the neighboring farm, and traces of the alley remain. All the lots had stables in the rear, which gave access to the lot. Of these six lots, five had houses built on them in the 1840s, though the house between 1263 and 1265 High Street no longer remains.

1267 High Street

This house, the western half of a duplex comprising #1265 and #1267 High Street, was built prior to 1850. Earlier deeds were not recorded. In 1854, George Keesaman, who had lived across the street, assigned the house to Richard Anderson to pay off his debts. His major creditors were Richard Anderson, Stees, Brandt and Strock, and Dan Stees. In 1855 the house was sold at a sheriff sale to J. Strock

1267 High St.

and John Brandt, who sold it in 1857 to Adam Freese (1831–1881). George also owned a shop. In 1856, the goods in the shop were auctioned off, and then the outbuilding was sold for $666. Personal possessions were also put on the block; sold were his wagon and sulky. After everything was sold, there was $1,583 and his creditors got $.47 on the dollar.

Adam Freese, from Massachusetts, was a teacher from 1853 to 1867, as was his neighbor three doors up, Charles Ringwalt. The recessed door on the right side of the house would indicate that perhaps two families lived here. Census records bear this out. In 1860, Ben Shatto and his family lived here. Ben had just bought a lot on North Street and was in the process of having a house built. In 1867, Adam sold the house to Susan Richwine, who had lived with Rudolph Krysher and his family for a number of years. Susan (1815–1888) lived with Thomas Kane, a laborer, for a long time. She boarded with him in several houses in Churchtown. In 1860, the earliest mention of them together, they were with Krysher. Perhaps it was a common-law marriage, but it was a friendship that lasted many years. In 1870, their boarder was John Booth, a carpenter, his wife and his baby son. It must have been interesting as Booth was a native of North Carolina, and the war had just ended five years ago. After Susan died in 1888, the house was sold at a public auction to Christian Baker.

Baker sold it to Margaret Westfall that same year for $350. Margaret rented the house to her daughter Emma Trostle, and before Margaret died in 1914, the house was willed to Emma's children.

Emanuel Trostle (1859–1929) and his wife Emma (nee Westfall, 1865–1945) lived here from 1888 until she died. Their eight-year-old daughter Margaret was killed on Tuesday, October 11, 1910. She was on her way to school that morning, and she and some friends were playing "sling," also known as "crack the whip." She was the end of the whip and was flung out into the path of the trolley run by the Valley Traction Company. There were some wet leaves on the track that day and the driver was unable to stop in time. Two other girls were nearly injured as well, hitting the side of the trolley. For years afterward, Emma never changed Margaret's bedroom; it remained the same as it was the day she died.

Mrs. Trostle was also the only pow-wower in the village at that time. Many are the children still alive whose parents brought them here to be "tried" for. She could stop blood and pain and relieve epilepsy.

This half of the duplex, being a three-bay, two-and-a-half-story, side hall house, is covered with vinyl siding. A kitchen extends to the right side, rather than to the rear of the structure, and has recently had its pent roof raised to accommodate a modern bathroom on the second floor. Its gable roof is covered with corrugated metal, and like #1265 (the other half of the duplex), the first-floor windows are 1/1 while those on the second floor are 6/6. The front entrance is ornamented with a five-pane transom and three-pane sidelights. The chimney of this dwelling protrudes through the roof between the two units. Interior integrity is poor due to extensive renovation, but the original pegged board construction is still visible in some areas. This house is said to have been haunted. Residents report having heard sounds of a young girl crying to her father coming from the crawl space that formerly existed above the kitchen. The door to this crawl space had a deadbolt on the outside. When the area was remodeled into the current second-floor bathroom, the crying stopped. Perhaps the child was Margaret.

1265 High Street

Originally, a log house was built on this lot. After selling his house across the road to George Keesaman in 1844, Michael Fissel (1815–1854) bought this lot from John Ahl in 1844 for $100. In 1847, he was assessed for a log house and shop. In 1850, he had a three-story log house and a two-story frame shop. The shop was on Old Stone House, next to #340. Michael, a coachmaker, was the township clerk from 1846 until 1851. In 1850, he sold this house to Henry Spahr for $600. Spahr gave his occupation as a speculator; in 1866, he was a produce broker. In 1849, he had been the township constable. In 1856 and 1859, Spahr was taxed for a two-story log house, but in 1862, he appeared on the tax list with a two-story frame. A common nomenclature change for a-sided log homes, "frame" had become a more fashionable term, although the sturdy, underlying log structures remained. This property remained in the Spahr family until 1910. One of the last craftsmen in the village lived here. He was Harvey Baker (1873–1947), who bought the house in 1910. In the summer, Harvey painted houses, but in the winter, he made and sold brooms in his basement until 1947.

A few lawsuits concerning Churchtown inhabitants were quite trivial, and in 1871, Henry Spahr's wife Anna and their 17-year-old son Milton were involved in one of them. In June of that year, the owner of the neighboring house (no longer standing), Jonas Wagner, accused them of stealing three quarts of cherries worth $1. Considering that a dollar was worth about a day's pay, that prices the cherries at $30 a quart in modern dollars. Jonas went to Peter A. Diller, the Justice of the Peace and filed a warrant, which was given to the constable, Joseph Darr. The case was heard in August, and James Burnett, Peter Baker, William Anderson and Levi Enck all had to take off work for the day to testify. Anna and Milton were found not guilty in a case that should never have gone to trial. (An interesting note about Joseph Darr—as constable, he was required to collect the county taxes as well. Three years later, he was arrested for embezzling $900 in taxes collected in 1871.)

In 1880, Spahr's daughter, Mary Ann, then 24, was a schoolteacher. When Henry died in 1910, he left everything to his wife, Anna, who sold the house and moved to Carlisle, where she died in 1918.

This three-bay, semi-detached house shares a wall with #1267. It is a two-and-a-half-story rectangular structure with side hall construction and a one-story extension in the rear. The exterior is currently covered with asbestos siding. The windows are evenly spaced, 6/6 on the second story and 1/1 on the first story.

1265 High St.

The gable roof is covered with corrugated metal, and a six-pane attic light is offset to accommodate the centered side chimney. The basement level is exposed in front as the yard slopes down to meet the street, and an enclosed cinderblock base now supports the 3-bay front porch with carved wooden railings on the first story.

Between #1265 and #1263 there once stood a house that was razed in 1915. Deeds for the property were not fully recorded. Henry Kline bought the lot from Ahl in about 1843. As early as 1847 a one-and-a-half-story frame house had been built, owned by Adam Whitcomb (1790–1868). He lived here until 1868. All of Whitcomb's children were in Ohio, so John Paul was the attorney who settled the estate. He sold the house to Jonas Wagner in 1868, and he rented the house to William Anderson, the barber, and his new bride, Susan Aulthouse, in 1879.

During his five years here, William's health deteriorated. He developed spinal meningitis, and his old war injury caused him to develop a constant head shaking and twitching of the arms. These were serious problems for a barber and his clientele dropped off as patrons feared for their safety with Anderson holding a razor.

Even buying a fancy barber chair in 1882 did not help. Dr. Hartzell treated him, but nothing could be done. In a medical report on Anderson's condition, it was stated that if he closed his eyes, he was unable to turn around, and if they were bandaged, he often fell forward.

Anderson found himself in hot water in the fall of 1884. The hotel on the town hill had been broken into on October 13, and the wife of the innkeeper, Thompson Reighter, swore that she saw Anderson and one other man prowling around outside. The next morning, they found where the pair of shutters had been tampered with. The arrest warrant was given to A.W. Plank, a Justice of the Peace who lived at #340 Old Stone House. Plank had Anderson arrested, and Levi Enck put up his bail. The case went to court in November, and Anderson was found not guilty. Shortly after this, Anderson moved to Dillsburg.

After Wagner died, his wife Mary sold the house to James Cook in 1910, who sold it to Joseph Gensler. Gensler sold it to Harvey Baker in 1915 for $85. The house was falling down, and Baker soon had it razed.

1263 High Street
This lot was sold to John Leidig in 1843 for $100. That same year, he built a brick home and sold it the following year to Mary Young for $450. John was a coachmaker, as was his neighbor at the time, Michael Fissel. Mary Young married Charles Ringwalt a few years later and, for many years, was a teacher. Mary (1804–1893) was the daughter of Mathias Young, who owned a large homestead west of the village. She inherited her father's house upon he died in 1839 but sold it to Anna

1263 High St.

Spahr and Hannah Eslinger. Her two sisters, Margaret and Sarah, never married and lived on Boiling Springs Road for many years. Another sister, Catherine, married Michael Morrett, Sr. and lived on a farm whose property was the field at the east end of High Street.

Here, the Ringwalts lived the rest of their lives. The lot to the west of the house was bought by Mary Young in 1844 and has never had any large structure built on it. Charles Ringwalt (1806–1887) was a teacher during most of the 1850s. His family, like a couple of others, came from Churchtown, Lancaster County. A long-time teacher, in later years, he became a day laborer, and about 1876, a mail carrier. He and Mary lived alone, having never had any children. Charles filled two local political offices. He was a constable from 1847 to 1849 and the township clerk for the years 1852 to 1854 and 1857 to 1858. George Enck was the executor for Mary Ringwalt, and in 1893, he sold the house to Ransome Babcock. Babcock died here the next year, and in 1896, his widow Myra sold it to Adam Hollinger for $435.

This is a common bond brick home, two rooms over two rooms, painted white with slate shingles that still cover the front face of the gable roof. The house is two-and-a-half stories high and three bays wide, with evenly spaced 6/6 windows and a centered door with transom. Windows are topped with lintels, and modern louvered shutters replace the original ones. The wooden cornice is ornamented with flattened triangular dentils. There are two interior chimneys, one at each end of the roof. A two-story rear wing extends from the back of the house. The center staircase, which formerly existed in the front of the house, has been removed, and the winding back stair from the kitchen is now used to access the second story.

1261 High Street

This lot was not sold until 1846, and by then, it already had a house on it. Levi Beelman, a chairmaker, bought it from Ahl for $550. In 1844, Ahl was assessed for only a two-story brick house, the one at the head of High Street; therefore, this house was built between 1844 and 1846. Beelman lived here only a year when he sold it to Elizabeth Miller for $535. She died in Indiana, and her administrator, John Murphy, sold it to Elizabeth Pipher and Hannah Shopp in 1856. Elizabeth was the widow of John Pipher, who had lived on a nine-acre farm at 1320 Church Street. When he died in 1846, and the heirs sold the property in 1856, Elizabeth bought this one. Here, she lived with her unmarried daughter, Elizabeth, and Harold Strock until she died in 1864 at the age of 73. In 1865, Elizabeth and Hannah sold the house to Rebecca Black, a widow living on Old Stone House Road. In 1870, the tenant was Frank Givler, a miller. He had a wife and five children living in this small house. Rebecca sold it to Joseph Gilbert, a painter, in 1876. He had been renting the

1261 High St.

house across the street. Sam Bishop, a Civil War veteran, bought it in 1880. He sold it to Fred Myers in 1884 and bought it back in 1885. Bishop lived in Mechanicsburg, and after he died in 1897, the heirs sold it to Margaret Miller in 1900 for $200.

The older men in the village remember Grant Miller, who lived here for years with his mother Margaret and her brother Frazier. Grant was an eccentric old man, the grandson of Peter S. Miller, who had a farm to the north of Gish Lane. Grant's yard here was always filled with old junk strewn everywhere. Every Halloween the local boys would sneak in here and find some large objects to spirit out and deposit somewhere in the village. The village kids also like to taunt old Grant by calling him names. He would chase the larrikins through the village, much to their glee, no doubt.

Margaret Miller had a brother, Zachary Taylor, who lived in various houses in Churchtown, always renting, until 1907. Taylor enlisted in Company A, 20th Pennsylvania Cavalry, in January 1864. He was taken prisoner at Lynchburg, Virginia, in June and paroled that November. He came home for Christmas on furlough before returning to the army. He returned to

Churchtown in the summer of 1865, and in September, he lost his right arm in a threshing machine. It was amputated five inches below the shoulder. Taylor was married twice and raised 11 children, somehow. In later years, he left his wife and was sued by her for non-support from 1916 to 1920.

In truth, a log house; this home is listed in the tax rolls from 1847 on as frame. The two-and-a-half-story building now has a brick kitchen attached to its left side. The log portion is rectangular, three bays wide, and the square kitchen has two bays. Both sections have a front entrance. Painted wooded lap siding covers the front and right sides of the house, while modern wood shingles have been applied to the other two sides. The gable roof is covered with seamed metal, with two interior chimneys. Spare and efficient, the building features no exterior ornaments save for a slight projecting pediment over the main entrance. Windows are 6/6. An old stone slab sidewalk leads from the street corner along the three-bay cement stoop in front of the house. As of 1993, this house still did not have a furnace, the heat being supplied by a kitchen stove and a small oil-burning room heater.

This is the end of High Street. Originally, it was surveyed to extend east into the field in front of you, but that part was never opened up, even though there was a road base put down. It was finally declared vacated about 1896. Turn left up Green Street and walk up that lane towards Route 174. Green Street was laid out in 1851; a petition from some of the locals expressed a need for it. Pass Walnut Alley on your left and look into the backyards of the houses on that side. Most of these houses were built in 1831. All of them would have had stables that sat at the back of the lots, outhouses, chicken coops and chickens scratching in the yards. Fences divided most of the yards from each other, as modern versions of those fences still do.

Now turn left onto Route 174.

1261 Boiling Springs Road
The first house, #1261 Boiling Springs Road, was built in 1831. The deeds for this lot can be traced back to 1750. It was part of the 797 acres that Richard Peters warranted in 1750. Two hundred acres of this was sold to Richard Steel in 1774. He sold it the next year to George Michael Wise, who sold it to his son, Jacob, in 1777. In 1784, Jacob sold 150 acres to Hartman Morrett and his son, Michael Morrett, sold one acre to Peter Livinger in 1824. In 1830, Peter sold this lot to Jacob Ritner for $42. Jacob was the son of the future Governor Joseph Ritner, and Jacob built the house on this lot. (Joseph Ritner was hired out as a farm hand for Jacob Myers, who lived on a farm just north of here, in 1790. He stayed for a few years until Myers moved to Newville. Ritner was Governor from 1835–1839. He had run for office in 1828 and 1832 but had been defeated. It was during his term the nation went through the Panic of 1837.

1261 Boiling Springs Rd. (2007)

Although no sheriff sales in Churchtown can be directly related to the Panic, the Great Depression affected thousands in the state.) Two years later Jacob sold the house and lot to William Morrett, a blacksmith, for $825, quite a substantial profit. Subsequent deeds for this lot have not been fully recorded.

By 1839, Dr. Jacob Sawyer was living here. He was a graduate of Exeter, N.H. and moved to Dillsburg in the early 1800s. He sold it in 1841 to Jacob Strock and moved to a farm along the Yellow Breeches in S. Middleton Twp. Dr. Sawyer moved to Carlisle in 1857 and died in 1859. Jacob Strock owned it until he died in 1852. In 1841 he was one of five people in the village to own a carriage, still relatively rare. The others were Jacob Morrett, Cary Ahl, Dr. Sawyer and Robert Sturgeon. In 1850, Strock rented the house to John W. Leidig, whose wife, Lydia Morrett, was a relative of his. Her brother Sam, a merchant down on the corner, lived with her and her two children. Later that summer John and Lydia bought her father's farm of 40 acres at 1251 Boiling Springs Road. This house passed to Jacob Strock's widow, Elizabeth. The Strocks owned a 131-acre farm next to the church, so although Elizabeth owned the house, she rented it out to her children. In 1860, Alfred Strock was living here. Elizabeth died in 1861 and the house was sold the next year.

When Henry Enck died in 1860, he left instructions in his will that the executors were to sell his other real estate and buy a house for his wife, Anna, not to exceed $1,000. This house was put up for sale by the Strock heirs in 1862, and the Encks, John, Henry and George bought it for $1,263. One thousand dollars came from their father's will as stipulated. The rest had to come from elsewhere.

Anna lived here until she died in 1882. Levi Enck, a butcher, lived here with his mother for a number of years and ran his business from a shop on the property. Levi got into one known legal scrape while living here. In 1866, when Levi was 17, his neighbor across the backyard, William Anderson, started pelting Levi with rocks. Levi went to James Burnett, the Justice of the Peace, and had an arrest warrant made, which was given to Peter Baker, Levi's neighbor, who was deputized to serve it. Anderson was ordered to keep the peace for one year or forfeit his surety. It stopped the rocks.

After Levi moved out, his unmarried sister, Katherine, lived with their mother until she died, and Katherine was given the house. Katherine lived here for years with her widowed brother, Hirem K. Enck, who was a huckster. With Katherine's death in 1923, the house was sold to her nephew, Norman Enck, son of Levi.

This house is a two-and-a-half-story brick house with a Flemish bond façade and a common bond on the other sides. The three-bay home features side hall construction, and a side porch with a balcony is part of the rear wing. The multiple gable roof is covered with seamed metal in the front and corrugated metal behind. The 6/6 windows are evenly spaced and flanked by solid wood shutters on the first floor. A Federal fanlight above the entrance is echoed by a centered three-pane attic fanlight on the east wall. This house is several feet taller than the rest of the houses in the 1260 block.

1263 Boiling Springs Road
This house was most likely built in 1831, but deeds prior to 1841 for this lot were not recorded. An Orphan's Court record of 1836

1263 Boiling Springs Rd.

mentioned a David Sollenberger, tobacconist, living here. According to tax records, he was not here in 1834. George Baish (1799–1862), a tailor, lived here from 1841 until he died. In 1844, George was a school director and, the next year township clerk. In 1858, the house was sold at a sheriff's sale to Peter Baker, but Baish continued to live here, renting from Baker. Peter Baker (1805–1892) was a township constable in 1860 and 1865. Baker lived here from 1863 until he sold it to Christian Baker in 1872. Christian Baker (1813–1899) lived here with his daughter Susan. About 1885, Christian's son John moved in with his family. After John and Christian died, John's son Clarence lived here with his new bride and his mother. Clarence had just recently come back to Churchtown. After graduating from school, he went to Franklin County for more schooling and then York County for a year. After two years in Illinois he came back home. He was a house painter and married in 1899.

This two-and-a-half-story semi-attached brick and frame house has five bays and a centered entrance. The multiple gable roof is covered with seamed metal and shelters the side porch and balcony attached to the rear ell. The windows are 1/1 in front, 2/2 and 6/6 in the rear, and adorned with projecting lintels. The three-bay front porch with a canopy and wood railing was probably added at a later date. The front door is topped with a transom. Remains in the attic reveal that centered internal chimneys previously existed at each of the three gable ends. Attached to the back of the rear ell is a one-room frame washhouse, which, as of 1993, was still used without electricity. Water was pumped from a nearby cistern and heated by a potbellied stove for washing. The interior staircase winds from the rear between the kitchen wing and the front parlors. The framework in the attic contains square-cut nails. In 1841 the house was taxed as a frame house, then in 1844 as a brick, then later as part frame-part brick. To the rear of the property sits a two-story frame barn.

1265 Boiling Springs Road
Peter Livinger sold this lot to Jacob Worst in 1830, and he built a small log house here. He sold it the next year to Abraham Paul. Paul owned the tavern lot #344 Old Stone House Road, where he lived; he rented this house out. Paul died in 1836, and on January 4, 1837, his heirs sold the house at a public auction to Mary Hymes for $298. Mary had been arrested for running a brothel in August 1827 with Tamzon Hymes and three others. Mary was fined 6 cents, but Tamzon was sent to jail for two months. Whether she continued this practice at house #1265 cannot be proved. Perhaps she reformed. She sold the place to William Sollenberger in 1840. Sollenberger (1798–1860) was a blind peddler, and it was under his ownership that the house became listed on the tax rolls as a "frame" house rather than its earlier "log" designation between 1842 and 1844. He sold the place in 1856 to Adam

1265 Boiling Springs Rd.

Givler, who rented it out for a year before selling it to Sam Kline (1799–1860). It would appear that Kline had a family boarding with him: the Zinns. Henry Zinn was a teacher with a wife and two young children. When the war started the following year, Zinn, then 24, raised a company. He later became a Colonel in the 130th Pennsylvania Infantry. He was wounded in the head at Fredericksburg on December 13, 1862, and died later that day from his wounds. His one son died that March while Henry was away, and his daughter died Christmas day, just twelve days after her father. She was seven. One son survived, George, born in 1861. Like his father, he became a colonel in the army. Henry's wife, Mary, then moved in with her mother-in-law and, in August 1864, hired an attorney in Washington, D.C., to get a pension. She later moved to Shippensburg.

In 1874, Sam's widow, Elizabeth, sold this house to Betsy Burtner. Betsy was 44 when she bought this house. She never married, and when she died in 1901, she left everything to the Lutheran Church.

This other half of the #1263 / #1265 duplex is one of several half-timbered houses that have been discovered in Churchtown during remodeling. Half-timbered buildings are constructed of square-cut wooden beams held together by wooden pegs in a mortise-and-tenon fashion. Most of the beams form tall rectangular compartments, sometimes braced diagonally by shorter beams and always stuffed with unmortared bricks. The bricks are not weight-bearing but serve as filler and insulation. The wooden beams are slenderer than logs, but seem to have been classified as "log" in the early tax lists for lack of any more suitable category. The current owner of this home spent considerable time removing the bricks in order to accommodate modern renovations. At least two other houses of similar construction also stand in Churchtown—#1285 Boiling Springs Road, built in 1831, and #1289 High Street, built in 1842. Both of these houses were extensively renovated in the first decade of the twenty-first century, and their interstitial bricks were also removed, leaving the empty mortise-and-tenon wood framework in place. #1265 Boiling Springs Road is three bays wide and rectangular, with two-and-a-half stories under a continuation of #1263's gable roof. Several rear frame additions have sloping shed roofs. Modern mid-twentieth-century window replacements are 2/2, with the sashes divided horizontally rather than vertically and are bipartite on the first-floor façade. The centered entrance has a fan-shaped window in the door itself rather than above it. This home is covered with aluminum siding. Off-center attic lights on the western wall suggest that a centered internal chimney once existed at that gable end. A stable once stood to the rear of the property.

1267 Boiling Springs Road
This lot was sold by Livinger to Sam Young in 1830. Young held it for a year but did

not develop it, selling it to Adam Bitner in 1832. Between 1832 and 1836, Bitner built a log house and slaughterhouse to the rear. He sold this to John Brannon in 1836 for $450. Brannon lived here for 13 years, and about 1843/44, the house's tax list designation changed from log to frame. He sold the house to James Weaver in 1849. In 1850, the tenant was George McAlwee, a shoemaker who lived here with his family and his two apprentices: Fred Goodyear, age 17, and Henry Pevins, age 21. Weaver sold it to David Vogelsong, a miller, about 1860 and he sold it to Moses Bricker in 1864. In 1860, the tenant was John G. Leidig, age 23, a clerk in one of the dry goods stores. Bricker rented it out (he owned houses all over Churchtown) for a year before selling it to David Diller. Diller was a merchant and tobacconist and may have run his store from the shop that sat at the rear. In 1868, Diller sold the house to Henry Knaub, a basketmaker.

Henry was born in York County in 1836. He worked first for his father until he turned 21 when he went out on his own. In 1858, he married Catherine, daughter of Solomon Diller, and the couple settled in Churchtown. At first, they rented a house owned by her father on Church Street. Ten years later, they bought this one. Knaub was a basket maker, his specialty being those made of willow. He had a large clientele throughout Cumberland County, his products reaching as far as Kansas. He continued at this until 1903, when he retired and then became an agent for the Western Medical Institute of Cincinnati. He and Catherine had two daughters, but they both died as babies. There were no others. Catherine was considered to be feeble-minded, and in 1919, she was committed

1267 Boiling Springs Rd.

to the State Hospital. When Henry died, John Nickey became trustee for the estate, and the house was sold at auction to Henry's widow in 1929 for $600. In the 1940s, Bill Hartz lived here. He had a machine shop in the back that had once been an old chicken shed. If you needed anything made or repaired you could bring it here.

This four-bay, two-and-a-half-story house has a centered German-style double front door. A gable roof protected by smooth sheet metal covers the front portion of the house, while a much lower-pitched gable tops a two-story rear ell. Windows are 2/2, with wood shutters on the front façade. The weatherboard exterior is now covered with aluminum siding. The two-bay canopy over the front entrances is supported by iron posts and railings. A pair of separated attic vents on the west wall suggests that the internal chimney on the east side was repeated on the west. A long, low shed or barn with many windows sits to the rear of the lot, once used as a chicken coop.

1269 Boiling Springs Road
Peter Livinger sold this lot to William Darr in 1830. Darr's wife was Margaret Diller, and she was the sister to David Diller, who later

bought the house at #1267. Darr built a log house here that year and sold it in 1832 to Daniel Wolf. Wolf died here, and in 1843, his heirs sold the house to William Brandt. Brandt (1820–1894) tore down the log house, and in the winter of 1849–1850, he built the frame house that now stands here. In 1850, William S. Reed (1810–?), a tailor, rented here. He had just sold his house on Old Stone House Road that spring and moved here with his wife and five children as well as an apprentice. The house went through many owners in the next few years. In 1852, it was sold to Daniel Stees, who immediately sold it to George Singiser, a merchant. George had a contract with William Firestine to sell this house, occupied by John Keeseman, for $805. But George died that winter, and his heirs sold it to William Firestine, a weaver, in 1853. In 1859, it went to Fred Goodyear (1833–1904) the apprenticed shoemaker mentioned above, and a nephew of the above Margaret Darr.

Living with Fred Goodyear and his family in 1860 was James Sibbert, a tailor, his wife and two children, plus his sister Elizabeth Sibbert and a girl, E.A. Zimmerman. James (1833–1905) was 5'5" and 100 pounds. He moved here about 1850 and was apprenticed to George Baish, who lived at #1263 Boiling Springs Road that year. In 1856, he married a widow and started a family. He joined the army, enlisting in Company A, 158th. After the war, he became a teacher and moved to Mechanicsburg.

In 1868, Goodyear sold the house to Catherine Richwine. Catherine (1815–1897) was the widow of Jacob Richwine (1807–1862). They had been living on a 20-acre farm along the York road, but after he died, she and her daughter, Elizabeth, sold it, moved

1269 Boiling Springs Rd.

to Churchtown and lived here for many years. In 1900, Lizzie was here and rented the rest of the house to Martin Goodhart, a grocer in town with six kids. Martin came to Churchtown in 1892 and lived in the village until 1903, when he bought the 42-acre Strock farm at #352 Old Stone House.

This three-bay, two-and-a-half-story house has a one-and-a-half-story rear section that spans the entire width of the building. Both sections have gable roofs of seamed metal. The front entrance is to the side of the façade and is surrounded by a mantle, transom and sidelights. Windows are 6/6, and above them is a row of 3-pane eyebrow windows. One internal chimney remains. The exterior is covered with aluminum siding.

1271 Boiling Springs Road

The next lot is actually #1271 Boiling Springs Road. Although no building stands here now, as early as 1832 there was a small shop here on a lot 33' by 30'. Originally log, it was later described as a frame building. This was part of a lot that Sam Hyer bought in 1830; he divided it in 1833 and sold this portion to Daniel Wolf. Daniel also owned the house next door that you just passed; this lot contained his shop. In later years, it was a residence/shop. Peter Henneberger bought the shop with the house and worked out of here until 1849. He sold it to George Singiser and 1850. George was a merchant, and how he used this building is not known. In 1852, George sold it to Jacob Weaver, a cabinet maker who lived at #1272 Boiling Springs Road. He worked here until the 1860s, and in 1864, his heirs sold it to his son John. John sold it to George Brindle in 1866. Brindle owned the store on the corner—perhaps this was used as storage. In 1877, it was sold to George T.B. Herman and became part of the property now known as #335 Old Stone House Road.

Some tenants were David Diller, the tobacconist; Edmund Eslinger, a shoemaker in 1860; Henry T. Enck, a cooper in 1870; and John Little, a blacksmith in 1880, among others. In the 1930s, the building, a one-story frame structure, was used by Lutz and Hoffman Funeral Home of Carlisle to build and store some of their caskets. Prior to Lutz, Frank Smith was the undertaker in town. He was here in the 1880s but his location is not known. Another undertaker was George Landis, but he moved to Duncannon in 1887. The building was torn down in the 1950s.

The Village Square
Only until just within the last few years have the local people started using street names within the village. Old Stone House Road was always called the town hill, and High Street was always just referred to as the back street. Old Stone House Road may have gotten its name from the stone house and former tavern that sits at its intersection with Lisburn Road, north of the village. Numerous other "old stone houses" also stand along the road further to the north, in neighboring Silver Spring Township. Whatever the source of its name, the road was laid out in November 1824 and follows closely the line between the lands of Jacob Wise and Peter Bricker. When the road was laid out, there was a cluster of houses around the crossroads; the name "Old Stone House" did not come into effect until the 1970s. Before that, this was Main Street.

Looking up Old Stone House Road and turning clockwise, in 1824, there was a log tavern at the top of the rise, a brick store just below that, and another store along Route 174 where #1279 Boiling Springs Road is. Across the road was Stoneberger's tannery and sundry buildings. A church and graveyard stood where the new church now stands; a school along the north side of Route 174, and this log store (now brick) where you are now standing. There were also some farmhouses, such as those of Michael Morrett and Jost aka. Joseph Strock, but these are now gone.

The square here used to be quite a lively place. In the late 1800s Churchtown had its bands of local musicians, both a cornet and string band. Some Saturdays the members would come here on the corner and give free concerts. In the latter half of the nineteenth century, politics was one of the passions that created friction among the villagers. Pole raisings were quite popular near election time. Men would gather and erect a pole at a prominent place, and from the top flew a banner with their presidential candidate's name. Mass meetings were also held here in the square. Some turned violent. A typical example was a Democratic meeting held here in 1879. While a speaker was addressing the crowd, some local Republicans started heckling the orator, which started a short fistfight between the Democrats and the outnumbered Republicans.

For decades, this was also a magnet for Halloween pranks. Circa 1900, Halloween lasted much longer than today. Two nights before Halloween was "corn night." Young men went out into the fields and swiped whole ears of corn, which they then threw at the doors and houses in the village. The next night was "cabbage night." This time, they took cabbage heads and did the same thing. In the 1920s and 1930s, one of the villagers that the boys picked on at Halloween was Grant Miller, who lived at #1261 High Street. It could have been dangerous because Grant had a shotgun, but perhaps this was half the fun—the challenge of not getting shot. The most memorable prank occurred one Halloween in the late 1920s. The morning after, the villagers woke to find the square filled with buggies, wagons, outhouses, and almost anything that wasn't nailed down. They completely blocked the trolley track; so massive was the jumble here that it was three days before the square was clear and the trolley could get through.

335 Old Stone House Road

Continue to walk up to the intersection of Boiling Springs Road and Old Stone House Road from Locust Alley. The shed that you are passing was used as a storage shed for the grocery store on the corner of #335 Old Stone House Road. Just by here is a concrete square slab. This was the location of an old hand-operated pump. It was taken out in the 1960s. The post office was moved from #1259 Boiling Springs Road to this building #335. The entrance was the first door down from Old Stone House Road. Turn left onto Old Stone House.

There were benches on the side of the store facing Route 174. For almost a century, they were always filled with old men on pleasant days. In winter the oldtimers were forced inside the store and found warm spots near the stove, spending countless hours looking out the windows, watching everyone who passed by. One of their jobs (or so they felt) was to chase the kids off the cemetery lot across the square. They thought it was disrespectful for kids to play there, even though the graves had been disinterred in the early 1900s. There used to be two hand-operated gas pumps in the village. One was here on the side of the building facing Route 174. The other was across the street at Roy Rank's store.

This lot is 33' by 200' and extends back to Locust Alley. It is part of the two tracts that Peter Livinger bought. One acre and 13 perches were sold by Abraham Paul to Livinger in 1823. This tract fronted both Old Stone House and Route 174. To the east of this tract lay 2 acres and 138 perches that Peter Livinger bought from R. Krysher in 1818, which was part of the 66 acres that Krysher bought that same year from Sam Goodyear and ultimately was part of the Adam Steel tract. This 2-acre tract also fronted Route 174. Peter surveyed the land into lots in 1829. On the survey map High Street was laid out, although it was not opened until 1842/3. Also laid out were Locust and Walnut alleys. The sale for these lots was held in March 1830; the people who bought them had to pay $15 to confirm the sale, with the balance paid by April 1, 1831.

The history of the earliest building on this site is uncertain. There may have been a log structure here as early as 1817, although using tax records, nothing can be proved prior to 1830. In 1830, Livinger sold this lot to Sam

Hyer, a merchant, for $330. The price indicates a lot with a building on it, most likely either a log or frame structure. Hyer sold it to William Murdoch in 1833 for $905. This much higher price suggests that a substantial building stood here by that time, most likely brick, not log. It may have been Murdoch who started the store here, although no license exists to prove that. In 1838 Murdoch sold it to Cary Ahl, brother to Dr. John Ahl. Cary Ahl definitely had a store on this site in 1838. That is the date for his first business license. He ran it for a year, but there was stiff competition in the village. Other dry goods stores were being run by Robert Sturgeon across the street, Peter Livinger (possibly at the Hyer place along Route 174), and Daniel Krysher (several houses up at #345 Old Stone House Road). Cary Ahl sold this store to Adam Reigel in 1839. The merchant enterprise known as Levi Reigel and Company ran a store here until 1851. In 1843, there were only one or two stores in the village that were allowed to sell liquor, but that was revoked the following year. In 1851, Adam Reigel died and his son Levi put the store up for sale. It was valued at $1,100, and the public sale was held on June 9, 1852. There were no bidders, and another sale was held on Oct. 23. They sold the business to George Singiser for $715. Singiser was a merchant and may have been leasing the store from Adam Reigel prior to 1850. They were also in business together in Mechanicsburg. George died three years later, leaving a wife and five young children. He owned two other houses in Churchtown when he died, which were soon sold. This one was kept for his family until 1860, when it was sold at a sheriff's sale to Amelia Morrett (she was the daughter of George Singiser)

335 Old Stone House Rd. (2007)

in 1861, and later her share went to George Brindle in 1864.

Amelia married William A. Morrett, a shoemaker, here at this house in 1856. One of the witnesses was David Devinney, who lived across the street. The other was her mother, Sarah. In August 1862, William enlisted in Company F, 130th Pennsylvania Infantry. He was discharged the next February because of a diseased heart.

George Brindle and his son ran a very successful store here from 1864 until 1875, when they sold it to George T.B. Herman. His son Harry bought it in 1914 from his father's estate, and in 1936, Riley Urich took over. This building, now a private residence divided into several rental units, served as a dry goods store well into this century.

From 1875, the store was run by G.T.B. Herman, who owned other houses in Churchtown. For most years, he did not live here; he may have had tenants above while he ran the store on the bottom floor. In 1879, Herman bought a pair of platform scales to set out front. Here, farmers could come in their wagons, loaded with hay, and have them weighed. Then there was the day about 1881 when Jacob Shopp came into town with a wagon loaded to the sky with hay. He turned the corner, but the load shifted, and several hundred bales of hay were flung against the store.

On Sunday, May 25, 1879, Churchtown was hit hard by a hail storm. Plank's house across the street (#340) lost 60 panes of glass; the hotel, 68; Dr. Hartzell, 66; John Kauffman on Church Street, 50; and many other houses lost smaller amounts. The next morning, Herman sold over 800 panes of glass before 8 AM and he had to send his son to Carlisle with a team for 14 more boxes. That was not enough and many people went to Mechanicsburg to get glass.

In May 1880, George brought his son in as a partner, and the firm was now called Herman & Son. George Sr. later moved to Carlisle, and his son ran this store. In November 1888, he was robbed. The thief first tried the cellar door but it was locked. He then bored a hole through the door and removed the pin holding the bolt. He took a gold watch, several pairs of boots, blankets, razors, etc.

This five-bay ell-shaped building has been renovated extensively over the years. Several entryways and display windows have been sided over, and the brick walls are now covered by aluminum siding. The doors and windows have all been replaced by modern ones. The roof is covered by seamed metal and consists of two gables joined at the corner in a hip. Today, the building is divided into several apartments. The most centrally located of Churchtown's community wells still sits near this store, along Old Stone House, although it has been sealed over.

337 Old Stone House Road

This lot, like all the others along this street up to High Street, has the same history as the

337 Old Stone House Rd. (2007)

previous lot, #335, up until 1830 when Peter Livinger sold most of these off. This property has always consisted of two lots, numbers 2 and 3, with the house on lot 2. Livinger sold these lots to David Diller in 1830, and in 1831, he built the house standing here now. Diller also owned a house at #1271 Boiling Springs Road (Route 174). He may have lived in this house and used the other as his tobacco shop. In 1835, the house was sold to Fred Watts at a sheriff's sale. Watts was a wealthy land speculator who bought a lot of houses at these sales to resell at a nice profit. He sold this one to Solomon Diller and Christian Richwine one month later. Solomon was David Diller's brother, and Christian Richwine was their brother-in-law. They rented it out for two years, then sold it to John Lutz in 1837. He sold it to David Martin in 1838. Martin ran a hotel here for a few years. David did not run the hotel himself; he owned several farms in the township. He had tenant landlords operate it for him. Only one is known so far, George Goodyear, who was here in 1850. In other years, this was rented out to different tradesmen. Martin sold the house in 1867 to Daniel Stees, who was buying and developing land on the other side of Route 174. He sold it in 1868 to George Brindle, Sr., who also owned the dry goods store next door. In 1874, Brindle sold it to David Goodyear. Goodyear owned this house until 1908 when he sold it to the Church of the Brethren Old Folks Home, who turned around and sold it to John Hoover.

This two-and-a-half-story, four-bay brick structure is attached to the old general store next door and extends the metal-covered front gable of that structure southward. This building still retains its common bond brick exterior, painted white, and has sawtooth soldiering at the cornice. Its front and side entrances are covered with hoods supported by corbels. The front door is topped with a transom. 1/1 windows have replaced the originals. There is a brick sidewalk underneath the concrete slab now here that was put in by David Goodyear in August 1880. Before that there were stone slabs which he took out.

339 to 345 Old Stone House Road

These four semi-Italianate row houses dominate the east side of the main street through Churchtown. Each brick unit has five bays, with a central hall and two-and-a-half stories. The structure as a whole is an excellent example of well-preserved nineteenth-century row homes. The units have "eyebrow" windows at the cornice, a portico surrounding the central three bays and 6/6 windows, coupled with sidelights around the front door. Only #339 still retains its shutters; #339 and #341 have intact lintels above the windows; only #343 has a bracketed cornice; and #345 has intricately decorated fascia. The units currently serve as single-family dwellings.

339 Old Stone House Road

This lot and the one to the south were sold to Adam Bitner in 1830. This lot went for $85 and the other for $70. It can not be proved through the tax records when this structure was actually built, but since they are all row homes and since #343 Old Stone House was built in 1831, we can assume that #339 and #341 were as well. All we can prove is that the houses were built prior to 1842, when they were both sold to Moses Bricker. Moses owned a number of properties, and these were rentals. In 1850, #339 was sold to William S. Reed, a tailor who had been renting on Route 174, and in 1854, he sold it to Isaac Lerew. Issac had married Mary Ann Goodyear, a daughter of Fred and Rachael. They lived all their married life in Dillsburg and rented this one out. Mary Ann died in 1859 at the age of 29. In her last illness, she was cared for by her cousin Susan. After she died, Issac married Susan. Issac sold the house in 1859 to William C. Brandt, a rake peddler. William, who usually rented the house, owned it until he died. In 1899, Sarah Brandt Hoerner sold her half-share to her brother Theo. Theo was living here by 1910. One of his boarders was Harry J. Gervin, 32, the manager of the knitting mill

339 (with 341) Old Stone House Rd. (2007)

that Theo was a major stockholder. In 1910, the mill went into receivership, and Theo was in charge of settling the affairs of the defunct company.

In 1880, Dr. Philip R. Koons and his bride were renting here. He had moved to Churchtown the summer before. He first studied to be a teacher, but in 1876, he began to study medicine in Carlisle. In 1879, he graduated with honors from Jefferson Medical College in Philadelphia and moved here. He moved to Mechanicsburg in 1886.

341 Old Stone House Road
The deeds for this house are sketchy. Moses Bricker bought it in 1842, along with #339. Sam and Moses Morrett bought it in 1854, and between these 12 years, it was owned by William B. Thomas, a teacher, for a couple of years after 1852. The Morretts rented it out for two years and then sold it in 1856 to Abram Goodyear, who sold it in 1867 to William Lehmer, who died in 1870. William's wife was Sarah Brindle, a daughter of George, Sr. The house was then jointly owned by Sarah, who married John Garver, a German Baptist minister, in 1872, and Lehmer's nephew, William Marcey. In 1913, Marcey, then in Kansas, sold his half to Sarah, and she sold the house to Murray Brownawell in 1921.

In 1880, the tenant was Adam Mountz, a pump maker, his wife, a daughter and grandson. Adam had limited education and learned pump-making at an early age. He later served as a musician in the Civil War, having enlisted in Company A, 1st Pennsylvania Light Artillery, in May 1861 and then in the 3rd Pennsylvania Heavy Artillery in 1864. He was 5'10" and about 160 pounds. Adam was wounded twice at Gaines Mills in 1862. One ball hit his right big

341 Old Stone House Rd. (2007)

toe, which had to be amputated, and the other went into his left ankle and lodged there. He carried the ball the rest of his life. The amputation healed well, but the wound on his leg opened every year and caused him a lot of pain. Mountz came to Churchtown about 1870, moved to Boiling Springs 1887–1889 and later died in Philadelphia.

343 Old Stone House Road
This lot was sold by Peter Livinger to George Lutz in 1830 for $56. Lutz sold it the next year to Ben Correll for $100. Because of this small price, it can be assumed that no brick house stood here when Lutz sold it. Correll, who owned the lot until 1838, built the house here, possibly in 1831. He also had a shop on the rear of the property. In 1838, Wm. S. Reed bought the house and owned it until 1850, when he sold it and bought #339 Old Stone House. While living here, Reed was a school director from 1846–47. Dr. Levi H. Lenher bought it in 1850 and owned it until 1872 when he sold it to Dr. Fred Hartzell of Lees Crossroads, this county. Lenher never lived here but rented it out to various tradesmen. Hartzell moved in here with his wife and three teenage children in 1872. For a while,

the village could boast three doctors, Hartzell, Lenher and Koons.

In March 1879, Dr. Hartzell met with a very painful accident. He had gone out to visit the family of Jacob Gates, who lived along the Harrisburg and Potomac Railroad tracks below Leidigh's Mill. He tied his horse to a tree on the opposite side of the tracks and went in. While in the house, Jacob warned him that a train was coming. Afraid that it might spook his horse, Hartzell raced out to get his horse and tried to cross the track in front of the train. The engine struck him and broke several ribs. The train also ran over part of his foot, and he had to have three toes amputated.

Death took two from this household in one year. Frederick's son Kempfer had moved to Carlisle and, on Memorial Day 1893, had gone boating with some friends on a creek near Carlisle. They were drinking, having a keg in the front of the boat. Kempfer was drunk, and as he sat on the keg, he began to rock the boat back and forth. Eventually, he tipped the boat and was the only one to drown, even though he was a strong swimmer. He was 28. He left a wife and several children. In 1894, Dr. Frederick died. He was very much in debt and the heirs were forced to sell.

343 Old Stone House Rd. (2007)

The first sale was set for February 9, 1895, but a great blizzard that day forced a cancellation. His wife Mary bought the house the next week for $1,257, and she sold it to her son Grant in 1897. In 1899, he sold it to Warren Zell.

In 1880, the house was rented to Philip Mountz, a brother to Adam next door. Philip was the recently elected constable and died the next year.

345 and 347 Old Stone House Road
This was sold by Peter Livinger to Adam Stonesberger in 1830 for $107. Stonesberger sold it that same year to Dan Krysher for $127. Dan also bought the lot now at #347 Old Stone House at the same time for $150. He had both of these structures built. Dan was a merchant; one of these houses was his residence, and the other was his warehouse. The earliest mention of Krysher with a retailing license is in 1833. He kept a store here for 17 years. In 1841, he was also the postmaster; his profit that year from both jobs was $4,000—quite a princely sum. In the 1850 tax schedule, he is listed as having two lots, with a brick house and a brick warehouse. In 1850, he sold both houses to Moses and Sam Morrett for $2,300. These two men, four years later, also bought #341 Old Stone House. In 1857, this house was sold to Rachael Butturf (1809–1894).

Meanwhile, Moses moved to Ohio in 1860 and never returned to Churchtown until a visit in 1888. Records would indicate that Rachael never lived here but rented it out. #347 Old Stone House was sold in 1858 to George Brindle, who later bought #335 and #337. George sold #347 to his son Cyrus Brindle in 1877. After the death of Cyrus in 1905, #347 was sold to the Knights of Pythias.

345 Old Stone House Rd. (2007)

These houses constituted the main business area for Churchtown from the 1840s through the 1880s. Many craftsmen and merchants plied their trade from these buildings, some of the trades being that of butcher, tailor, carpenter, shoemaker, blacksmith, merchant, doctor, hotel, and postmaster. Because they were rentals, it is almost impossible to know many of the tenants or exactly which house they lived in.

The architecture of #345 is described earlier, along with the other four Old Stone House Road row homes, all of which are similar in construction. #347 is a semi-attached brick house and the last in the line of the Main Street row homes. Unlike the other four, however, this corner unit has only four bays and no eyebrow windows. Windows are 6/6 above and 12/6 below and are crowned by lintels. The façade is a Flemish bond, and a two-bay portico covers the front entrance with a transom. The southern wall rises to form a parapet at the edge of the gable roof, and two lights flank its double interior chimney. Rear extensions have shed, and flat roofs, and the ends of five wooden beams can still be seen flush with the brickwork on the rear wall of the ell.

349 Old Stone House Road

This house stands on the lot that John Ahl bought from Peter Livinger in 1842. John sold the land north of Locust Alley but kept this half-acre lot for his home, which he built by December 1842. That is the first mention of it in the tax records.

John Ahl came from a family where both his father and grandfather were doctors. He was born in Franklin County to Dr. John Ahl. He studied with his father for a few years, then graduated from Washington Medical College in Baltimore in 1838. The first few years were spent in Penn Township, but about 1842, he moved to Churchtown. He took over the responsibilities of Dr. Jacob Sawyer, who had moved to South Middleton Township in 1841. Dr. Ahl stayed here until about 1854, when he moved to Brandtsville and bought a mill along the Yellow Breeches. In 1856, he was elected to Congress and served one term. He died in Newville in 1882.

Ahl owned this house until 1850, when he sold it to George Bricker. George was the son of Joseph Bricker, who owned several extensive farms and a mill along the Yellow Breeches. George sold it in 1852 to his sister Juliann

347 Old Stone House Rd.

349 Old Stone House Rd. (2007)

Bricker, and she to her other brother Moses Bricker in 1859. Moses owned other homes in Churchtown at the time, but his residence was a farm south of the village. Not until 1862 did he move into the village when he went into the iron forge business. This house he rented to William Diller, a carpenter, in 1860 who later built and lived in the house at #1290 High Street. Bricker sold the house at #349 to Henry Paul in 1966. Henry, a son of Abram Paul, must have been well-off financially. While living here he was one of three people in Churchtown to own a piano and a gold watch. A gold watch was worth almost a third of the average worker's annual wages. Paul sold the house to Sam Plank, inventor of the Plant Shifting Beam Plow, in 1869. Sam lived here until he died. With him was his wife, a least one domestic servant, and, at times, his daughter-in-law and her sons. Sam died here in 1880, and the next year, his widow Rachel sold the house to her son Sam C. Plank for $2,000. That year, there was a spate of break-ins in Churchtown, and Rachel's house was not spared. One Friday night in August, while she was away, thieves broke in and stole some eggs, two pairs of shoes, a bonnet and a basket. There were at least two thieves, and one of them was barefoot, based on the prints found in the dirt outside. Sam C. Plank sold the house to Jacob Hoerner in 1883 for $2,500. Jacob died in 1885, and his family inherited the house.

This two-and-a-half-story ell-shaped brick building now serves as the parsonage and fellowship building for the Church of God next door. Its façade is a Flemish bond with six bays. The two entrances, one to each half of the building, are centered side-by-side and covered by a two-bay cantilevered hood. The entrance to the parsonage section is ornamented by a fanlight transom and an arched molded casing decorated by corner rosettes. It appears that the other door, not decorated at all, was originally a window and that the hood replaced a three-bay canopy over the original door and the windows on each side of it. Windows are 1/1 in front and on the sides, with some windows in the rear and sides that are 8/12, 12/8 and 6/6. Windows on the two elevations facing the street have lintels ornamented with corner rosettes. A 10-pane semicircular attic light bisects a split interior chimney. The multiple gable roof is made of seamed metal, painted red to match the church. A cast-iron fence surrounds the side yard.

351 Old Stone House Road: Churchtown Church of God

This church is built on a lot that John Ahl sold to Sam Bricker, Dan Stees and John Brandt, trustees and elders of the Church of God, in 1849. Ahl stipulated that no building would be erected on his lot (#351) on the north or east side of the church lot within ten feet of the boundary line for 99 years. As you can see, there are as yet no buildings.

351 Old Stone House Rd. (Church of God)

This two-and-a-half-story rectangular brick church, built about 1853, has Gothic arched stained glass windows and an open octagonal cupola beneath a finial steeple. The sanctuary wing forms the southern half of the building, with its gable end facing the street and its southern eave turning up slightly in a Flemish sweep. Attached along the entire northern side is a perpendicularly gabled wing containing offices and Sunday School rooms. The façade of the multiple gabled structure is five bays wide with a centered entrance, which is crowned with a wooden Gothic arch ornamented with dentils. Strap hinges support the door. The molded wood cornice continues the dentil motif on the front and sides of the building, and painted seamed metal covers the roof. Windows in the extension wing are 6/6 with protruding brick sills and crowned with lintels, some of which feature a zigzag motif. The stained glass windows on the side of the sanctuary also have lintels with zigzag ornamentation instead of the Gothic arches on the front of the façade. The church was formerly known as the Bethel Church of God and is listed as such in the 1872 Beers Atlas. The small Bethel cemetery lot, dating back to at least 1872, is located along Old Stone House Road to the south, on the southeast corner of the intersection with Route 74.

353 Old Stone House Road

The early history of this lot has not been recorded but can be surmised. Part of the Wise warrant, it was sold to Rudolph Krysher in 1818. Owned by him as late as 1849, this part of the land was sold to Jacob Morrett (1786–1858), while the rest stayed as part of Krysher's farm (which was sold to Jacob Baker, then John O. Dill). The lot that this house sits on was comprised of three smaller lots that Jacob Plank bought. Two of the lots he bought from the heirs of Jacob Morrett in 1858. This house was built about that time. The other lot came from John O. Dill in 1868. Jacob (1793–1879) and Mary Plank lived here for many years. In 1860, he was a retired farmer, and he had four of his children living here, from ages 16 to 29. One of these was David, age 21. David, who was 5'7" and about 160 pounds, was a coach maker in the village, and when the war began in 1861, he enlisted that May, responding early to Lincoln's call. He joined Capt. Henry Zinn's Company, which became part of the 7th Pennsylvania Reserves. The unit was shipped down to Washington that summer. On July 16, David was on picket duty near Tenleytown. He became drowsy and lay down against a stump to rest, his musket loaded. When his relief approached, guilty that he had been caught napping, he jumped up and, in the process, discharged his gun, the ball tearing into his left hand. Three of his fingers were only held on by a piece of skin, and these were amputated. He was sent home soon afterward on furlough and never rejoined his unit, being discharged. Rumors floated around town that he had done it on purpose,

353 Old Stone House Rd.

but since he was not yet sworn into the Army, there would have been nothing gained by it. But David's career as a coachmaker was over, and since he had little education he was in a dilemma. During the war he left Churchtown and went to Carlisle and studied to become a doctor, which he did in 1865. But doing this left him heavily in debt, and his creditors chased him for many years. He never could get caught up on his bills. He moved to Bedford County in 1865.

One day in the spring of 1879, a reporter from the *Carlisle Volunteer* came to Churchtown to interview Jacob. It was an extensive article that ensued, and much of the early history of Churchtown that we now know is a result of that interview. Three weeks later, Jacob was dead. After Jacob's death, his wife Mary continued to live here. Her children had all moved out, so her sister, Eliza Reifsynder, who was 13 years younger, came to care for the old woman. This was in 1880. Mary died in 1890 at the age of 90 and the house passed to her heirs. The house was valued at $950, and when it came time to bid for it among the many heirs, only her daughter Catherine did so. She bought it and then sold it the same year to her sister Annie, the wife of Rev. Kremer. It was sold in 1916 to their daughter, Gertrude.

This two-and-a-half-story brick house has a Flemish bond façade and side hall construction. Windows are 6/1 with lintels, and the three eyebrow windows at the cornice have six panes each. Some side windows are bipartite, and their lintels have corners at each end. A transom and six sidelights surround the recessed front entrance, although block glass has replaced the original panes. A modern aluminum awning protects its one-bay front stoop. The cornice is trimmed with dentils, and the gabled roof is covered with seamed metal. A two-story frame addition off the rear south wall has a sloping shed roof. One external chimney still stands along the north wall. Several side windows and doors have been bricked over. Also on the property is a frame garage with wood siding and a seamed metal roof. The single-family home is now owned and rented out by the neighboring church.

Continue along the street to the imposing home at the top of the rise. Along the left is a row of homes built after 1946. This ground is known as Allen Heights and was developed by Harry Lichtenberger in 1946. Years ago, it was all open fields, once owned by Rudolph Krysher in the 1840s. A deed from that period mentions some buildings here, but whatever they were, they were torn down by 1872. There was formerly a United Brethren Church at the corner of Old Stone House and Brandt Roads. It was torn down in October 1893 by the Rev. Hauck and a crew of local workmen. There was some controversy involved in the reasons for its razing, but the local villagers have forgotten it. All that remains is the cemetery, east of here along Brandt Road, and

361 Old Stone House Rd.

a low wall made of random sandstone, which separates the church lot from #361.

1299 Brandt Road
It isn't easy to date this house. It sits on part of a 38-acre warrant to Jacob Bricker in 1792 patented as "Hope" in 1804. After Jacob's death it passed to Joseph Bricker. Joseph died in 1822. He was an extensive landowner. Not only did he own several farms in the area, but he had two houses in Lewistown as well. His favorite sons got the best farms. Joseph Jr. had to settle for what was left, which included this ground. Joseph, Jr. got a 145-acre farm, and in 1843, he sold his sister Mary Ann 156 perches from it for $100. Mary Ann sold it to Jacob Neisley in 1854. Jacob owned a lot of land in this area, and to go with this 156 perches, he bought an adjoining 33 acres. The house may have been standing at that time. In 1864, the property was sold to John E. Eberley, and he sold it to David Neisley in 1869. Neisley owned it until 1893, when he sold it to Jacob K. Neisley and he to John K. Paul in 1897.

Marking the southern boundary of historic Churchtown, this imposing Georgian brick farmhouse with barn and outbuildings once functioned as a profitable pig farm. The five-bay, two-and-a-half-story house features brick parapets at the eaves of its multiple gable roof. 1/1 windows below and 6/6 windows above are framed by solid wood shutters and capped by lintels and rows of vertical stretchers. A three-bay front porch covers the centered front entrance and is supported by four round columns. The north entrance features a covered stoop with built-in wooden benches flanking the door. A side porch with a balcony runs along the southern side of the rear ell, which is sided with German lapwood siding. The roof is seamed metal, and the cornice is filled in with a smooth, sloping plane of brick, which slants inward to meet the front wall of the house. Each gable end supports a centered chimney. The original exterior bricks were red but were later covered with yellow brickface, perhaps reminiscent of the yellow bricks manufactured in Mt. Holly. This brick face is now painted over. Within, the house features a full Georgian plan with double parlors and a central stair. In the basement is a wine or root cellar with a ceiling of vaulted stone. A summer kitchen to the rear has been remodeled and connected to the main house, but features such as the fireplace and pig-fat rendering stove remain intact. Detached outbuildings

1299 Brandt Rd. (2007) (faces OSH Rd.)

include a large frame bank barn with a metal roof and cut stone foundation, a small smokehouse, and a farrowing house.

Cross over the road and walk back toward Churchtown. The houses on your left are all recent additions, standing on what was once the farm of Rudolph Krysher. His house is the first that we will come to.

352 Old Stone House Road

This property was, at one time, part of the 66 acres that Rudolph Krysher bought from Sam Goodyear in 1818. Seventeen acres on the opposite side of the road were split off, while seven acres that comprise much of Churchtown were divided into lots during the mid-1800s. This house, at least the original log part, was the fourth house built in what is now Churchtown. In the history section of this walking tour, a mention was made of a house raising in 1812. This is that house. It took two days in the fall to put it up. This farm stayed with Krysher until he died in 1854. Krysher's executors sold the land after his wife's death to Jacob Baker and John Dill in 1863 for $5,980. But one of the executors refused to hand over the deed, as he refused to be bonded. Baker and Dill then had to go to court and get a petition to allow the executors to sell the land without being bonded. This was granted; the deed was turned over, and the money was given to Krysher's estate. Baker later sold his interest to John O. Dill in 1868. Dill sold off part of the lands. One lot went to Jacob Plank on Old Stone House, and much of the land that lay along High Street was sold into lots, many of which were never built on until the middle of this century. In the hailstorm that struck Churchtown in 1879, Dill lost his wheat crop growing here. In 1882, the house

352 Old Stone House Rd.

caught fire and was saved in the Churchtown fire described later in the description for #328 Old Stone House Road.

Rudolph Krysher (1775–1854) and his brother, David (1784–1857), were some of the shakers and movers in Churchtown from 1815 until 1857. Rudolph married Rosanna Goodyear, from the same family who owned large tracts around Churchtown. He died without heirs. David also married and raised a large family. Their sister Mary (1785–1849) married Abraham Paul (1790–1836), who owned the tavern and developed some of the lots along Old Stone House Road. Another sister, Catherine, married Peter Livinger, and Elizabeth (1770–1824) married John, a son of Leonard Wolf, an early land patentee. Another brother, John, had a son, Daniel, who, with his uncle Rudolph, ran a store for a while in the village, down by the corner of Route 174 and Old Stone House Road.

Rudolph came to this area prior to 1815, that year being the first recorded deed for him. He bought and sold different tracts of land around Churchtown, at one time owning as much as 200 acres. In 1817, he was assessed for a one-acre lot and house, 150 acres of farmland, two horses and two cows. By 1823, he was the postmaster for Churchtown; this job he held for many years. For a few years in the 1820s, he went into the store business with his brother David. Later, he farmed for his living. He was politically active. Some of the elected posts he held were township clerk, 1841–1844, and Justice of the Peace, 1845. He served as administrator for many estates, witnessed countless wills and deeds, and generally played a very active role in the community until he died. Since he and Rosanna were childless, he willed two large bequests to the United Brethren Church, which lay just across the road. In 1849, he gave 54 perches of his land to the trustees so that a church could be built.

This two-and-a-half-story frame and log house was constructed in two sections, both complete by 1848. The original four-bay, two-pile portion (1812) has two front entrances and a delicate ribbed wood motif repeated both inside and out in the door surrounds, window frames, and fireplace mantels. The entrance on the north end of the façade is topped with a pediment supported by corbels. Inside the other entrance, to the south, a winding rectangular side staircase dominates the entry hall, and twin fireplaces grace the northern walls of the two lower and two upper rooms. The twin interior chimneys meet in the attic to form a single chimney protruding through the roof. Two lights frame the merger. A narrow rear staircase from the first to the second floor sits behind the front staircase. Floors are random pine planks, and beams are secured with square-cut nails. The three-bay, two-pile addition sits to the south of the staircase and adds four more rooms, two above and two below, to the structure. The rear room on the lower level features a built-in corner cupboard, wainscoting, and crown molding.

Windows in both sections are 2/2 and evenly spaced within each section, although not on the structure as a whole. The second floor in both sections has a much lower ceiling than the first. Cellar entrances are external only. Several one-story frame additions extend from the rear of the structure, and outbuildings on the one-acre lot include an old wooden shed or garage, a modern garage, and a small smokehouse. An old iron hand pump still stands over a cistern, and a wrought iron fence surrounds the yard.

350 Old Stone House Road
The lot that this house sits on was formerly two separate lots, each with a frame house sitting on it. In 1813, Peter Livinger bought from Jacob and Anna Wise a lot that went from the north boundary of Krysher's land up to High Street and westward to what is now the second alley off High Street, next to the Adam Gensler home. Here, he built a log house about 1814 at what is now #348 Old Stone House Road. In 1842, Peter sold this lot, one acre, to Ben Correll for $470. He reserved for himself a piece of land, 38' by 200', where his log house stood. There was also 10 feet reserved along the north boundary between Livinger's land and Paul's land. This strip became High Street a couple of years later.

If you were to visit here in 1840, the people you would meet formed a tight-knit group of families. Facing the house, to your left, would be Rudolph Krysher's farm. He lived with his wife and sometimes boarders that he regularly took in. In front of you lived Peter Livinger in his log house. He and his wife were also childless. Peter and Rudolph were brothers-in-law. To your right, on the other side of High Street, was the log tavern and home

350 Old Stone House Rd.

owned by Mary Paul. She was Rudolph's sister. Down near the intersection was the store run by Robert Sturgeon. Behind these homes stretched empty fields. Their development into lots was still several years away.

Ben Correll built a house on his lot in late 1842. He owned it until 1848 when he sold both lots to Dr. John Ahl. Ahl sold these lots that same year. One lot, 38' by 200', went to Detrick Coover for $1,000. A house had already been built on the lot. This house sat on the now-empty lot to the right of the house at #350 Old Stone House Road. Coover, who never lived here but rented the house out, sold it to George Brandt in 1856. Brandt was a retired farmer and lived here with his daughter, Matilda, and George Greybill. George sold this lot to Matilda and Maria Goodyear (wife of Fred) in 1872. They sold it to Peter Hartz in 1873. Peter (1813–1887) lived here with his two unmarried sisters, Mary and Catherine. The family were Dunkards. When Peter died, their brother, Henry, was forced to sell the house to pay Peter's debts. It was sold at a public auction held on Saturday, November 12, to the Hartz sisters for $625. The house was described as a two-story frame house with a frame stable and a yard planted with fruit and ornamental trees. Peter's personal effects were also sold that same day. The next month, both sisters made out new wills, willing the house to the other should one die first. Mary died in 1901, and Catherine in 1904. The house burned about 1936, taking with it both houses on the lot at #348, as well as burning the rafters at the house still standing at #350.

The present house at #350 was built about 1848 when Ahl sold the lot to Mary Belshoover. Her husband, George, had drowned in the Yellow Breeches in 1846, so she sold his farm and moved into town. The first mention of the house is in the 1850 tax records as a two-story frame. Mary lived here with some of her children by a prior marriage; John Gross and his wife Jane and his brother Christian Gross were here in 1850. Mary died here in 1857, and her heirs sold it to John McClure in 1859. He was a farmer who lived here until he sold it to Elizabeth Harlacker in 1867. She was a widow and lived here until 1908 with her daughter Catherine and granddaughter Ida Naugle.

This two-story rectangular frame house, now covered with aluminum siding, has undergone extensive renovations. Like many early homes, the spacing of the windows and entrance is uneven. Two large picture windows have replaced the windows on the lower level of the façade. A row of five eyebrow windows light the upper level of the home. The gable roof is shingled, and the positioning of modern chimneys and attic lights suggests that the home may have had up to three chimneys, one at each gable end and one in the rear.

348 Old Stone House Road

This modern house sits on what was formerly two house lots, all buildings long gone. This current home was built in 1948. This land is part of the tract that Peter Livinger bought from Jacob Wise in 1813. He built a log house that stood here until about 1936, when it burned down. There was also a second log house on this lot, which Peter rented out. It doesn't show up on any maps but is mentioned in his estate. In 1860, Henry G. Stephens, a merchant, was renting the other house. That year, Stephens bought some property at the bottom end of High Street. Peter was another one intimately linked to his community. He was township clerk in 1840, supervisor in 1843, and constable in 1844–1847 and 1850–51.

Peter died here in 1862 and his widow Catherine the following year. There were quite a few heirs on the Krysher side that had to be placated. On December 15, 1863, there was granted a Writ of Partition and twelve men were appointed to view the land. They were Moses Bricker, George Strock, H. G. Stephens, Adam Gensler, David Mondorff, Michael Longsdorff, Hiram Enck, Jacob Goodyear, Daniel Goodyear, Peter Baker, Thomas Kane and Henry Bowman, all residents of Churchtown and men we will mention in this history. They agreed that there was no way that the lot could be divided and so the heirs were to appear in court in October 1864 to accept or refuse the estate. On October 25, only two showed up to bid on the property—John Paul and Mary Diller. After several bids, it went to John Paul for $425; $343 of this went to pay off all the other heirs.

Paul sold it to Daniel Wonders in 1868, and he to Elizabeth (nee Diller) and Stewart Johnson in 1872. Stewart was a Civil War veteran from Company C, 195th Pennsylvania Infantry, and Company F, 101st. Stewart must

348 Old Stone House Rd.

have had a pinched nerve because his left eye and face twitched constantly. He stood 5'6" and weighed 112 pounds.

Elizabeth sold the house to Anna (nee Diller) Spahr (a granddaughter of David Krysher) in 1885. She and Henry Spahr lived at #1265 High Street; this one they rented out. Anna sold it in 1908.

The second part of this lot, 38' by 200', is part of the one acre that Livinger sold to Ben Correll in 1842. That one acre was part of two tracts that Livinger had bought: 80 perches came from the 1813 sale from Jacob Wise, while the rest were part of three acres and 42 perches that Peter bought from Rudolph Krysher in 1818.

Ben sold this lot to Peter Ahl in 1842. Ahl had a two-story frame house built here. The house was sold that same year to Joseph Beelman, who lived here until about 1848. In 1846, Joseph gave John Beelman a power of attorney to sell the house, and he then moved to Ohio by 1848. John Beelman sold the house to Leah Diller in 1848. Leah was the daughter of Martin Diller, who, in 1844, had bought the lot behind her house. Leah never married and, in later years, shared the house with her widowed sister Rebecca Black and her daughter Salome. Rebecca died in 1886, and Leah in 1895. She left the house to Salome Black, who died in 1909. The house was then given to Susan Diller and Laura Smith. The last doctor to live and practice in the village, Doc Sam Smith, lived here for many years. He was the husband of Laura Smith and moved here about 1894/95. After he left town, the villagers had to go to either Boiling Springs or Carlisle. The house burned down with the other houses about 1936, the second fire to hit it. The first was in 1882.

Turn left onto High Street. This road was opened in 1843, which was when some of the first houses were built along here. Until well into this century, this was the main road through town, not Route 174. The traffic from Carlisle came from the bottom of High Street up to here, turned left onto Main Street (Old Stone House) and then right at the square.

All the houses along this part of Old Stone House that you just passed have lots that reach 200' back to the first alley on your right. Continue past that alley until you come to the first building on the left. This lot that you are passing has apparently never had any buildings built on it until early this century. In the large garage that you pass, Lloyd Hair used to make grandfather clocks in the 1950s. He was probably the last craftsman in the village.

1285 High Street: The Knights of Pythias Meeting Hall

This lot was first sold to Ben Correll by Peter Livinger in 1831. He held it until 1843, when it was sold to George Brindle, Brindle to Martin Diller in 1844, and then back to George Brindle in 1860. Cyrus Brindle, his son, bought it in 1877. Cyrus died in 1905, his wife in 1906, and the lot reverted to the estate

1285 High St. (Knights of Pythias Hall)

of George Brindle, who had died in 1882. His executors sold it in 1906 to the Knights of Pythias Lodge, as well as the house at #347 Old Stone House Road. The Knights of Pythias were established in Churchtown prior to 1881.

This hall was built in 1909. Its formal opening was in June 1910, when it hosted the annual convention of the Past Chancellors Association of Cumberland County. About 125 members from all over the county converged on Churchtown, most by trolley, that Tuesday night. A visitor described the building as being two stories with a basement surrounded by concrete sidewalks. The first floor was a public hall. The second floor was the Castle Hall with the armory and ante-room. It was furnished with fine carpets, oak swing chairs and desks, and a hanging chandelier, and the walls and ceiling were freshly painted.

However, the hall was used for other community functions. Strawberry and ice cream festivals were held here, as well as locally produced plays.

The Knights of Pythias meeting hall until recently, used to double as the meeting place for the Crossroads Bible Church. Since this book was originally published, the Crossroads Bible Church has relocated to a newly built log building of its own at the "turkey foot" intersection of York Road, Locust Point Road and Williams Grove Road. Unlike the surrounding houses, the eave wall of this rectangular frame building faces the street in the Greek Revival fashion. A seamed metal gable roof covers its two-and-a-half stories, and its front façade is three bays wide with a centered entrance. Windows are evenly spaced, 2/2 in front of the first story and 1/1 on the second story and the sides. The original wood siding has been covered with vinyl.

1287 High Street
This lot is part of the land that Peter Livinger bought from Jacob Wise in 1813. He sold this lot to Ben Correll in 1842, who sold it to John Davis Zell in 1843 for $65. Zell (1812–1860), who was born in Lancaster County but moved here in 1835, came from a family of masons, and he was probably the actual builder of this house. The house is not listed on the 1844 tax records but is a brick house in 1847. Therefore, it was built 1844–1846. (The tax records were usually recorded in December of the preceding year. If a house was not listed in 1844, that means that by December of 1843, it had not been built). Zell lived here with his family and an apprentice until 1853, when he became bankrupt, and Moses Morrett, who handled the estate, sold the house to John Diller. The house had to be readied for sale, and we know that Elizabeth Burtnett was paid 50 cents to clean it, and Henry Richwine was paid $1 to whitewash it. John Zell was married to Rebecca, daughter of John Gensler. She was the sister to Adam Gensler who lived next door. After selling this house they moved to Boiling Springs Road into a house that her father bought for them.

1287 High St.

John Diller held one local office: he was the inspector of elections in 1849. John (1803–1882) married Mary Krysher (1804–1882), and their daughter, Anna Spahr, bought the Livinger log house on the lot you just passed on Old Stone House Road. In 1860, John rented his house to his son David B., who was a tinner. David had a wife and two children and needed a bigger house. It appears that John, a cooper, then rented in the shoe shop next door and lived in the rooms above. When John died he was in debt to the amount of $600, owed mostly to relatives. The house had to be sold. When his widow died soon after him, their son-in-law, Henry Spahr, became the executor. The house was sold at a public auction on Saturday, October 28, 1882, to Levi Enck for $700. Enck was a butcher living at #336 Old Stone House Road. He bought several houses in Churchtown about this time and rented them all out. All of John's tools and machinery in the tinner shop were willed to his son.

Levi only kept the house for 2 years before selling it to George Fisher in 1884. George was married to Mary Bricker and they lived here until their deaths, Mary in 1892 and George in 1893. They had no children so the house passed to their siblings and their kids.

There were a lot of heirs. Henry Bowman was appointed executor, and he sold the house to William Albert. Albert had it for 12 years but was forced to sell it at a sheriff's sale, and it went to Fred G. Burtner in 1906. Burtner sold it to Wilbur Brandon in 1922, and he to Harper Zell in 1926. After 70 years it was back in the Zell family, Harper being the great-grandson of John D. Zell.

This is one of three brick houses on High Street. It displays a Flemish bond pattern, and its cornice is ornamented by two rows of bricks whose corners slant outwards to form a sawtooth pattern. A roof of seamed metal covers its two-and-a-half stories. The bricks are painted white, and the façade is three bays in width. A centered entrance with a light transom is surrounded by evenly spaced windows, 2/2 below and 6/6 above. Lintels crown all openings. Twin chimneys protrude near the edges of the gable roof. A one-and-a-half-story frame kitchen with a steep shed roof and a one-story enclosed side porch (covering the entrance to the cellar) has been attached to the rear of the structure. Internally, the staircase is on the left side of the front room, and random-width pine plank floors remain uncovered. A large fireplace stands exposed in the western wall of the cellar. Wooden outbuildings include a two-seater outhouse and a chicken house now used as a shed.

1289 High Street

These two houses, #1289 and 1291, close to each other, mark the western limit of Peter Livinger's land bought in 1813. The first recorded deed for #1289 is from Ben Correll to John Machlan in 1842. Machlan, a shoemaker, was probably the one who had this house built, originally as a shop. In September

1289 High St.

1842, he sold the lot and house to Adam Gensler (1819–1887), also a shoemaker, for $200. The original house may have been just one-and-a-half stories, with living quarters above the shop. Gensler lived here with his wife and two young children until he had a new house built next door at #1291 in 1850. #1289 became his shop, which he shared with the tenants who rented the rooms above. In 1860, John Diller lived here with his wife. In 1870, the tenant was William H. Russell, a shoemaker who had formerly owned a house on Boiling Springs Road but had been forced to sell it. He moved from here back to the house that his father-in-law, John Cocklin, bought for him just months before Cocklin died. In 1880, the house and shop were rented to George Landis, a carpenter and undertaker.

This two-and-a-half story, two-bay brick house, formerly a shoe shop, has been enlarged by additions into a single-family residence. The brick portion of the house forms the entire 30 ft. front façade, extending back for 16 ft. and upward to just above the tops of the second-story windows. The west side of the house is stuccoed over diagonal wood lathing, while the east side is exposed brick and aluminum siding. Actually, extensive renovations in 2004 have revealed that the addition immediately above and behind this single-pile portion is of half-timbered construction—i.e., a framework of squared mortise-and-tenon beams originally stuffed with stacked, unmortared bricks in the interstices. The bricks, which were non-structural and served only as an unfortunately-moisture-retentive insulation, were removed by the renovator and tossed endlessly out the windows into a metal dumpster (clunk! . . . clunk! . . . ca-clunk!) over some time, that seemed (to neighbors like this editor) much longer than it actually was. However, the wood beam framework remains intact. The lost art of half-timbering was apparently utilized with some frequency in Churchtown and greater Monroe Township in the early to mid-1800s. This house is one of three known half-timbered houses in the village, the others being #1285 and #1263 Boiling Springs Road. A log house at #497 Criswell Dr. also seems to have a half-timbered addition, evidence of which can be seen exposed in the basement stairway. Until recently, the house at #1289 High Street retained its 6/6 windows and 3/6 attic lights. The gable roof is covered with metal. Two one-story additions have been built onto the rear of the structure. It appears that the other story was added to the brick shop after Gensler's death.

1291 High Street
This house was built between 1850 and 1852, but I think 1850 is probably correct. In the summer of 1850, Adam Gensler was living here with his wife and two small children plus Edwin Eslinger, aged 19, a shoemaker, his sister Jane Eslinger, David Clark, 23, another

1291 High St.

shoemaker, and Simon Messinger, brother of John Messinger who lived across the street at #1288.

In 1850, Gensler, a shoemaker, employed three men listed above. He paid them $15 per month in wages, which compared favorably with most other trades. They produced 100 pairs of boots and 500 pairs of shoes that year for a total gross sales of $1,000.

In 1860, he still employed three men, and their wages were now $20 per month. His materials cost him $900. His crew produced 156 pairs of boots valued at $468, 332 pairs of shoes at $520 and other work worth $1,400. His net profit after all expenses and wages was about $760. Compare that to the annual income of his workers at $240.

This rectangular two-and-a-half story frame house with three bays and a gable roof was built in 1850 on what was originally a lot of Gensler's, to the west of his stone shop at #1289. In this house, the unevenly spaced door and windows currently have no ornament, and the windows are 2/2 on the sides and 6/6 in front. Attic lights have 6 panes, and there are two chimneys. Two one-story additions with pent roofs have been added to the rear of the structure. A stable was added in 1856; now, a wooden garage sits at the rear of the property. The home is now covered by vinyl siding, but when this book was first written, the exterior brick of the original shoe shop remained exposed at the base of the front façade (like a water table) and along the foremost section of the eastern elevation, from ground level to just above the 2nd story window. The upper portion of the front façade was stuccoed, as was the western elevation, while the remainder of the eastern elevation sported asbestos shingle siding. The roof was, and still is, seamed metal.

1295 High Street
Walking down to 1295 High Street, we see beyond it a town lot that Adam Gensler owned. There was an apple orchard here until recently. It stretched from the field behind the Diller house at #1287 to a former baseball field. Formerly, all this land down to the end of High Street was part of the Wise patent for 199 acres, 66 of which was sold to Sam Goodyear, who sold it to Rudolph Krysher in 1818. Krysher sold this lot to Gensler in 1850 for $100. The deeds for the lot that #1295 sits on have not been fully recorded but can be reconstructed. It was part of Krysher's farm that was sold to Jacob Baker in 1863, who then sold it to John O. Dill. The first recorded deed was from Dill to Michael Brandt in 1869. He died in 1882, and his heirs sold it to Adam Gensler in 1884, and Adam sold it to his son Joseph that same year for $200. According to tax records, this house was built in 1888 by Joseph Gensler.

A two-and-a-half-story rectangular frame house with three bays and a two-story rear wing, this house features German lap siding and matching peaked lintels with carved

1295 High St. (2007)

scrollwork. The cornice of the seamed metal gable roof is adorned with simple wood molding. The 2/2 windows, almost evenly spaced, are framed by wooden shutters that are partially solid and partially louvered. A canopy covers the centered door and front stoop, probably an addition. An older roofed side porch spans the length of the front wing on the right side. One internal chimney remains on the west side of the house, while the east chimney has been rebuilt externally.

Just past this house to your left, in the farmer's field, there once stood the town baseball field. Here, the Churchtown Nine took on the teams from other towns in the area. The ball field is long gone.

1301 and 1305 High Street
Continue down High Street past the empty lots on your left. All of this land was once part of the Jacob Wise patent, part of which was sold to Sam Goodyear and later to Rudy Krysher in 1818. John Dill sold off chunks of this land over the years, but several of these lots were never fully developed until recently. John Messinger owned one of these lots, and Charles Hoffman, who lived across the street, owned another for many years. #1301 and #1305 High

1301 High St.

1305 High St.

Street are modern ranch houses that sit on some of these lots. As such, descriptions of them are not included in this history. Huffman's lot passed through a number of owners between 1887 and 1903 when William Shumberger bought it for $150. Shumberger was a young man just getting into the lumber business. He moved to Churchtown from Leidigh's Station because he thought here would be a better location for wholesaling and retailing lumber. He built a structure here and tradition has it a sawmill as well. In 1914, Luther Arnold bought the lot and building. Luther, who lived across the street at #1302, built a blacksmith shop on this lot. It was a one-story frame barn-like structure with a high ceiling and open at the top. Luther died in 1931, his wife in 1935, and the heirs sold the lot to Monroe Township in 1936 for $300. For years, the township kept a horse-drawn grader there.

Just before you get to the next house, #1311, there is a hedgerow of shrubs. There was at one time an alley that ran through here to the alley at the back of these lots. To the east of this alley there once stood a house, now gone. This lot was sold by Rudolph Krysher to Sam Waggoner in 1849. I don't think he ever built on it, and in 1854 he sold it to George Bricker, who sold it to Anthony Baird (1800–1871) that same year. Baird, a native of Germany, had at one time owned a house just across the street from 1839 to 1845, but it is no longer standing. In 1856 Baird was assessed for a small one-and-a-half story log/weatherboard house, and here he lived with his family until he died. After he died, he willed his house to his daughters, Eliza Ann and Rebecca, as long as they remained single. Rebecca died single prior to 1883, and Eliza married John Ulrich. She sold the house to Adam Gensler in 1888. In 1880, Solomon Rider lived here. He was a carpenter with a wife and five children. The house was torn down between 1888 and 1895.

1311 High Street

The deeds and the history of this house are not complete. In 1858, John Swanger was listed as a tenant and not a land owner. It is possible that Swanger bought the lot in 1859 and had the house built on it in 1859/60. In 1860, Swanger was living here with just his wife, Nancy. There were no children. In 1860, he sold it to Henry Stephens, a merchant who was renting at the time from Peter Livinger on Old Stone House Road. Stephens sold it to William H. Miller in 1861. Miller was a cooper and, in 1862, the township constable, and had been renting a house at the time from Francis Meneer at #1304 High Street (no longer standing). But Miller lost his house because of back taxes, and it was sold at a sheriff's sale in 1862 back to Stephens. At the time, the house was described as being a 22' by 16' two-story frame with a cooper shop.

The house was not the only thing that Miller was to lose. William was from the Newville area, and after the death of his first wife, Eliza Diller, in 1849, he remarried and drifted to Churchtown about 1857. He at first rented from Peter Miller, who owned a tenant house, probably along Boiling Springs Road near his farm. Miller was a lady's man, and his relationship with Peter's young daughter Margaret caused the village tongues to wag. It appears that William and Margaret had a habit of going to evening church together, oftentimes not getting home until eight or nine o'clock. They had to pass William's home along the way, and more than once, Mrs. Miller caught William with his arm around Margaret, and there were a few fights over his behavior. Money was tight for the Millers, with a young family to feed. Mary took in washing to help, but it wasn't enough, and they still lost their home. That year (1862), William joined the army for the bounty offered. He came home in June 1863 and ten weeks later went in as a substitute for Wilson Beidler. It paid him $450, all of which he gave to his wife. This time, while at Culpepper Court House in Virginia, he got frostbite on his feet in December 1863. For the rest of his life, he could not wear leather shoes without cutting away the leather part that came into contact with the diseased part of his foot.

1311 High St.

Two weeks before he came home in the summer of 1864, his wife, who had in the meantime moved to Shiremanstown, sold all the household furniture, put the kids out with neighbors, and pocketing all of William's military pay and bounty, eloped to Illinois with her lover, Frank McGuire. Apparently, she was not entirely blameless. Although they went to Illinois separately, it had all been prearranged. William came home to find everything gone. He moved back to Churchtown without his kids, and in the winter of 1865 while visiting his brother in Plainfield, met Mary Lusk. She became pregnant and, much against her mother's wishes, married William. The only problem was that William was not divorced from his second wife, Mary. So, as far as can be known, Miller was Churchtown's only bigamist. His second wife also remarried, and no legal action was ever taken. When Miller heard that his wife had gotten remarried he assumed that she divorced him, and she thought likewise about him. There was no hassle until William died. William stayed in the area until 1871 when he moved to Ohio. After he died, both wives tried to claim a pension as his legal widow. In the investigation that followed, it was determined that wife two was his legal widow, and she got the pension. Wife three was forced to abandon her claim.

In 1867, Henry Stephens, who had moved to Lower Allen Township, sold the house at #1311 High Street to Peter K. Diller and he to Sarah Ann Diller in 1869. Sarah was living here alone in 1880, aged 70. After she died, her heirs sold the house to John Eichelberger and he to Sarah's son, William Diller, in 1889. William's heirs sold it to Howard Diller in 1911. Howard had a son, Wilber, born in 1897, with infantile paralysis. One leg was deformed, permanently bent and crossed over the other. The children of Churchtown used to go to a swimming hole called the "seven foot," and "Wib," with his deformity, was able to float on his back all day, to the amazement of his friends.

The original part of this house is a two-story, 22' by 16' wood structure. A two-story ell, two rooms deep, was built onto the southwest corner of the house. During this century, two one-story additions were built. The house has been extensively renovated.

1315 High Street
Since the original edition of this book was published, this house was demolished and replaced with a modern, one-story home.

The original house at #1315 High Street was a two-story wood frame building, five bays across, with a centered front door. Pink asbestos siding covered its weatherboarding, and scalloped trim adorned the cornice. A one-story cement block addition was attached to the southern elevation. This house actually occupied two lots, and at one time, there was another house to the east of it. The earliest that the house can be searched is for John F. Lutz. In 1856, John Lutz was assessed for

1315 High St.

19 acres and a stone house. In 1959, he had two 2-acre lots, one with a frame house and the other with a log house. So, it would seem likely that this house was built about 1858. In 1860, the house on the left was rented to Joseph Darr, a butcher, while John Lutz, age 23 and son of John P., lived in the frame house with his wife. In 1893, Lutz sold the houses to Susan Diller. Susan was the recent widow of Daniel Diller. Daniel owned part of the old Casper Diller homestead along York Road, and after Daniel died in 1861, she moved into town. Susan sold this house to her daughter, Amanda Kinert, in 1870. The eastern part of this lot was part of land that Henry Greybill sold to John Swanger in 1859. Swanger sold it to Sam Morrett in 1866, who sold it to Amanda Kinert in 1868.

Amanda's husband John, 27 years older than she died in 1904 in the county home at Huntingdon County, and she married Robert Wilson in 1911. He died in 1913 at the County Hospital Asylum. For the rest of her life her main source of income was Wilson's war pension, as much as $27 a month. One resident remembers Amanda, who, as a little old lady in her eighties, after a storm had broken off some branches, was out there dragging them up the street, having sawn them into pieces with a cross-cut saw.

Continue left onto Church Street. This street was formerly the main road into Churchtown before Route 174 was built in the 1950s. The trolley line that went from Carlisle to Mechanicsburg passed through Churchtown along this stretch of Church Street. It traveled the whole length of Church Street, from its intersection with Boiling Springs Road down through here and on past the Mennonite Church. This road was dirt until after the trolley line was taken out.

1323 Church Street
This house caught fire after the first edition of A Walking Tour of Churchtown was written, and the remains were subsequently razed.

The next property we come to is #1323 Church Street, upon which a green-sided house sat until recently. The history of this lot goes back to the Jacob Wise warrant of 1776 for 50 acres. In 1802, Wise sold seven acres of it to Peter Bricker. The alley to the east of #1311 marks the eastern boundary of these 7 acres. When Peter Bricker died in 1804, much of his land went to his son, Peter. In 1813, Peter, Jr. sold Jacob Strock 10 acres, of which these seven were a part. In 1840 Jacob sold his son George 92 acres, which included this land. Strock sold it to Henry Greybill in 1853. In 1853 he had 77 acres and a brick house which still stands along the York Road. You can see the barn and outbuildings across the fields from here. In 1859 Henry Greybill, who owned much of the land south of Church Street, sold this piece of it to John Swanger. It went from #1311 down to what is now an abandoned house formerly at #1327. It was sold back to Greybill in 1860 and then to Cyrus Brindle

1323 Church St.

in 1863, who then sold it the same year to Catherine Morrett. She sold it to her son Sam Morrett, and it was he who probably had the house built between 1865 and 1868. Morrett had enlisted in November 1862 into Company A, 158th Pennsylvania Infantry, but deserted that same month. He was a constable for a number of years during the 1870s. He also ran a stagecoach line from Churchtown to Carlisle via Boiling Springs. It was a daily service with arrival in Carlisle at 9:30 a.m. and leaving Carlisle at 2:30 p.m. for Churchtown. He carried the mail on this stage route. His only competitor running the stage line was Peter S. Miller, who lived on a farm at the north end of town. Morrett kept the house until 1876, when he sold it to Christian Baker. Baker was buying properties all over Churchtown and renting them out. In 1880, David Nelson, a laborer, was living here with his wife and 4 children. In his younger days, prior to the war, David had been a butcher. He enlisted in 1864 in Company F, 209th Pennsylvania Infantry, for nine months. At the time, he was 5'4" and 125 pounds. David claimed that during a night march in front of Petersburg in March 1865, he fell over a stump and injured his hip, which worsened as he got older and made it hard for him to do manual work. After the war, he did some tobacco farming, which became very popular in Monroe Township at that time, and later found work as a day laborer. Dr. Hartzell was his family doctor, but after Hartzell died in 1894, Dr. Sam Smith took over. There was little that could be done, although nowadays, chiropractics could have cured him. His back became weaker, and for long spells, David was unable to work. He eventually got a pension from the government for $12 a month and supplemented this with some work at the lime kilns as a burner.

Tragedy struck in August 1880. David's son, Lee, 17, was working with a threshing machine, feeding it, when he got his hand stuck in it. It was badly mangled, and Dr. Hartzell was called, as were two doctors from Carlisle. Lee lost two fingers from the hand. In 1882, Elder Nelson, a son of David, bought the house for his parents. Nelson, who was single, died in Leadville, Colorado, in 1891, and the house reverted to his mother, Amelia. When David died in 1906, Amelia was left to fend for herself. In the days before Social Security, widows found it hard to survive. All the income that Amelia had was the interest on $330 of her own money, which she claimed came to $25 a year. Her children were not well off, but she was able to claim a widow's pension, and on this, she survived.

Before the recent fire that destroyed it, this two-and-a-half story frame and brick house, three bays wide and one room deep, retained 2/2 window lights. A one-story frame kitchen sat off the southwest corner of the house, and attached to the kitchen were two twentieth-century frame additions. The gable roof of the main structure was covered with metal. The exterior was covered with asbestos siding.

1327 Church Street
The fifteen years or so between the original writing of this book and its third printing have seen many changes to Church Street. This house, too, has been dismantled in the interim and no longer stands.

Walk past the mobile home to where an old house was, until recently, hidden behind the shrubs abandoned since the 1960s. The history of the lot follows #1323 until 1874. It appears that the house at #1323 was built first, and then by 1870, this one was built, since in 1871, Sam Morrett was assessed for two frame houses on a half lot. In 1874, Morrett sold this house to Simon Diller, a minister, keeping the one at #1323 for two more years. The deed describes the lot with a house and stable. In 1879, Simon sold it to Oliver Diller. Oliver, 30 when he bought this house, was a son of Joseph Diller, a farmer along the York Road. Oliver was a day laborer while living in Churchtown, and he lived here with his new wife and their daughter Clara, born in this house in Feb. 1880. In 1884, Cornelius Smyser bought it and rented it out. In April 1892, Smyser moved into Churchtown and lived here for two years before selling it to Ben Bowman. Bowman sold it back to Smyser in 1906.

Cornelius (born 1837) had served in the Civil War in Company B, 165th Pennsylvania Drafted Militia. He was a mason prior to the war and followed this trade for years afterward. By the time he moved to this house, he was suffering from rheumatism to the extent that he had difficulty taking off his coat or raising his arms above his head. He stood 5'3" and weighed about 160 pounds.

The house that stood here was a two-and-a-half-story, four-bay rectangular house with a two-and-a-half-story rear ell and a

1327 & 1329 Church St.

one-story extension. Exterior features of this house included German style twin entrances, centered, with transoms, and molded projecting lintels above the doors and windows. A two-bay porch with square posts sheltered the front doors. The front portion of the house had 6/6 windows and was sided with clapboard, while the rear ell windows were 2/2, and that portion was sided with elaborate German lap, similar to that of the 1877 house at #1281 Boiling Springs Road. The gable roof is covered with metal, and the cornice returns still retain their molding.

To the west of this house, there once stood another house, torn down in 1970. It was a two-story frame house with four rooms and an out-kitchen. There was also a barn behind the abandoned house that had since been torn down. And behind all these houses there once ran an alley, no longer open, which gave access to the stables in the rear of the lots.

1341 Church Street: Churchtown Mennonite Church

Keep walking up Church Street until you get to the Mennonite Church at #1341. The two houses that you are passing are modern houses built after 1950. The church was built in 1885. Sitting at the western end of Church Street, it stands apart from the rest of nineteenth-century Churchtown. This church is a rectangular building of common bond brick. The meeting hall is three bays wide and four bays long. The tall 4/4 windows are flanked by solid wooden shutters and crowned with lintels. Fenestration is not quite even. The original front entrance, centered between two windows, has been bricked over and replaced by a rear extension and entrance, which were added in the early 1900s. The remains of the front entrance suggest that it may have been like the old side entrance, recessed in a molded wood casing and crowned by a transom and lintel. One of the windows on the western wall has been transformed into another door. The gable roof is covered with painted asphalt shingles. The churchyard contains only a few graves.

Turn back and walk into Churchtown. To your left is what was once a 75-acre farm. The old house that you can see was the farmhouse for this tract. The main part of this land was a 62-acre parcel that began right before you, stretched to the west of York Road on your left, up to the crest of the hill on the horizon

1341 Church St.
(Churchtown Mennonite Church) (2007)

and over to the first road that you see snaking its way up the hill on the right. Part of a patent to Jacob Wise in 1774, it was sold to Peter Bricker in 1775. His son, Peter Jr., sold it to Thomas Weakley in 1851. John Ahl bought it in 1854, and Cyrus Brindle in 1856. In 1878, he sold the farm to Juliann Morrett, the wife of Michael Morrett, Jr. The farm was rented out, as the Morretts owned another farm east of Churchtown where they lived. Juliann died in 1892, her husband in 1893 and the farm passed to their two children. The interesting thing about her estate was the types of claims against it, most of them not allowed. Her one son was a doctor, and he tried to sue the estate for his services in looking after his mother. The auditor of the estate thought it was rather cheeky, and the claim was refused. Then, there was a note from P. A. Goodyear against Michael for $600. Juliann was his co-signer. Nevertheless, when Goodyear tried to get his money, the auditor cited a law that stated that "a married woman can not make a valid contract of guaranteed suretyship." The farm was bought by Isaac Enck and is known as the Enck farm to the older inhabitants.

1320 Church Street
Walk down to the first house on the left. Passing a lot before you get to the house, there once stood a livery barn here. It was part of the 75-acre farm. The house at #1320 Church Street sits on a 155-perch lot, which was once also part of the 75-acre farm. Fifteen acres of it was part of the Thomas Rankin warrant of 1769 for 120 acres. This was sold to Jacob Wise (not the same Jacob who started Churchtown but perhaps a first cousin), who patented it under the name "Weissenfeld" in 1774 and sold it to Peter Bricker, Sr. in 1775.

Six of these 15 acres became vested in Peter, Jr., and he sold them to William Line in 1814. Line sold the land to Jacob Strock in 1815, and his son George bought it from him in 1840, along with the 10-acre tract mentioned for #1311 High Street and #1323 Church Street. Strock sold this tract to Greybill in 1854, and he sold it to Cyrus Brindle in 1862 for $1,200.

The other 9 acres had been sold by Bricker to John Pipher in 1812. Pipher was a tailor, and it was probably he who had this log house built in 1812. He died in 1846, and his family continued to live here until 1856 when his heirs sold the land to Henry Greybill. Elizabeth took her share of the money and bought a house at #1261 High Street. Cyrus Brindle bought these 9 acres at the same time as the above 6 acres. He had 62 acres from an earlier purchase, which adjoined these two tracts, and all three tracts became a 75-acre farm. In 1863, he sold 155 perches from the 9 acres to Catherine Morrett for $1,200. This tract included the Pipher house. Catherine was the widow of Joseph (1822–1860) and later married James Burtnett. In 1874, Catherine Burtnett sold this lot to John Kaufman (1808–1882). She died three years later. John was a farmer, and this was his farmhouse. Here, he died, and his heirs sold it to his wife Mary in 1883 for $550. When Mary died in 1892, the heirs held onto it until they sold it to Susan Diller of York County in 1896. Susan was the wife of Sam Diller, and their son Louis, who lived with them, was a schoolteacher. Susan also bought a house at #348 Old Stone House Road with Laura Smith.

This house can be dated without any doubt to 1817, when John Pipher was listed with nine acres and a house. Earlier tax records just gave acreages with no mention of houses.

1320 Church St.

But, since he owned no other land, he would have needed a house as soon as he moved here. It could date even earlier than 1812, but not by much. The right half of the house is the log part. As late as 1900, it was still just a two-story log house. The frame addition was built about that date, based on some newspapers stuffed into the walls of the addition.

This two-and-a-half-story house faces the road in the same manner as its neighbor, #1316, with a long wall, complete with a double-decked "side" porch serving as the front façade. The 3-bay wide front elevation is the original 1800s log structure, with the main entrance being centered in this section. Shuttered windows are 6/6 on the first floor and 2/2 on the second floor, with most windows retaining their wavy nineteenth-century glass. The gable roof is covered with corrugated metal. The exterior is presently covered with a mixture of aluminum siding and board-and-batten.

The interior features exposed hand-hewn log walls with cathedral-style notching, open-beamed chestnut wood ceilings, original random-width plank floors, and an enclosed stairway (which protected one against drafts). A main beam measuring 30 feet in length runs the length of the original log structure. The interior workmanship appears to be of German origin, with American Chestnut wood used throughout the structure. The house is one of the few remaining in this area, built entirely of chestnut wood due to the blight of 1804.

Original to the house are the board-and-batten doors used in the attic and cellar way, wooden pegs or treenails used in various beams of the house, original door hardware, and wrought nails or T-heads used throughout the plank flooring.

One of the community wells was on this property and served those who lived at this end of High Street. While all houses had a cistern, wells were infrequent in this village. This lasted until the 1940s. No outbuildings remain, but there is a stone foundation which may have been a shop for Pipher's tailor business. In the 1880s, the property served as a horse farm and had a livery stable. Sheep were also raised on the property. In the 1920s, the house was used as a boarding house. From 1901 to 1930, the Valley Traction Company ran the trolley through Churchtown. The track beds remain on the property. In the 1960s, the house was rented out, and the owner, Percy Jumper, lived behind the house in a trailer. He is well remembered for his daffodils, which he grew in gardens on the property and sold to motorists as they traveled along Route 174. The present owners report that a benign poltergeist has been with them since they possessed the house and have been most pleased with the restoration of the property.

1316 Church Street

The next house, #1316 Church Street, marks the southwest corner of the Hugh Gibson warrant of 144 acres. This warrant passed to Rudolph Miller, who, in 1787, sold the land to Jacob Myers. Myers sold it to John Wolf in 1789, and he sold it to Frederick Goodyear. Frederick had been a soldier in the Revolution and served in the same company as Hartman Morrett, who also moved here. They were from Lancaster County, and Fred moved here in 1790. (Fred's brother, Ludwick, also moved here and bought a large farm to the northwest along York Road and adjoining this farm. The first stone house on the right, north from the intersection of Routes 74 and 174, was built by his son Jacob Goodyear in 1817.) Frederick died in 1814 and this land passed to his sons Fred and Daniel. It remained in the Goodyear family until 1853 when it was sold to Daniel Stees. The Goodyear home was a two-story log house. When Fred Goodyear died in 1849, his widow Rachel (1794–1870) had this brick house built and lived here until a short time before she died. She died in South Middleton Township at the home of her daughter. Rachel was the daughter of Casper Diller III, who owned the land just to the west of the Goodyear tract.

When the heirs of Fred Goodyear sold his land to Stees, this small lot of 155 perches was carved from it for Rachel's use. She did not always live alone. In 1850, just after her husband's death, she had Eliza Beetman, 19, and Mary and Daniel Goodyear living with her. After she died, the house was sold to Fred Goodyear, Jr. in 1872. Fred was at one time a shoemaker and later a butcher, and the shop may have been on this lot. He had served in the Civil War, enlisting twice. He was in Company A, 158th Pennsylvania Infantry, in 1862–63 and then as a sergeant in Company F, 101st. He was 5'8" and about 140 pounds.

1316 Church St.

His wife was Maria Brandt who has been mentioned earlier. By 1877 he had given up butchering and become a huckster. In later years, he was a day laborer and, shortly before he died, a butcher again. His poor health was a big factor in his changing jobs. In 1884, at the age of 50, he first noticed his rheumatism. The next year, he became dyspeptic, and most of his teeth were gone. He became badly nourished as a result, and by 1890, his eyesight was failing. He died here in 1904, and the heirs sold the house.

The brick farmhouse, probably built in 1849/1850, is a two-and-a-half-story rectangular structure with a gable roof and a Flemish bond façade. Unlike other farmhouses in and around town, the long wall of the house, complete with a side porch and balcony, faces the street. Windows and doors are evenly spaced within each section of the façade. Windows, now 1/1 replacements, are crowned by lintels, and a transom tops both front entrances. The roof is covered with seamed metal, and two internal chimneys remain, one at either gable end. Inside, original wall plaster, hardwood floors, and door latches remain. A modern addition extends from one side of the house. No outbuildings remain.

1310 Church Street

The next house along this side of the street is unique in Churchtown. The house was built for Kathryn Enck with $1,500 from inheritance on the front of the old Farenbaugh/Enck property #1288 Boiling Springs Road. Later, when the Route 174 bypass was built, it went through this property and separated the new bungalow from the older farmhouse. Kathryn closely supervised the building of the house and lived in it for only a short time. Not long after moving in, her brother Vance Enck, who lived on the farm across the backyard, was left to raise his children by himself when his wife left him. Kathryn, who never married, moved in with him, and for many years this house was left vacant until she rented it out.

This two-story bungalow was built in 1936 using the Sears Craftsman plan. Its façade is three bays in width, with a side entrance and a three-bay portico. The gable roof with extended eaves is covered with painted seamed metal, and its front and rear dormers are also gabled. The original bipartite windows are 6/1. The walls still feature the original plaster, and a variety of woods are found in the woodwork, including yellow pine flooring, fir moldings, and chestnut kitchen cupboards. Outbuildings include a two-seater outhouse with a metal roof and original tongue-in-groove siding.

1316 High Street

Cross over the street and walk towards its intersection with High Street. A hundred years ago, these yards had buildings on them. So much has changed. Just past the last alley before High Street there once stood a shop which was used by the owner of the house now at #1314 High Street at the other end of the lot. Continuing down to the corner, what was until recently a vegetable garden and is now a new house, #1316 High Street was once a blacksmith shop owned by Jesse Rinehart in the 1860s and 1870s. Rinehart employed two men most of the time he was here.

Turn left up High Street. There once stood two houses before the one at #1314. The first stood opposite #1311 High Street and was owned by Jesse Rinehart and, after he died, by his wife, Sarah. They had a son, George, who served in the war from 1862 until 1865, first in Company A, 20th Pennsylvania Regiment, and later in Company F, 130th. After the war, he moved to Allegheny County. In 1874, Sarah Rinehart was assessed for an old house and shop. Sarah's heirs still owned the house as late as 1918, when it was torn down. One of the few Churchtown wells that date to the nineteenth century is on the property. There was also, at one time, a hogpen at the rear of the lot. The next lot also had a house on it built by Anthony Baird, a mason, in 1841. Baird bought this lot from Rudolph Krysher in 1839. He owned a number of lots on the lower end of High Street and may have been the builder of the houses on most of them. The house that once stood here was a one-story

1310 Church St. (2007)

1316 High St. (old-style new house) (2007)

frame house with a later half addition. There was also a shop at the rear of the lot, and this may have been what is now a frame garage. Baird sold this lot to Dr. Christian Bush in 1845 and he to Jacob Strickler (1802–1873), a druggist, in 1848. Stickler rented the house to Anna Sibbert, age 50, who lived here with her daughter and granddaughter. Strickler sold it to Issac Mishler in 1851. Issac's wife was Mary Ann Brandt (1816–1867). Her sister, Elizabeth Kline, lived just three houses up, and a brother, William, lived in Churchtown. Mishler sold the house to John Stammel in 1860.

Stammel was born in Germany in 1826. Prior to coming to America in 1851 he served for five years in the German army. After he landed in Baltimore, he lived there for six years before moving to Churchtown. He was a shoemaker for many years. Stammel served in the Civil War for three months in 1865 in Company F, 101st Pennsylvania Regiment. He was then 5'8" and 150 pounds. He married soon after he arrived in 1851, and they had ten children, but all of them died young but two. Stammel was from Waldeck in Prussia, and it is interesting that in 1870, his apprentice, Jacob Althoff, was from there as well. Was he writing back home, bringing people over? In 1860 Stammel employed two other shoemakers, whom he paid $25 a month, $5 more than what Adam Gensler of #1289 High Street paid his shoemakers. They made 40 pairs of boots that sold for $630. His materials cost $310, while his net profit was $430.

John's wife Anna died in 1879 and he married Margaret Richwine, a daughter of Christian, in 1880. After he bought his farm outside of Churchtown in 1880, he continued to rent the house here until he sold the lot to Warren Zell in 1896 for $175. Stammel was forced to give up shoemaking because of his health. He got rheumatism about 1889, and in later years, John lived with his son Hermes. In 1910 he was an invalid and was so until he died in 1912.

The recently built home that now stands here at "the point" formed by High and Church Streets is the first of its kind in Churchtown: a new house built in the old style. The architectural descriptions of the homes featured in this book were used to do a statistical analysis of building features for nineteenth-century Churchtown. This analysis, in turn, was the basis of new zoning guidelines adopted by Monroe Township to preserve the historic character of the village and its surroundings. The design guidelines are to be applied to new developments adjacent to Churchtown as well as to village infill. Based on how compatibly this newcomer fits in with the original village homes around it, the guidelines seem to be serving their purpose.

1314 High Street
This lot was bought by Anthony Baird from Rudolph Krysher in 1849. That same year, he built this house, a two-story frame, and lived here. The upper half addition is a later add-on.

1314 High St.

The next year, he sold the house to Henry Rife. Rife then sold it to Charles Huffman in 1857 for $425.

Charles Huffman (1820–?) was a cooper from Germany who lived here with his wife. His employees often boarded with him. They had a frame shop to the rear of the house in which they worked and sold their products. In 1870, Charles had two coopers working for him. One was from Maryland, but the other was from the same German state that Huffman was—Hesse Darmstadt. Interestingly, both Huffman and his neighbor Stammel were recent immigrants, and one would assume that a lot of visiting went on, both delighted to have someone to speak their native tongue to. There were other German immigrants in the village as well.

In 1876, his first wife having died, Charles married Catherine, 20 years younger than he, with a daughter Carrie; Charles had no children of his own. Charles became financially strapped and fearful of losing his house. He sold it to his brother John in 1876, and John sold it back to Catherine. Charles also owned several lots in the village, one across the street and another on West Street, and these were also involved in the transaction. Charles and Catherine lived here until she died in 1886. She then willed all her real estate to Charles. It was meant to give Charles a place to finish his days, but Catherine died in debt. Charles tried to get her estate to pay for her doctors' bills and tombstone but it was not allowed because the auditor claimed that a husband was liable for all the bills of his wife. The man who had her mortgage, John Wetzel, forced the estate to sell her property. The first sale was in November 1886, but the weather was bad, and there were no bidders. In December, it was sold again, and this time, Wetzel bought the house. Wetzel sold the house to Evan Sheaffer in 1887 for $500. He was from Silver Spring Township and died here in 1916. The house was then sold to Richard Enck.

Charles had a rough time with his neighbors. Village life was not always peaceful; over the years, the passions that flared between people tended to be forgotten. Charles' nemesis was Simon Richwine, who lived next door. The first time that the harassment from Simon boiled over into a lawsuit, Simon was 25. His cohort, James Rinehart, was the 18-year-old son of Jesse, a blacksmith who lived on the corner. These two boys and others used to taunt Hoffman by throwing rocks against his house. On many occasions, the boys would sneak into Hoffman's yard by opening the gate. They would then steal the boards that Hoffman used to border his flower beds. In June 1878, the two boys got carried away. One night, they broke into his carriage house and vandalized his spring wagon by cutting off the curtains, drilling holes in the woodwork and breaking the wagon's shaft. They then stole his wagon rubber and singletree. Hoffman was fed up and had the boys arrested. A trial was held, and the two men were found not guilty.

In March 1884, Hoffman found four pigeons missing. He suspected that Simon had decoyed them into his yard, killed and eaten them. Simon was arrested in May but again was found not guilty.

This two-and-a-half-story frame house is fairly square and, until recently, sat on a large triangular lot that included "the point" now comprising #1316 High Street. The house has undergone numerous renovations. It appears that it may have originally had 3 window bays across the front, but aluminum siding and a large picture window on the first floor have reduced the number of visible bays to 2. The gable roof is covered with modern shingles, and a portico with a concrete base spans the width of the front façade. Windows are 1/1. Outbuildings include an old frame garage with vertical weatherboards and 9-light windows.

1312 High St.

1312 High Street

This lot was sold by Rudolph Krysher to James Wiley in 1843. That same year, a two-story frame house was built. Wiley sold it to Henry Richwine in 1847, and Richwine owned it until it was sold in 1879. Henry (1816–1887) was a fence maker as was his son Simon. Henry lived here with his wife and five children and Rachel Burtnett. In March 1879, Henry and Lydia sold the house to their daughter Louisa Jane Kreiner, and she sold it back to Lydia. The family lived here until 1911 when Lydia's heirs sold it.

This two-story frame cottage at one time served as a tenant house for the manager of the hosiery factory down the alley. The square-shaped building is three bays wide, two piles deep, and has a gable roof. Two one-story extensions with sloping shed roofs extend from the rear. A front porch extends the width of the front façade over a concrete base. Windows are 6/6, and fenestration is uneven. The roof is covered with seamed metal, and the walls of the house have aluminum siding, although a mixture of wooden clapboard and German lap siding remains beneath the portico. No outbuildings remain on the property.

1306 High Street

At one time, this lot consisted of two separate houses. The western lot was sold by Rudolph Krysher to Joseph Baker prior to 1848. In 1849, he lost the house because of back taxes, and it was sold by sheriff's deed in 1849 to Dan Krysher. It was listed as a one-and-a-half-story frame. Krysher rented the house to Margaret Leidig, age 57, and her two children, both in their 20s. Krysher sold it to Rebecca and Joseph Black in 1852. Joseph died not long after, and Rebecca, who eventually moved in with her sister, Leah Diller, on Old Stone House Road, sold the house to Daniel Goodyear. He sold it in 1861 to Elizabeth Kline. Her heirs sold the lot to William C. Brandt (1820–1894) in 1885 for $284. In 1895 the heirs of Brandt sold the house to Michael Burgard for $51. The deed specifically mentions a one-and-a-half-story house here. At that price, it must have been all but falling down.

The eastern half of this lot was sold by Krysher to Joseph Baker in 1845. In 1846, he sold it to Adam Baish. 1847 is the first mention of a house owned by Baish. It was a two-story frame. If this is the house referred to in the 1850 tax lists, then it was empty in 1850. Baish, who never lived in Churchtown, sold it to Francis Menear of York County in 1854, who then sold it to Michael Brandt in 1868. Brandt sold it to Michael Burgard in 1884. In 1860, the tenant was William Miller and in 1870, Frank Winebrenner. By 1895, these two lots were combined. When this actual structure currently standing here now was built is not yet known. The appearance of the siding and corner boards and the fact that there are two separate basements suggest that the two houses here were converted into one long building. In 1895, Burgard was taxed for one house and one small house. He was a grocer, and his store was here. In 1913, he was taxed for two lots, one with a frame house (#1288 High Street) and the other with a frame house and store building. The tax records do not indicate over the years if these buildings were combined.

Michael had a daughter, Tura who was blind, but she loved to garden. On nice days, it was not unusual to find her outside, stooped over, feeling the ground with her fingers as she planted or weeded. It amazed people. When they closed the store about 1925/6, this building was then a feed mill for a few years. Later it stood empty for several years before it was turned into apartments in the 1940s.

This two-and-a-half-story frame rectangular building is now divided into units and serves as five row homes that are rented out. In all, the building has 18 bays and is 2 piles deep. Porches extend along the entire width of the front and rear façades, although sections of the rear porch have been closed in as extra rooms for some of the units. The wooden siding is a mixture of clapboard and German lap, and the gable roof is covered with corrugated metal. Fenestration and entrance arrangements are irregular. Windows are 2/2 and 1/1. To the rear of this property sits a shed covered with wide-board German lap siding, which houses the only rooster left in town.

1302 High Street
The deeds for this lot are not complete. It was sold to George Longsdorff in 1851 by Rudolph Krysher. In 1856, George sold it to his daughter-in-law, Mary Longsdorff, for $143, which may indicate that it was still just a lot. It was not on the tax assessments until 1859, owned by Michael Longsdorff. Michael, who had just been re-elected township constable in 1864, died that summer and Mary lived in this house until she died. In 1870, she shared the house with John and Mary Cook and their family. By 1885, William Mundorf, a carpenter, was the owner. Prior to 1882, he carried the mail from Churchtown to Carlisle

1306 High St. (2007)

1302 High St.

by stage, but he sold that to Charles Henry in March. Mundorf lost this house, and sheriff's sale sold it in 1889 William Beetem. Beetem sold the house to George B. Lutz and Lutz to Adam Burgard in 1895 for $700. Burgard died here in 1906, and his wife Agnes sold it to Joseph Gates in 1908. Gates sold it to Luther Arnold in 1914. Arnold also owned the blacksmith shop across the street. The house was listed at the 1889 sale as a two-story weatherboard home, 34' by 33', with a one-story attached kitchen, 12' by 12'. It was sold for $400. In 1900, Robert Wilson lived here alone. Robert had served in Company D, 7th Maryland Regiment, in the Civil War and lived off his pension. He came to Churchtown in 1877 and worked for George Plank as a machinist. He also lived with him for a few years. He never married until he married the widow Amanda Kinert in 1911. He was 64. He died two years later at the County Asylum.

This two-and-a-half-story frame house is five bays wide, with 5 over 4 construction and a central staircase. Like #1295 High Street, this house is also covered with German lap siding and the same ornamented peaked lintels crown its windows and doors as that home displays. This style of lintel is also seen on other frame houses in the township. The gable roof is covered with seamed metal. Sheltering the centered entrance is a three-bay front porch supported by carved wooden posts. (The original porch was a one-bay stoop.) The windows are 2/2 and evenly spaced. One of the three chimneys remains. The attic light in each gable end is offset, with 4 panes. The rear porch has been enclosed. Wooden outbuildings include a 3-seater outhouse and a small shed/garage.

(rear of) 1301 Church Street
Walk to the lot past the alley. This property has an interesting history. The land was part of the Wise patent, which was sold to Sam Goodyear, who sold 66 acres to Rudolph Krysher in 1818. This lot was sold to Peter Zell in 1841 for $75. Zell (1784–1863) was a mason who built the only stone house here in the village. It was two stories and 20' by 25' and was built during the summer of 1841. Zell sold the house to Catherine (nee Krysher) Bashore in 1854 and moved to Danville, Ohio, where he died. Peter Zell was the father of John D. Zell, also a mason. Living here with Peter were his wife and five children, all in their twenties and thirties. All three sons—Adam, Sam and Peter Jr.—became bricklayers, and they built many of the brick homes in Churchtown in the 1840s and 1850s.

Catherine Bashore lived here until 1869, when she sold it to Jacob Bomberger. Bomberger had rented the house out to a John Herman, one of the clerks in a dry goods store here in Churchtown. He sold it to John Bobb in 1871 and Bobb to Issac Sheaffer (1822–1882) the same year. Isaac Sheaffer was a fence maker. His son Jacob did not follow that trade, but instead, found a job with Bell Telephone putting up the new-fangled telephone wire in New York City. In May 1880, Jacob was 24, stout and partly deaf. He had just been paid on a Friday when someone followed him from the bank and, in the cover of darkness, knocked him over the head with a club. Jacob was killed, robbed, and his body thrown into the North River. He was found the next day, and the body was shipped here to Churchtown. Dr. Hartzell did the autopsy and confirmed that he had been murdered. (The telephone lines came to Churchtown about 1882.) In the summer of 1882, Issac was building a fence on the property of John Hoover, who lived in the Township. While pointing the rails, he had a heart attack and died instantly. He was found with the axe still in his hands. Mrs. Sheaffer continued to live here with her two granddaughters until the heirs sold the building to the Allen Knitting Company in 1902 for $400. The company used the stone house for storage. In 1910, the company went into receivership. Alfred Musselman held the mortgage, and it was sold to him at a public sale in 1911 for $575. The old stone house was razed shortly after 1913.

Just past the stone house was the lot owned by Solomon Diller. His lot stretched from Church Street to High Street. Here is a stone platform that is all that remains of the old Monroe Fire Company engine house. The township fire company still owns the lot (20' by 31') and the platform. The engine house was a two-story frame structure with swinging barn doors in the front and a personnel door to the left. It was a small structure, wide enough to fit two vehicles comfortably. There were the two pumpers that the fire company used. The Little Red Bull and the other one are now on display in the Monroe Fire Company building on Peffer Road. The township had to fight to get the two pumpers back. When the building was torn down, they were given to another fire company to store. They renovated them and kept them for many years. When Monroe got its new building, they wanted the pumpers given back. Reluctantly, they were.

There were stairs inside which led to the second floor, and there was just one big open room. For years, men gathered here to play cards. In the 1930s, they had a pool table in there, which left room for very little else. Behind the firehouse and to the right, there once stood a hall. These buildings were built a few years prior to 1872. The engine house was torn down in the 1960s. Just past this lot at #1296 High Street is a modern Cape Cod-style house sitting on a lot that many years ago had a very small two-room house on it. "Pappy Rupp" lived here for a while in the 1930s.

The lot surrounding the fire company lot was part of Solomon Diller's lot that he sold to his daughter Ida in 1883. Ida then sold it to David Devinney for $50 in 1892.

1296 High St.

1290 High Street

This house marks the western limit of the 4 acres that Abraham Paul bought from the Kryshers in 1816. From here up to Old Stone House Road was undeveloped land until 1848. That was when John Paul bought three undivided quarter shares of the Paul inheritance. He developed this land into lots, which were all sold in either 1848 or 1849. This lot was sold to Jacob Richwine in 1848, and he sold it to Adam Gensler, the shoemaker across the street, in 1854 for $95. Gensler sold it to William Diller in 1886. The 1889 tax assessment lists Diller with a new house and shop, so this home was built in 1887/1888. Diller (1830–?) was a carpenter and had rented in Churchtown since 1863. At age 57, this was his second home. William and his wife Margaret raised a large family. There were two sets of twins born to them, one set in 1860 and another in 1870. The set born in 1860, William and Katie, both died in September 1863, five days apart. One of the twins born in 1870 died in 1872, just 11 days after a seven-year-old sister died. The other twin survived. In earlier years, William had filled several local offices. He was a tax collector in 1865 and the township auditor in 1874.

This two-and-a-half-story L-shaped frame house has 3 over 2 construction with a central staircase and a full gable roof over the rear wing as well as over the front portion. There is no basement under the rear kitchen wing, and attic and wall inspections indicate that it was constructed slightly later than the rest of the house. The arrangement of the entrance and windows on the four-bay front façade is not quite even; the door and the windows of the eastern portion (two-bay) are evenly spaced, while the left-most bay is wider, setting its first

1290 High St.

and second-story window somewhat apart from the other openings. The small front foyer, which separates the two front rooms from each other, is trapezoidal so that the entrances to each room are at an angle. The structure of the house remains fairly intact, but cosmetic renovations now mask many underlying details on both the exterior and interior. The 2/2 sash windows of the front section were formerly ornamented with peaked wooden lintels, perhaps similar to those on #1295 High Street, just across the street. But vinyl siding now covers the exterior frames of all but one window (in the rear) and a rear attic light (now a vent). The second-story window above the front door, formerly lighting a closet above the stairway, has been sided over. The roof is covered with asbestos shingles, the cornice is sheathed with aluminum, the front door has been replaced, and its light transom sided over. Nothing remains of the original three chimneys except for two brick portions still inside the attic and one first-floor mantelpiece. The back porch (in the crook of the ell) has been walled in, and a covered wooden deck has been added onto the end of the rear wing. Inside, the rear corner staircase in the kitchen has been removed, although its second-story flight into the attic remains. Most original interior door and window frames remain except for those in the kitchen. A doorway from the first floor (east) front room into the kitchen has been boarded up so that the central staircase can no longer be circled. The interior doors in the lower story have been removed, while those in the upper story remain, as do uncovered pine plank floors and some horsehair wall plaster. The nails used in the frame of the house are square cut.

1288 High Street

This lot and the one next to it were bought by John Messinger from John Paul in 1848. Messinger, a carpenter, built this house in 1848/49. In the 1850 tax assessment it is listed as a two-story frame with a shop. Perhaps the shop sat on the adjoining lot. In 1850, John, age 24, lived here with his wife, three young children, all under age five, and three other boarders, all of them carpenters. In 1851, he sold the house to his mother-in-law, Sarah Gross, and bought the brick house now at #1284 High Street. John's wife was Catherine, the daughter of Jacob Leidig and Sarah. After Jacob died in 1832, Sarah married Henry Gross and had one other child. She bought several houses over the years in the village. She sold this one back to Messinger in 1857 and moved to Old Stone House Road. John sold this house to his mother, Barbara, the next year.

The reason for the sale of this house back to his mother and the sale of his other house to his brother-in-law in trust for his wife is evident from his financial situation. Early in the 1850s, John had gone into partnership with John Burns and set up a distillery. For whatever reason, the business failed, and by 1857, they owed money all over town.

1288 High St. (2007)

John Paul forced bankruptcy in 1859, and everything was assigned to him, but since the houses were no longer in Messinger's name, they were safe from the auction block. John lost everything. His household furnishings went to George Leidigh, who gave them back to his sister Catherine. Nineteen barrels of liquor were taken to Baltimore and sold. The hops, corn, malt, oats, etc. were also sold. The still house was fixed up by Ben Shatto before it, too, was sold. Paul realized $989 from all this, and the creditors got back 25 (cents) on the dollar.

His mother, Barbara, was the widow of John Messinger who had owned a farm in the township. After he died, she moved into Churchtown to be near her sons. Simon was living just across the street with Adam Gensler. She had two daughters, Mary Landis and Julia Ann Lehman. Barbara lived here alone until she died in 1875, and in 1876, her heirs sold the house to Michael Landis, a former cattle broker and horse dealer. Michael's wife was Mary Messinger, the daughter of Barbara. Michael, a blacksmith, owned a home on Old Stone House Road and rented this one. Landis sold it to Michael Burgard in 1911, the same man who bought houses further west of this one along High Street. There does seem to be some confusion with this lot and the one to the east. Sarah Gross is listed with a brick house in 1853, but in 1859 Barbara Messinger is listed with a two-story frame and carpenter shop. Also, in the 1872 map of Churchtown, this house is not listed, but there is supposedly one on the lot to the right. The 1872 map does have some errors, and this may be one of them.

This two-and-a-half-story frame house has three bays with side hall construction. It has been covered with vinyl siding. The gable roof still retains its seamed metal covering, as does the shallow shed roof of the rear wing. Unlike #1290, the ornamental casings of the door and windows were not sided over. The 2/2 windows of the front façade retain their wooden pediments, and two corbels support the projecting pediment over the entrance. A nine-light ransom and three-pane side lights frame the door. Rear windows are 6/6. A wooden garage sits at the rear of the property.

The lot next door was sold by John Messinger to his wife Catherine in 1858. Catherine held it until 1891, when she sold it to the Knights of Pythias, who sold it to Michael Landis in 1895. This lot is also mentioned in the will of Barbara Messinger. She willed it to John since he had erected a carpenter shop on it. She also said that it was entirely fenced in, all the way to Paul's alley at the rear of the property.

1284 High Street
To the left of the present house there once sat an early house. The now vacant lot was sold by John Paul to James Burtnett in 1849, and a one-and-a-half-story frame house was built that year. Burtnett sold it to George Morrett in 1851 and moved to #1266 High Street. Morrett sold it to William Diller in 1855. The house went through a lot of owners in the next forty years, but it was all these transactions that enabled all the adjoining lots to be identified in the deeds. The owners of this house were William Diller 1855, Sam Plank 1863, George Kaufman 1867, Joseph Harman 1869, George T.B. Herman 1871, Catherine Bashore 1872, Susan Burgard 1875, Andre Staley 1878, David Kimmel 1880, William Althouse 1882, Susan Krysher 1892, and Charles Bogar 1899. Jacob Wolf bought it in 1904, and Harvey Rinehart in 1907. Harvey lived here until he died in 1934. His wife, Lillie, died in 1939, and the heirs sold it to Velma. She lived here until she died. By that time, in the 1960s, the house was literally falling down around her. After she died, the house was torn down (ca. 1975), and the land was sold for taxes in 1980.

The brick house at #1284 was built for John Messinger in 1851. John Paul bought the lot from his mother's estate in 1848. He sold it to John Messinger in 1851. In 1857, Messinger sold it to his brother-in-law George W. Leidich to be held in trust for his wife Catherine Messinger.

George Leidich was a miller who lived along the Yellow Breeches. In 1848, he was apprenticed to Jacob Goodyear, his brother-in-law. During the war, when General Ewell was at Carlisle, a picket line was formed near Leidich's house. Ewell sent out an order that if any goods were smuggled or removed from the mill where Leidich worked, he would burn it to ashes. In 1865, Leidich helped renovate the Junction Flouring Mill and he bought it in 1881.

In 1860 John Messinger lived here with his family and two other men, both 19 and

1284 High St. (2007)

both apprenticed carpenters. Four years later John's son, David, then 18, left home to join the army. He enlisted into Company A, 20th Pennsylvania Infantry, and became a Corporal. In 1870 John had yet another apprentice with him, Harry Brubaker, as well as his wife and two children. As a carpenter, John's work took him all over the township, including nearby York County. He built barns, among other things, and in July 1871, while working on a barn in York County he took a bad fall from the roof and was badly injured. It was a long, painful wagon ride home.

John lived here until he died in 1877. In 1881 Mrs. Meneer was living with his widow Catherine. They, too, were victims of a crime spree that hit Churchtown in the summer of 1881. On August 7th, while they were at church, the house was robbed. Catherine always kept an extra key to the front door on the inside of the cellar door. The thief found the key and ransacked the house. All he took was a purse with $20 that belonged to Mrs. Meneer. The thief was never caught.

David came back to Churchtown in 1888 and moved in with his mother. Now divorced, he was suffering from tuberculosis and a spinal disease. He was emaciated, being 5'4" and only 94 pounds. He was a complete invalid; the only income he had was a pension of $12 a month. Dr. Hartzell, whose office was just up the street, treated him, but by 1890, he knew David's case was hopeless, and it was just a matter of time. David died in 1892; he was only 46. George B. Lutz, the local undertaker, took care of the funeral. After he died, Catherine lived solely on his $12 pension. When she died in 1900, the house was sold by her heirs to John Fissel.

This two-and-a-half-story common bond brick house has 3/3 side hall construction. The cornice of its metal-covered gable roof is ornamented with two rows of dentils, and the entrance is graced with a dentiled entablature and flanked by a pilaster. The 1/1 windows are topped with carved wooden lintels and have louvered wooden shutters. A roofed second-story balcony tops the side porch. The left side wall of the kitchen (rear) at one time collapsed and was repaired with cinderblocks, painted reddish-orange to match the brick. Interior integrity remains good. The random pine plank floors are exposed and well-preserved. The winding rectangular staircase continues to spiral gracefully from the second story to the attic, although curiously, its last stretch of stairs is so close to the stairwell ceiling that one must bend over considerably to get to the small attic door.

Continue up High Street to its intersection with Old Stone House. To your left is a vacant lot, #1282, once owned by John Paul. A wooden structure with iron bars on the window sat to the rear of the lot, which may have been a shop since he was a butcher. The 1865 assessment lists Paul with a brick house, which you are walking to, a one-story log house with a shop, and a frame slaughterhouse. Was the slaughterhouse on this lot? This frame shed collapsed under the weight of snow in the first few years of the twenty-first century and then demolished, had beaded weatherboard, a crude cinder block foundation, and barred windows.

346 Old Stone House Road

The frame building that you are passing to the rear of #346 Old Stone House Road's main structure was a butcher shop. The garage was built in 1952.

Turn left onto Old Stone House Road. This brick home was the former John Paul residence. It sits on land that his father, Abraham Paul, bought from the Kryshers in 1816. That was a 4-acre tract that went from High Street to the present Route 174 and from Old Stone House Road back to #1290 High Street. John Paul bought 2 acres of this land in 1848 from his father's estate for $1,300. He had this brick house built sometime between 1848 and 1849. He owned it until he died, and his heirs sold it to Mary Niesley in 1897.

In 1850, Paul was living here with his wife, two children and a domestic servant named Lydia Zinn. His oldest son, George, would later join Company I, 195th Pennsylvania Infantry. A butcher like his father, he became the regimental butcher but hurt his back during the war and had to wear a truss for the rest of his life. After the war, he returned to Churchtown but soon moved to Ohio for three years. He returned here, married Rebecca Brindle, and in 1873, moved to Philadelphia, where he and his brother J. Otis went into the wholesale grocer business.

By 1860 John Paul had moved to the west end of High Street but rented this house out. For several years, Paul was a peddler, but in

346 Old Stone House Rd. (2007)

1863, he went into butchering, a trade he and his sons followed for decades. For 14 years, he was in business with Henry Bowman, who lived at #1259 Boiling Springs Road. The tenants in 1870 were John Pipher (1819–?), a cooper, his wife and six children. In 1880, the house was let to George Keeseman, age 68. Keeseman, in earlier days, was a butcher. In the 1840s and 1850s, he owned some properties on the east end of High Street. Ever since then, he had been renting. By 1880 he had also changed vocations, becoming a tinner. He lived here with his second wife, Julia, and their three young children. He fathered his last one at 62 but never lived to see her grow up. He may have been the tenant when this house caught fire in 1882.

This Flemish bond brick house is two-and-a-half stories, with three bays and side hall construction. The metal-covered roof is hipped in front but gabled at the rear, similar to the roof of #335 Old Stone House Road, another corner building. The 6/6 windows are not quite evenly spaced and are crowned with lintels. The recessed entrance is set between two pilasters supporting an entablature. A transom and three-pane sidelights frame the door. Connected to the pent roof of the rear porch is a frame summer kitchen, also with 6/6 windows, projecting molded lintels, and wood siding, some of which are plain weatherboard and some of which is German lap. A carriage house sits at the rear of the yard. The brick sidewalk around the two street sides of this building is made of yellow bricks manufactured in nearby Mt. Holly Springs and bears the "Mt. Holly" logo. The bricks were made between 1892 and WWI. They were made with white clay but glazed a golden color with russet flakes.

344 Old Stone House Rd. (2007)

344 Old Stone House Road
This may be the most historic structure in Churchtown, or at least the most interesting. Tradition states that it was built by Jacob Wise in 1804. Another source, a biography of Jacob Plank, states that there were three houses in Churchtown in 1812. The first actual mention of it is in 1816. So tradition may actually be very close to the truth.

This lot was part of Wise's patent for 199 acres. Jacob Wise, Jr. bought 4 acres of this land and, in 1815, sold it to his brother-in-law, William Line, the village schoolteacher. Line then sold it to the two Kryshers, who sold it to Abraham Paul in 1816 for $1,500. The deed specifically mentioned a "messuage." The 1817 tax assessment listed Paul as a weaver. There was at least one outbuilding on the property, and this may have been his shop. Paul eventually used this house as a tavern, and the first record of this is an 1822 license that Paul got. Paul was forced to give up weaving because of his poor health. The house was listed as sitting on the "great road leading from Middlesex to the York Road." This road, now known as Old Stone House, was surveyed in 1824 and possibly built the following year. It may have been just a wagon trail prior to that. There must have been some wagon road that connected the tavern with the flowing traffic of movers along what is now Route 174.

After Mary Paul died in 1849, this property was rented out for a year. In 1850, David Stuckey, a plow maker, was renting it. Later that year, it was sold to Peter Goodyear, and in November, his five-month-old daughter died here. The 1853 tax records list him as a tavern keeper with a two-story log house and a shop. In 1854, he sold the place to Charlotte Allgeier for $1,550. She sold it to Sarah Liggett in 1859, and the deed called the place the "Churchtown Hotel." By 1877, the name had been changed to the "Monroe Union Hotel."

Sarah, the daughter of Jacob Lehman, was married to Thompson Liggett. It was the money from her inheritance that went into buying this hotel. Thompson died in August 1862, and 8 days later, her one-year-old daughter Sarah also died. She was left with three children to raise. Sarah moved out and moved in with her mother on Boiling Springs Road, but she rented the hotel out. In 1862 the landlord was John Dickover; he also carried a liquor license. He stayed until 1864, when Jerry Hanen took it for a year. In 1865, George O'Donell ran it, and in 1866 A.J.

Morrison. Morrison also had a liquor license and kept stallions as well. By 1870, Augustus L. Hursh, age 28, with a wife and three children, was here.

Augustus found himself in trouble because of some apparent poor judgment. In January 1874, Jacob Shopp made out an affidavit accusing Hursh of selling liquor to minors. In April, a second complaint was lodged by Shopp, and this time Hursh was forced to trial. The minors involved were Adam Gensler Jr, 14; David Kauffman, 12; George Plank, 15; Clarence Goodyear, 8; Theo Brandt, 19; Jacob Sheaffer, 13; and Solomon Kauffman. The warrant was given to the constable, Sam Morrett. Many of the fathers regarded Hursh as a nuisance, and they testified against him. Shopp tried to force Brandt to enter bail because the rumor was that Brandt was going to flee the state. But he stayed. At the trial, Hursh pleaded guilty to selling liquor without a license and was fined $50. He was found not guilty of selling liquor to minors.

Hursh moved to Dillsburg, and in April 1879, John B. Floyd took over. In April he took out the old pavement around the hotel and put in a new concrete one. Then, in May, the hailstorm damaged his building, and he had to replace 68 window panes. He stayed only a year, and in March 1880, Jeremiah B. Swartz, 31, took over the lease. He had been running a hotel in New Kingston prior to moving here. He and his wife had no children, but they had two servants to help them: Old Dan Humer, age 76, and Hannah Anderson, 22. They also had two boarders: one worked in the dry goods store while the other was Sam Eckert, a plow maker in Samuel Plank's factory. In October 1881, Swartz moved back to New Kingston, and Amos Bruner took over. Bruner was here when the hotel caught fire in 1882. His stable burned to the ground, destroying a buggy inside and a spring wagon sitting outside it. He built a new stable that same June. In February 1883, he left for Mechanicsburg, and Thompson Reighter moved in, having been renting a house on Boiling Springs Road. It was his wife who accused William Anderson of breaking and entering the following year. In 1894, Alex Goodhart took over from Harry Richwine. Prior to this, Churchtown was a dry town. What the men did instead was go outside, buy the beer, and bring the kegs back to the village. There was no law to prevent that. Goodhart got the first liquor license for Churchtown in 1894, and they had it for a long time. Sarah's heirs sold the hotel to R.D. Anderson in 1897. He then sold it to Arthur Rupley that same year. Goodhart stayed as an innkeeper until about 1900. Sometime prior to 1910, Norman Enck moved in and ran the hotel. His bartender was Thomas H. Miller so the liquor license must have been still in effect. In 1915, Rupley sold the hotel to Lizzie Brownawell.

Adjoining the house on what is now the sideyard stood a butcher shop, slaughterhouse and barn. The butcher shop went from the street all the way back to the alley. The Pauls worked here for years and, later this century Hobart Souders. About 1945, all three buildings were torn down.

During the Great Depression, the WPA dug several cisterns in Churchtown. One was in the graveyard lot down on the square. The other one was here. Not only did they provide water for fighting fires, but they also created jobs for a while.

This two-and-a-half-story traditional log and frame building is currently a single-family residence, and the apartment that once occupied the rear frame ell has been converted into additional living space. The current, carefully restored structure has a five-bay, two-pile layout with a central entrance and stairs. Windows are 2/2 with some 6/6 on the sides and are crowned by peaked lintels with ornamental scrollwork (different from those found on High Street). First-floor windows have solid wood shutters, while those above have louvered blinds. The spacing of façade windows and the door is uneven. The glass-paned door is recessed and framed by sidelights, with a larger peaked lintel matching those of the windows. German lap siding covers the walls, and the cornice is adorned with dentils, both on the front façade and the rear wall of the house. At one time a porch wrapped around two sides of the hotel, and although the marks can still be seen, it was recently taken down. The painted metal covering the gable roof is seamed vertically in front and horizontally in the rear. A summer kitchen joined to the back porch of neighboring #346 sits corner to corner with #344. Very little of the early interior features remain, other than some six-panel doors.

340 Old Stone House Road

Walk down to #340. The yard to the left of that house once contained a plow factory operated by Sam Plank, who invented the Plank Shifting Beam plow. The lot that this shop stood on belonged to Michael Fissel. Fissel (1815–1854) was a coach and wagon maker, and he had a small shop here. In 1850 he employed two men at $18 per month. Sam Plank bought the lot in 1853 and several years later enlarged it and it became his plow

340 Old Stone House Rd. (2007)

factory. In 1860 he employed 4 men at $23 per month. He paid about the best wages around. In 1860, this shop made 120 plows valued at $1,560, 65 grain cradles at $325, 10 wagons at $275 and other work at $1,350. His materials cost him $1,400. Plank's net profit was $900, four times that of Stammel, the shoemaker down at the "point" end of High Street. In 1870, Plank's son Albert was running the shop. He employed two men, and they made 300 plows and 50 cradles. In 1880, Albert still employed only two men. The average work day for the men was 12 hours, for which skilled workers got $1.50 per day while unskilled workers got $1. The plow shop also caught on fire in 1882 but it was saved. Plank later moved away from plow-making because he could no longer compete with the large factories, which underpriced him.

The house lot was part of the early Paul land. Sometime prior to 1839, Rudolph Krysher bought it, and in that year, he sold it to Cary W. Ahl for $149.[17] Ahl sold this lot to his brother, Dr. John Ahl, in 1844, and in 1845, Ahl sold it to Robert Sturgeon, a mer-

---

17. The Ahl family became quite wealthy. In 1859, Cary, with three other men, bought the Ege Forge and foundry in Boiling Springs and Cary was the last one to operate it. Cary also became president of the Harrisburg and Potomac Railroad, a position he held until he died in 1885.

chant who also owned the house to the right of this one. It was sold to George Singiser in 1852 and by his heirs to Sam Plank in 1853. The house was not built until 1858.

Jacob Plank, the father of Sam, was the inventor of the Plank plow. He came from Lancaster County in 1810, accompanying his employer, Peter Gerhart. Jacob was apprenticed as a wagon maker, but because of the heavy demand for plows, he abandoned that trade for the more lucrative plow business. In 1812, Jacob left Gerhart to work for George Lutz, west of Churchtown. On his way there, he passed through this village and helped William Line build his new home, the third one in Churchtown. After he left Lutz in 1815, he worked for Adam Stonesberger in Frankford Township until 1817. Stonesberger moved to Churchtown in the Spring of 1818. Jacob eventually settled in South Middletown Township and lived there for many years. On his property, he built a large plow-making shop. His son Sam learned the trade from him and later moved to Monroe Township, where he opened his shop and built both wagons and plows. In 1844, Jacob moved near Sam, buying a neighboring farm. Sam sold out in 1852 and moved to Churchtown and bought the Singiser place next door, at #338 Old Stone House Road, when it came up for sale in 1852. Sam trained and employed a number of men in making plows and wagons. In 1860, he had two employees living with him. In 1870, Sam did not live here, but his son Albert did, with his family and Sam Eckart, a Civil War veteran and an assistant postmaster to David Devinney. Sam Plank had bought the brick house at #349 Old Stone House Road. There he died in 1880.

Sam was elected to several local offices. He was a school director in 1854–55 and was instrumental in healing the rift between the school board and the Mt. Zion Church trustees over some land that both claimed to own. He was also a Justice of the Peace in 1860 and 1865. Sam was very involved in the life of his village. He bought land and developed it into lots, settled many estates, served as a guardian, and witnessed countless documents.

Sam retired in 1879, but his son Albert carried on the family trade. Sam invented the Plank Shifting Beam Plow while Albert patented four new plows, all variations and improvements on his father's plow. Albert lived here for many years. After his father's death, Sam C. bought the house at #349, and Albert bought this one in 1881 for $1,800. A two-month-old son died here in 1870, as well as his first wife in 1874. This house was hit hard during the hail storm of 1879; 60 window panes were broken. Albert sold the house in 1895.

Albert's son Hermes got into a bit of trouble with some friends of his. One October night in 1886, Hermes, 18, along with Grant Miller, 19; Jacob Messinger, 22; Abraham Nelson, 17; John Zell, 16; and James Lerew, went over to the Ridge School, which lay outside of the village and began harassing those inside. Apparently, the people inside were part of a singing school. The boys spent some time outside making a general nuisance of themselves, but they were recognized by those inside and arrested later that week. The parents of the boys got together with those who filed the complaint and it was agreed to settle outside of court. There were probably a few thrashings administered.

In 1910, Maria Williamson, 76, and her husband, Thomas U., lived here. Thomas was a Civil War veteran, having served for 10 months in 1862–3 in the 158th Pennsylvania Militia. Thomas died in 1909 at the age of 80, a physical wreck. A medical exam in 1902 described him as 5'7" and 140 pounds. His eyesight was failing, all but one tooth was gone, and he had two broken ribs that never healed from a fall in 1877.

From 1936–1944, Squire John Nickey lived here with his two unmarried daughters. Cora was an accomplished musician and she taught piano. Her sister Alma was a schoolteacher at Mt. Holly. Squire Nickey used to get very upset over the football games that the local boys used to play on the grounds of the old cemetery on the square. He would often march down and chase the boys off. This was not the only way that they upset the Squire. The town hill[18] was always a favorite spot for sledding in winter. It was also the main road through town. After a few hours sledding the road became so slick that cars could not make it up the hill. And so Nickey would come out and chase the sledders off. Squire Nickey was also very influential in the village, and the story is told that when the people wanted to put electric lights in town, he said that they didn't need them, and that was that.

This frame house was built by Sam Plank in 1857/58, who was then living in #338 next door. He sold that place in 1859 and may have moved here. This house is a two-and-a-half-story rectangular clapboarded structure with five windows across the front and a two-story Queen Anne-style bay with tripartite arched windows on the south side. The front entrance is covered by a hood supported by corbels and pilasters and is crowned by a transom. The gable roof, covered with seamed metal, is ornamented at the cornice by ornate molding and double corbels. The evenly spaced, shuttered windows are 3/1, and the two-story bay window features an elaborate triangular dentil motif at the cornice. The side porch is supported with wooden pillars, arranged in sets of three at each corner. A wrought iron fence surrounds the yard.

338 Old Stone House Road
Before you get to the house you pass what is now the side yard for this home. There once existed a frame structure here that was used as a shop by Sam Plank and, after he built a new plow factory on the lot south of #340, as a men's social hall. Later, in the 1910s, it was a small restaurant before being torn down.

This lot for #338 was sold by Abraham Paul to Adam Stonesberger in 1823 for $200. Stonesberger was a blacksmith who also owned property across Route 174. He may have had this house built as early as 1824. The 1824 road docket for Old Stone House Road shows a house on this site. In 1828, he was the owner of a store with Robert and David Sturgeon as the tenants. The 1832 tax assessment lists him as the owner of two improved lots. Stonesberger got into financial difficulties, and he assigned this property to George Brindle and Daniel Hollinger in 1834. They sold it to Robert Sturgeon the next year for $700. Sturgeon died in 1845, and his heirs sold it to his son, Henry, who sold it to George Singiser in 1852 for $1,600. George agreed to sell the property to Sam Plank, who had just moved into the village from the township, but Singiser died before the contract was executed. The matter was settled in Orphan's Court, and Plank bought it for $1,580. Plank bought this house and the two adjoining lots, one to the left and one to the right. It was probably at this time that he built the adjacent

---
18. Old Stone House Road.

shop on the left. In 1857, Sam began construction of a new home at #340 and sold this house to David Devinney in 1859. Devinney lived here until he died in 1895. He had a number of occupations over thirty years, some of which were postmaster, druggist, owner of an icehouse, and confectioner.

The first mention of Robert Sturgeon is on the 1828 tax schedule, where he is listed as a merchant with his brother David. In 1835, Robert bought David out and ran the store himself. The store occupied the first floor, with living quarters in the rear and above. Robert died in 1845 at age 50. After he died, the store was run by Jacob Paul from 1846 until about 1848. In 1848 a writ of partition gave Henry Sturgeon the whole property but stipulated that he was to pay his mother and two sisters $571 each. Henry moved to Carlisle and rented the store to George and Christian Brandt. George was 31 and had a new wife, just 18. They had no children. Christian was his younger brother. He had a wife and baby in 1850. Christian may have lived in the rooms above the shop on the adjoining property at #336 (or he may have lived with his brother—this point is unclear). Sturgeon sold the store to George Singiser in 1852. George had been a merchant in Churchtown since at least 1847, renting out the store across the street. When this one became available, he bought it but died soon afterward.

David Devinney was first listed in the tax records as a store helper in 1858. He was then 35. He had moved to Churchtown about 1855 and, in 1859, bought this place. The small shop to the left (no longer standing) was his confectionary store and possibly the same building where he operated as a druggist and tobacconist. The rear of this building was his living quarters. In 1871, David became insolvent, and his creditors, M.L. Hoover and George Butturf, sold off his effects. The store lot next door went to Levi Enck.

For 25 years, David was the postmaster of Churchtown, and his office was in the front part of his house, the same as the store. His place became an agricultural curiosity shop. Every summer, local farmers would bring in the largest or earliest of some fruit or vegetable and others would try and top it. Sort of like show and tell, with bragging rights.

The only known murder in Churchtown occurred right here on Saturday, June 17, 1893. Frank Hosler was one of a party of young Churchtown men who were in the habit of bringing a keg of beer from Carlisle and drinking it here since Churchtown was unlicensed. This Saturday night, Hosler became quite drunk and was in a fighting mood. He had a grudge against several people and left with a loaded revolver to get square with them.

He first went to #1269 High Street to the residence of Emanuel Trostle. Here, he stopped and rapped on the door and asked to see George, Emanuel's younger brother. Emanuel refused to let George go out and this angered Hosler, who forced his way into the house. Hosler was thrown out and the door was locked to prevent his getting back in. Hosler was impotent with rage, and before walking away, he broke a window pane. Emanuel, watching Hosler through the window, was showered with glass. Hosler walked to the hotel where there was a group of young men standing around laughing. He pointed the revolver at them and said if they didn't stop laughing at him, he would shoot them. He then walked down here to the post office. Here, he met Warren Zell and began

338 Old Stone House Rd.

to reprimand him for not helping him clean up the Trostles. Zell tried to ignore him by walking away, but Hosler grabbed him, and the two began to scuffle. Hosler pulled out his revolver and fired at Zell but missed, and the ball struck Sam Eckert, who was sitting on a bench here in front of the post office. Eckert got up and walked into the store, said that he had been shot, and then walked up the street to the residence of Dr. Hartzell.

Hosler was not aware during all this that he had shot anybody, and maddened by his failure to kill Zell, aimed the revolver at him and fired twice, but the gun did not go off. Zell was able to disarm him, and about this time, Hosler learned that he had shot Eckert. He became frightened and ran away, hiding in a clover field. That night, a posse went looking for him at his father's farm outside of Churchtown, but Frank was not found. Sunday morning, Hosler went home, and Constable Morrett came and arrested him. He was taken to Carlisle by buggy and placed in jail.

Dr. Hartzell examined Eckert that morning. The bullet had entered Eckert above his navel and went out near his spine. Dr. Koons, then of Mechanicsburg, was called in, but the case was hopeless. Eckert was then removed to his room at the hotel. He was conscious all day Sunday and, knowing that he had not long to live, made out his will and funeral arrangements. He had several nieces in Chambersburg. He began to hemorrhage and died Monday at 10 a.m. He was 67. Eckert had come to Churchtown in 1867, having served in the Civil War in Company K, 135th Pennsylvania Infantry. He was a mechanic and worked at Plank's plow factory for many years, as well as being an assistant postmaster for David Devinney. For a while, he lived next door at #340 Old Stone House and later boarded at the hotel, where he died. It is stated that until recently, his bloodstains could still be seen on the wood floors.

Frank Hosler was 23. A good student in his younger days, he became a bad apple and a source of trouble for his parents. Some put it down to the dime novels he loved to read. He imagined himself as a desperado and, for some years prior, had been carrying a concealed revolver. After his incarceration, his mother sent word to the sheriff to keep an eye on Frank as he might try and commit suicide, but Frank was there for his trial in September. There were two cases against him. Trostle sued him for assault and battery, to which Hosler pleaded guilty and was fined $1. On the charge of murder, he also pleaded guilty and was sentenced to 15 years at the Eastern Penitentiary in solitary confinement.

Frank was sent to the penitentiary on October 3, 1893. His description upon entering was a man of 5'6" and 146 pounds with brown hair and eyes. He had a bruise on his right hand from a pistol shot. He'd left school at seventeen after ten years of education. Frank was pardoned on May 29th, 1896 and moved back to Churchtown. He was married the following year and got a job selling books. He lived for many years at #314 Old Stone House Road.

In March 1879, David Devinney took an extensive trip out to the Midwest, where he looked at buying some farmland. Dan Bowman looked after his post office during the month-long trip. He bought a 160-acre farm in Lee County, Illinois, but David never moved away. Two years before he died, David took a ten-day trip to the World's Fair. Jerry Bowers was left in charge of the drugstore. When David died in 1895, his only heir was Marcus, who was mentally disabled. Marcus continued to live here, but the house was rented out.

Marcus had income from the rent of the farm in Illinois, $12 per month, plus the rent from this house, $5 per month. Until 1903, D.K. Paul was his guardian. Paul was responsible for the repairs to this house; in 1897, a new roof was put on and repaired three years later when new shingles were added. Marcus did not live here but was boarded out until 1907. A.C. Devinney became Marcus' guardian until the former died in 1917. In 1907 Marcus came back here to live, living with Eli Shearer, who ran a restaurant next door. After Eli's death, his widow Maria continued to live here until 1917. For the next eight years, there were four renters. Irvin Winand rented here, and he was paid $57 every six months to board Marcus and do his washing. Marcus, now middle-aged, used to sew dishcloths that he would sell all over town. In 1919, Mary Comp moved here, and Marcus had to go live with Emma Engle up the street. He became sick in November 1920 and the following year was taken to the country home, where he died in 1928. After Marcus died the house passed to the heirs of David's brother Augustus, and they sold it in 1930.

This two-and-a-half-story, four-bay brick structure features Flemish bond brickwork in front and common bond in the rear. Shaker shingles are still on the gable roof under the metal, and there is possible mortise-and-tenon construction in the back, with pegged construction in front. A window separates the two front doors. The porch columns are cast iron, and a cast iron hook hangs from the porch roof directly above a door that leads straight down into the basement (possibly for lowering ice). Windows are 9/6 and 6/6. The two-over-two construction of the rear wing of the house suggests that this was the original portion. A brick bake oven protrudes from the back wall, and a hand-operated pump still stands in the side yard.

Four of the five original fireplaces still stand, and two of the upstairs fireplaces have candle closets. Original woodwork remains throughout except for one room, and two bedrooms contain original chair rails and shaker pegs. The floorboards are random-width plank pine. The front portion of the house has a three-story staircase, while the rear staircase into the kitchen has beaded boards on its wall.

336 Old Stone House Road

This lot was always part of #338 until David Devinney sold it to Levi Enck in 1872. As mentioned earlier, he was forced to sell it to pay his creditors. Levi's wife, Mary Bryan, was related to David Devinney's Catherine Bryan. When Levi bought this lot, there was a small shop already standing, which can be seen from the side of the house, and when the main house was built, it was incorporated into it. The shop may have been built as early as 1850;

the main house was built by Levi's brother, Issac, in 1873. In 1878, Levi sold the house back to Catherine Devinney and then rented it back from her.

Levi was a long-time butcher and resident of Churchtown. The first mention of him is in the 1869 tax assessment when he is listed as a tenant butcher with a shop at the corner of Green and Church Street, now Green and Boiling Springs Road. He lived with his mother and family at #1261 Boiling Springs Road and ran his business from the shop at the rear. In 1869 he married Mary J. Bryan and apparently married into money. After his house at #336 Old Stone House Road was built, Levi and Mary spent the rest of their married life here. Levi and Mary had a large family, but three children died while living here: Mamie in 1875, Lillie in 1876 and Champie in 1877, aged 2, 8 and 6, respectively. In 1879 a butcher shop was built on the rear of the property, which Levi operated until he died in 1922. In later years, he also did some auctioneering. He was an auctioneer at the estate sale for Levi Gates, who lived across the street at #1276 Boiling Springs Road. Gates died in Feb 1894 and the auction was in April. Levi Enck's nephew, Elmer, had married a daughter of Gates, and this may have been the reason that Levi was the auctioneer. Levi was also the township constable in 1872. Mary Enck died in 1890. Shortly before she died, Mary bought back the house to give Levi a home for the rest of his life. After she died, Levi remarried. In 1923, his heirs sold the home to his son, Norman Enck. Norman was also a butcher, and most of the villagers just called him Butch Enck.

In 1900, the conditions for preserving meat were a little primitive. The butcher's

336 Old Stone House Rd. (2007)

idea of a refrigerator was a barn completely closed up so that no air could get inside. In winter Enck's employees would cut ice from the Yellow Breeches at Leidich's Station and haul it back to Churchtown. Devinney had an icehouse next door, and here, the ice was stored and covered with sawdust, which kept it for a while. Norman Enck did a lot of business at the Carlisle Farmer's Market. To get there at 5 a.m., he had to leave Churchtown at two in the morning. On cold mornings heated bricks would be put in the wagon to warm cold feet.

In the front of the house, there used to be benches. There was little entertainment in Churchtown save the socializing that went on here at all hours of the day. So strong was the pull here that many men, no sooner had they gotten home from their jobs in the city, would rush here before supper and loaf. It was a wonderful way to unwind. This corner was also a trolley stop and, in later years, a bus stop for all the school children.

When putting in the flower gardens at the rear of the property in 1988, the owner, Joan Fields, with the help of none other than Kevin Vanderlodge, who boarded here, came across what appeared to be the trash pit for the house at #338. There were numerous druggist bottles as well as broken plates and crockery. In the days prior to trash removal, that's where most rubbish went; almost all the homes in Churchtown have yards full of "treasure."

When the state widened the road through Churchtown in the 1950s, the residents tried to get the state to buy this house and tear it down. It sits on a dangerous corner, creating limited vision. But the state refused, and the house remains.

This two-and-a-half-story, five-bay frame house sits on the southwest corner of the town square. The 4-over-4 house features a Georgian floor plan, symmetrical fenestration, and a recessed entrance surrounded by a transom and sidelights. The original wood shutters are solid on the first floor and louvered on the second, and the remaining original windows are 2/2. The gable roof is covered with seamed metal. Attached to the rear of the house is a summer kitchen with 6/6 windows. This may be the part that dates to the 1860s. There is an L-shaped back porch. The house has undergone numerous renovations, including the replacement of the pediment over the front entrance with a one-bay portico (the early 1980s) and the removal of the muntins on the lower sashes of the first-floor windows to create a 2/1 look from the original 2/2 windows. The wooden clapboard has been covered with aluminum siding. To the rear of the property sits a garage built in the 1930s on the site of the former Butcher shop.

Turn left onto Route 174. This road may have been laid out as early as the 1750s. In the early 1800s it was known as the Forge Road, leading to Ege's Forge near Boiling Springs. Later it became Church Street, Water Street, then Boiling Springs Road, but with the widening of it in the 1950s, it is now Route 174.

The trolley ran along here during the first three decades of this century. The tracks were on the northern side of the street and were taken out in 1930. Looking down Route 174 towards York Road, aka Route 74, you can see where Church Street veers to the left. The main trolley line followed Church Street, but a spur went to the right and around the houses before joining up below town. This was where the trolley from Carlisle passed the trolley going to Carlisle.

1272 Boiling Springs Road

This is the white house just to the left of the brick house on the corner. This house and all those down to the corner of the diagonally situated Union Alley were part of 7 lots developed by Samuel Diven in 1849. This land, a triangle formed by Route 174, Union Alley in the rear and Old Stone House Road to the east, was part of the patent in 1814 by Jacob Wise, Sr. 144 perches; it was sold to Jacob Wise, Jr., who sold it to William Line in 1816. He sold it to Ferdinand Edelblutes, a carpenter, who moved to New Cumberland after selling it to Rudolph Krysher, who in turn sold it to Abraham Smith, all in 1816. Smith sold it to Adam Stonesberger in 1817 for $970. Sometime prior to 1812 a two-story log house was built here with a blacksmith shop, while a bark shed and tanyard with 23 vats were added a few years later. One of the town wells was also located here. Jacob Wise, Jr. was a blacksmith, so it was he who likely improved this lot, and Edelblutes may have been the carpenter for him. Edelblutes was living in Churchtown by 1811. He was sued by Joseph Bricker, a farmer south of Churchtown, in 1812 for failure to repay a $200 loan. Perhaps the money went towards building the house. Other houses that Edelblutes probably did the carpentry work for are #352 Old Stone House Road (1812) and #1320 Church Street (1812).

The first mention found for Adam Stonesberger was in 1815 when he was living in Frankford Township, about 8 miles north of Carlisle. He was primarily a wagonmaker, but he also dabbled in wooden plows and grain cradles. The wooden plow was a holdover from an Old German belief that an iron or metal plow hurt the soil, giving off a poisonous energy that harmed the plants. While progressive farmers were using the latest metal plows around Churchtown, there were still some who clung stubbornly to their beliefs.

Adam stayed in Frankford Township until 1818, when he moved to Churchtown to take up business on the lot he had bought the year prior from Smith. He was successful here, and in 1823, he bought the lot at #338 Old Stone House from Abraham Paul. Here, he built a two-story brick store, which he rented out.

In 1830, Adam bought one of the new Livinger lots across the street from the store. He then sold it to Daniel Krysher. Financially, Adam became overextended, and in 1834, he assigned his property to George Brindle and Daniel Hollinger, his largest creditors, who sold off the two lots to pay Stonesberger's debts. The tanyard lot went to David Martin and Thomas Williamson for $1,350. Adam moved on and may have died in Ohio.

David Martin owned a hotel in Churchtown, and numerous other properties in the township, so the running of the tannery was left to Williamson. He, too, got into financial difficulty and in 1841, David Martin bought out his share at a sheriff's sale. In 1842, he sold it to Sam Diven, and seven years later, Diven divided it into seven lots. Most of the outbuildings were torn down,

1272 Boiling Springs Rd.

and homes were erected along the street. In 1848, he bought a strip of land from Frederick Goodyear, which became Union Alley the following year. This alley runs behind the properties. In the early 1800s, a well was dug behind the house at #1272. It was a community well, and when Diven sold this land by lots, one of the stipulations was that the owners of lots one through five would have free access to the well on lot two.

Sam Diven was born in York County in 1813. He became a tanner early in life and later moved here, where he followed the same trade. After selling all the above lots, he moved to Mt. Holly Springs prior to 1855. There, he became a merchant and introduced the first steam saw mill ever used in that area. In 1868, he moved to Harrisburg and became a brickmaker and builder. He died in 1886.

The date that this house was built cannot be proved. It sits on part of lot two of Diven's addition, the lot including the brick house on the corner. This house may have at one time been a frame shop that had been converted into a house. The 1850 census apparently puts a family here: one Jacob Weaver, a cabinetmaker with a wife and two children and Edwin Quigley, his apprentice. However, in 1856, the owner of this lot, George Wunderlich, was assessed for a brick house and a tinner shop. What can be proved is that it was a house by 1869. That year, Christian Niesley and Tobias Kauffman sold to John Plank a house 24' by 16' on part of lot 2. This lot was originally owned by George Wunderlich, who sold it to W. H. Russell in 1865. Russell sold it to Niesley and Kauffman in 1866. When Plank bought it, he rented it; in 1880, his son George lived there. George was a machinist who worked at the machine shop around the corner of Old Stone House Road. Living with him and his family were his brother Clarence and three male boarders, all machinists, as well as a female domestic servant. During the early years of this century, this house was a bake shop and later a hat store.

In 1900, Harry Landis lived here with his family. He was a grocer next door at #334 Old Stone House Road and a Civil War veteran. He served for four months in Company I, 195th Pennsylvania Infantry, in 1864. Born in Churchtown, he lived his whole life here, renting at various locations in town. Harry stood 5'8" and about 150 pounds. He was bald on top and grey around the sides. He later developed cataracts in both eyes and went to Baltimore for an operation, but it was a failure as he was unable to read even with glasses. In 1922, he suffered a stroke on his right side, and for the last three years, he needed constant attention.

The house is reputedly haunted. In the 1930s, Ruth Waggoner, a widow, with her mother and two young girls lived here. They rented from the owner for $8 a month. Being the widow of a minister, Ruth had no income except for the generous gift of $21 a month that another man gave them from his retirement. One of the then-young girls remembers several eerie happenings. There was a picture that hung on a wall in an upstairs bedroom. Some nights, that picture would come off its nail and slide down the wall until it hit the floor. The grandmother also saw an older woman descend the stairs to the kitchen door, lift off the latch from the inside and go outdoors. The story was told to them of a woman who, about 1900, had hung herself in the attic.

The two-and-a-half-story house is attached on both sides to the neighboring brick houses. Its façade is three bays wide and is covered with aluminum siding. The upper windows are 1/1 and are set in thin, molded casings, while picture windows have replaced the lower windows. The arrangement of the windows and door is uneven. Two-story and one-and-a-half-story extensions with sloping shed roofs are attached to the rear of the structure. A number of outbuildings stand in the yard behind the house, including a frame stable or carriage house, an outhouse, and two small sheds. The outside was extensively remodeled after Mabel Gibb bought it in the 1940s. The front entrance was originally in the center of the house between the two windows. It opened into the living room. There was a doorway that led to the backyard in the rear of the kitchen, and the kitchen was the width of the house. To the right of the living room was the dining room and the only way into that was from the kitchen. There was no doorway between the two front rooms. The stairs to the second floor were in the kitchen, steep and narrow. In the front of the house had been a large store display window to the left of the door. Gibb had that taken out, removed the central door and put in the door now used on the right of the house.

1274 and 1276 Boiling Springs Road

The owners of #1274 have always bought all of Diven's lot three and the back half of lot four. This duplex was built between 1850 and 1852. The first buyer of #1274 was George Wunderlich in 1850, a tinner. He also had the shop next door. In 1850, George employed two men at $23 per month. These were the best wages in Churchtown. The men did not only tinwork but also worked with sheet iron. They produced tinware valued at $650 that year. George lived here with his wife and three young children. Prior to selling it, George moved out of the township and rented the house out. His tenant in 1860 was Jacob Goodyear, age 42, his wife Susan and their seven children. William Russell bought it in 1865. While living here, Russell was a Justice of the Peace in 1869 and an election inspector in 1872.

In January 1873 Jacob Shopp had Russell arrested for forgery. His father-in-law, John Cocklin, went on bail. Apparently, Russell was forging certificates upon which he obtained money from Lodge 215 of the I.O.O.F (International Order of Odd Fellows). For some reason, Shopp later agreed to drop the charges if Russell would pay the costs of the prosecution to date, which he did.

Russell was forced to assign his house to John Paul, who sold it to Russell's father-in-law, John Cocklin, in 1873. But John died that year. Perhaps he knew he was dying when he bought the house because he willed it back to his daughter, Mary Russell. The Russells rented the house out; in 1880, Mary's mother, Anna, was living there, as well as her sister, Caroline Work. Mary Cocklin's heirs sold the house to Sam Kline in 1891. Three years later, he went bankrupt, and Fillmore Faust, his assignee, sold the house to David Goodyear, who sold it to Ephraim Baish in 1895.

Eph was from Franklintown, York County, prior to moving to Churchtown in 1895. He was an old veteran who served two enlistments. He was captured at Chancellorsville on May 3, 1863, the battle where Stonewall Jackson was mortally wounded. Eph was paroled 11 days later and rejoined his regiment. He was wounded at the Wilderness May 5, 1865, having been shot in the ribs and arm. After he recovered, he was wounded again in October 1864, shot in the hand.

Eph lived the rest of his life here in Churchtown. He was a short man but heavyset, being 5'5" and 165 pounds. He and his wife lived alone; one night in April 1912, Eph had a stroke and was paralyzed on his right side. That same night, his wife fell trying to help him and broke her collarbone. He died a few weeks after the stroke.

The #1276, half of the duplex, was built in 1850 by Sam Diven. John Murphy, a Justice of the Peace and saddler, bought the lot in 1850 for $520. The deed states that he was to get half of a brick house on lot four plus all of lot five, on which there was a frame stable and frame shop. However, he only got to use

1274 & 1276 Boiling Springs Rd.

half of the shop (then a shoemaker shop) as Diven reserved for himself the other half of it, 23 feet in front and 25 feet in back. Murphy had a young apprentice living with him—Levi Gates, age 18. Murphy also had two other men working for him. He paid $16 per month. Murphy sold the house to Sam Smith in 1854. Smith was a saddler, as was the man who bought the house in 1859 (from William Bentz), Levi Gates. Levi may have continued to live here those years before he bought it, working for Sam Smith.

Levi was born in York County and came to this area as a boy. He was apprenticed to John Murphy and followed this trade until he died in 1898. Levi served in the war in Company F, 101st, in 1865. He was described as being 5'6", 188 pounds, healthy-looking and corpulent.

His son Addison learned the trade from him and, after working with his father for many years, moved to Boiling Springs, where he was a harness maker for 25 years. As a young man Addison got himself into some serious trouble. In 1881, when he was 20, he got Lizzie Sweger pregnant. Lizzie was from Perry County and was working for Theo Brandt as a cook. When she realized she was pregnant, she confronted Addison. Addison procured some ergot from a druggist outside of Churchtown and told her to take it, hoping to induce a miscarriage. Lizzie went back to her mother's in Perry County and took the medicine there. It made her very sick, so she stopped taking it and came back to Churchtown. In August she went into the household of David Devinney as a cook. She took more of the medicine there and again got sick. In September, she had Addison arrested, and his father, Levi, went on bail.

Devinney, a druggist, went on bail for Lizzie. The trial was not held until August 1882. One of those to testify for the prosecution was William Anderson, the barber who lived on High Street. He said that he met Addison in the fall of 1881, and Addison mentioned that he had gotten into a baby scrape with Brandt's cook. Anderson told him to try and get out of it and then Addison admitted to getting some medicine. Addison was found guilty. His lawyer filed for a new trial, which was granted. In April 1883, Addison was found not guilty. Lizzie's mistake in this case was admitting that after the ergot did not work, she went to another druggist to get something to abort the child.

Levi had other young men as his apprentices. One was his son Harry. Harry learned the harness trade and then went to work for his uncle Sam at Shippensburg. (Sam Gates, nine years younger than his brother Levi, had lived with Levi in the 1860s and learned harnessmaking from him). Harry moved from his uncle's business to Indiana to work for his uncle Harry, the manager of a harness factory. Levi's son Philip (1865–1903) refused to be a saddler. Instead, he went to various academies and became a teacher. He taught three terms here in Churchtown before moving to Iowa, where he died. He was only 38.

In 1860 Levi employed two men at $20 per month. They made 30 sets of harnesses valued at $470, 40 collars at $90, 12 bridles at $36, 5 saddles at $75 and other work at $300. His materials cost $430. His net profit in 1860 was under $100. It was a lean year for Levi.

One of Levi's employees in 1860 was his brother Sam. Sam stood 5'5" and was about 125 pounds. In 1865, he joined the army and became a sergeant in Company I, 195th.

He got a hernia while in the army and had to wear a truss ever after. After coming back to Churchtown, he married Caroline Goodyear in 1869 and moved to Shippensburg.

After Levi's death, his heirs sold the house to his daughter Cora and her husband, Elmer Enck. Elmer (1864–1940) was originally a cooper, but in 1893, when he was 29, he was appointed postmaster at Churchtown and held this position for 16 years. The post office was in the old saddler shop, and here, he also ran a cigar store. Elmer's uncle was Levi Enck, the butcher, who lived just up the road at #336 Old Stone House Road. Elmer later sold this house to his daughter, Ida, so it remained in the Gates family for over 120 years.

This common bond brick duplex is composed of one three-bay unit with a rear ell and a second unit to the east with a two-bay side extension. The front entrances stand side by side in the center of the main structure and are flanked by fluted pilasters and crowned by transoms and fan-shaped wood panels trimmed with dentils. The eastern extension has a third front entrance, also with a transom, that is crowned by a lintel and a row of vertical stretchers. The 1/1 windows are also trimmed with lintels and rows of stretchers above them. The stretcher rows are part of a yellow-white brick-face exterior that covers the older red bricks underneath, much like that on the farmhouse at #1299 Brandt Road. The two-and-a-half story structure as a whole has a multiple gable roof covered with seamed metal. A side porch off the western unit has a flat roof with entablature, which is supported by square columns. Attached to its roof is a frame summer kitchen with 1/1 windows, wood siding, and a steeply sloping shed roof. The extensions attached to the rear of the structure are in a variety of shapes and sizes.

Levi Gates put in a new brick sidewalk here and at #1278 in August 1880. It may still lie beneath the concrete.

1278 Boiling Springs Road
This house was originally a shoe shop, then a saddler shop, and finally a post office before becoming a private residence. From the deeds it would seem that two owners split the use of this shop. The Levi Gates used the right half of the house while the owners of the lots to your left, lots six and seven, were allowed the use of the left half. A deed for 1851 specifies this. Sam Diven sold to George Brindle, a trustee for Mary Ann Natcher, lots six and seven and the southwest corner of lot five, 34' by 25'. It was then a shoemaker shop.

Sam Lehman bought the house and two lots from the Natcher heirs in 1877 and, in 1882, sold it to Albert Plank. Plank rented the house out and after he moved to Carlisle, sold it to Annie Cooper in 1895. At the same time, the Coopers also bought Plank's blacksmith shop at #330 Old Stone House. Annie's husband, William, went bankrupt and was forced to assign the two properties. They were both sold to Daniel Bentz, her father, of York County in 1898. Bentz died in March 1899, and this house was sold at auction in September to George Zell, a barber, for $250. George sold it to Warren Zell in 1905.

In the early 1930s John Brownawell lived here with his wife, a daughter of George Zell. She was a redhead who always wore her hair piled high on top. Somebody burned a large cross in his side yard one night because they disapproved of some alleged activity of his wife. The cross smoldered for several days and was quite a sight for the schoolchildren who passed it.

This three-bay frame house with a two-bay side extension has 2/2 windows. The roof of the extension is slightly lower than that of the main house, but both roofs are gabled and covered with seamed metal. Each section has a front entrance. That of the larger section is topped by a transom, and protected by a canopy that is supported by two corbels. A side porch attached to the west wall of the building appears to be a modern addition, but the summer kitchen attached to the rear of the house seems to be original. Outbuildings include two outhouses and a garage. At one time, there was a frame stable attached to the west wall but this has been torn down.

Keep walking until you get to the intersection of Union Alley and Route 174. This triangular piece of land was lots six and seven in Diven's additions. Looking up Union Alley, to your right was the old Wise patent, and to your left was the Hugh Gibson patent, which the Goodyear family later owned. The boundary line lay to the right of the alley, and if you turn around, continue down Church Street.

Lots six and seven, now empty, only ever had a frame stable built on them. Brindle bought them in trust for Mary Ann Natcher. In 1855, he also bought for her the lot to the north where the modern ranch house and garage now sit to the rear. Daniel Stees bought that land from the Goodyear heirs in 1853, part of 151 acres that Stees later sold off. Mary Ann was the widow of Gabriel Natcher, a millwright, and the daughter of John Jacob Lehman (1787–1849). Gabriel (born 1819) left Mary Ann to raise four young children after his early death. In 1850, Gabriel and his family may have been living on the second floor of the shop at #1278. He had an apprentice with him, Peter Pifer, age

1278 Boiling Springs Rd.

20, from Germany. That same year, Gabriel was arrested for fraud on a complaint by A. Keeney. It was settled out of court. Two years later, he was arrested for larceny but was found not guilty.

Mary Ann also had a brother, Sam, who was a landowner in Churchtown, and her sister was Sarah Liggett, who owned the hotel on Old Stone House Road and other property in Churchtown. When their father Jacob died in 1849 he was against his daughters getting money; he preferred instead that they invest in real estate. Two of his daughters, Nancy and Elizabeth, were directed by his will to buy land in Monroe Township. Sarah and Mary Ann did the same. These lots here were sold by Mary Ann's heirs to her sister Sarah in 1873 and by her to her brother Sam in 1877. Sam sold them to Albert Plank in 1882. Even as late as 1882, the sale still included half of the shop, i.e., #1278, on lot five.

1280B Boiling Springs Road
This house was apparently built by 1882. It does not appear on the 1872 atlas. It sits on a part of the Goodyear land that was sold to Daniel Stees. He sold this tract to George Brindle in trust for Mary Ann Natcher. In

1280B Boiling Springs Rd. (2007)

1882, her heirs sold the house to Albert Plank for $465.

Two houses occupy this property at the junction of Union Alley with Boiling Springs Road. #1280B is a two-story, four-bay, square-frame house that sits along the alley. Its German-style double front doors are surrounded by molded wood casing and crowned by pediments. The arrangement of the 2/2 windows is symmetrical. The gable roof is covered with seamed metal. A one-story extension attached to the house in the rear, also with 2/2 windows, appears to be original. A modern canopy with wrought iron posts has been added over the front doors. #1280A is a modern ranch house and sits to the rear of

1280A Boiling Springs Rd. (2007)

the property, in front of a large wooden stable now used as a garage.

1279 Boiling Springs Road

Cross back to the south side of Boiling Springs Road and walk back to #1279. This tract was part of the 4 acres that Abraham Paul bought from Rudolph Krysher in 1816. In 1823 he sold to Sam Hyer, a merchant, a piece of land 60' by 174' for $100. Hyer built a two-story brick house, brick store room and frame warehouse on this lot and the one to your right (#1281). This second lot he bought in 1825 for $100. An alley bounds both lots to the rear, and #1279 has one on the east. These alleys were opened in 1824.

Sam was a merchant here for ten years, but he got into financial difficulties and was forced to sell this property at a sheriff's sale. At the time, the house was described as a two-story brick house, 42' by 36', with a kitchen attached, 23' square. The property was sold to Adam Kyle in 1833. Kyle was also a merchant and lived here until 1838. In 1838, the lots were sold to John Ahl. Dr. Ahl rented these buildings to his brothers Peter and Cary Ahl, and they ran a store here for two years. Peter then bought Cary out and ran it alone for a year until John sold the house to Sam Zeigler in 1841. Zeigler sold it to Richard Anderson, a blacksmith, in 1845. Anderson lived here, but his shop was across the street, where he had bought lot one in Diven's addition, where there was a blacksmith shop. In 1850, eleven people were living in this house. Richard, his wife and five children and four of his employees, all young men who were originally from out of the township. In 1860, Richard lived here with seven children and three employees.

In 1850 Anderson employed five men in his shop at $16 per month. In 1860, he still had five men, and the wages had gone up to $20 per month. They made 2,000 horseshoes at $500, 150 sets of plow irons at $900 and wagons worth $1,000. He was quite successful.

In 1862, Anderson sold this place and lot one in Diven's addition to Henry Bonholtzer for $2,600. Bonholtzer was forced to assign the house to Harry Saxton in 1871 to pay his debts. The house was described as being a two-story brick house, 32' by 32', on a lot 116' by 150'. It came with a stable, wash house, wood house, bake oven and hog pen. Saxton sold it to Daniel Harris, and Harris sold it to Christian Baker in 1876. From 1862 until 1876 there were a number of owners who rented the house out. Some tenants are known. In 1870, William Diller, a carpenter, lived here with his family. He later bought a lot and built the house at #1290 High Street

While living here in 1868, Diller became a principal participant in an ugly brawl. He, William Green and John Zell took a decided unliking toward George Yohn for reasons which have been forgotten. From April until September of 1868, they would harass, insult and annoy him every chance they got. On September 5th, those three, plus George Arnold, Michael, Harry and George Landis, found him in the village and beat the heck out of him. This probably took place on Old Stone House Road because most of the witnesses at the ensuing trial were from the houses around David Devinney, who was one of the witnesses called. Anyway, Yohn, after being severely kicked, managed to get away, and as he was being chased along the street, he looked behind him and saw all of them yelling, "Kill the sonofabitch." Two days later,

1279 Boiling Springs Rd.

all of them were arrested and brought before Sam Plank, where bail was entered. The trial was in November. Green, Landis and Arnold were found guilty, but Zell and Diller were innocent. The case was dropped after those parties paid the costs.

In 1880, Warren Zell, a scion of the well-known Mason family, lived here. He was a blacksmith and worked across the street. He was the foreman in Plank's machine shop. It was Christian Baker who divided the lot in 1877 by selling the western half, 33' by 152', to Joseph Farenbaugh, who owned a house across the road. He sold this house in 1881 to Fred Asper, a local farmer. Fred died in 1899, and his widow lived here until 1908. The house went to her daughters Mary and Emma. Mary died in 1917, and Emma in 1918.

#1279 was probably the sixth house built in Churchtown, built in 1823/24. The two-and-a-half story, four-bay single-family house was originally brick but was later covered with permabrick and then aluminum siding. Formerly, the house had two German Georgian front doors, but the current owner has removed one. The gable roof is metal, and the overall condition of the building is good, although the integrity, due to alterations, is poor.

1281 Boiling Springs Road

This house was built in 1877 when Joseph Farenbaugh bought the lot from Christian Baker. When he died in 1878, the house was rented out to Harry and Sarah (nee Farenbaugh) Landis. They bought it from the heirs, Catherine Farenbaugh and Kate Plank, in 1881. Harry was one of the participants in the above mentioned brawl, a son of Michael Landis, and a Civil War veteran. As a young man, Harry was employed as a farm laborer. In February 1877, while he was quarrying stone, he got a hernia. He tried manual labor until 1888, but by then, he was wholly incapacitated, being unable to stand on his feet longer than an hour at a time. He tried many of the trusses available, but none worked. In 1888, Harry went bankrupt and lost the house to his mother-in-law, Catherine Farenbaugh. She and her widowed daughter Kate Plank were living here in 1900. In later years, Harry moved back in, and they lived there with their invalid daughter, Nettie. Sarah died in 1929, and the house was sold to Earl Gross in 1931.

This two-and-a-half-story, five-bay wood frame house is covered with German-style wood siding. The metal gable roof has wood shakes intact, and the cornices are trimmed with dentils. Brackets across the front of the house are set in pairs, and the glass in the windows may be original (very distorted). The house has an arched wooden front door and a small transom over the side and back doors. The basement foundation is of limestone. A side porch was added in the 1930s. There is a summer kitchen to the rear of the house, and outbuildings include a wooden outhouse and a one-and-a-half-story stable with a stone foundation. The outer integrity and condition of this residence are good.

1281 Boiling Springs Rd.

Interior integrity is also good. All doors have original porcelain knobs and locks, with outside doors possessing brass knobs and back plates. The interior doors are four-panel. French doors separate the kitchen from the den, and large, solid, folding doors exist between the formal dining room and the living room. Windows are raised by pressing a small lever in the side of the frame. The front staircase is completely enclosed, and a back set of very narrow stairs connects the master bedroom to the kitchen. The floors are comprised of original wide planks, unfinished, and covered with carpets. The interior woodwork is all original wide plank, with curved woodwork around doors and windows and plain mantelpieces. The walls are old plaster and wallpapered. An original large brass light graces the living room.

1283 Boiling Springs Road

This lot and the one to the west, #1285, mark the northwest corner of the 4 acres that Abraham Paul bought from Rudolph Krysher in 1816. The alley to your right, next to #1285, follows the western border all the way back to High Street. Paul sold this half-acre lot to John Rider, who had this house built that same year. Rider appears on the 1832 tax assessment with an improved lot. In 1836, he sold it to Sam McAlpine. The history of the owners after that is not quite complete. McAlpine died in Connecticut in 1875, leaving only a son, John and two daughters. Somehow, the house got assigned to Christopher Quigley, his wife Elizabeth (1807–?), and her children Edmund and Carrie Quigley Spangler, who, in a 1930 deed, were all listed as McAlpine's heirs and assigns.

Christopher Quigley lived here in 1850 with his wife and their three children. Also living with them was Rebecca Williamson, age 79. Chris was still here in 1860 but he died by 1870; Elizabeth lived here with her children until she died. Henry Quigley was living here in 1861 when he went into the army. He served three enlistments in the war. In June 1863, he mustered into Company D, 20th Pennsylvania Cavalry, for seven months. He re-enlisted in July 1864 into Company I, 195th Pennsylvania Infantry, and was later transferred to Company B. Carrie was a schoolteacher and may have taught at the school up the street. She later married Christian Spangler, and they had no children. Living with Carrie and her husband for many years were her two brothers, Henry and Edmund. After Christian Spangler died in 1904 it was Henry's pension of about $12 a month that paid for their food and fuel. Henry was receiving a pension for a hernia, paralysis of the fingers and failing eyesight. When he died, Carrie tried to get a pension as a sister, but the claim was denied, so she and Edmund had to make do as best they could.

This two-story single-family residence has three bays and a metal gable roof. The front and sides of this Flemish bond brick structure have been covered with aluminum siding. A one-story frame addition with wood siding was added to the back of the originally rectangular building. The interior stairway is extremely narrow.

1285 Boiling Springs Road

This was part of the lot sold by Abraham Paul to Sam Hyer in 1825. Hyer sold this lot to Jacob Wolf in 1831. That same year, Wolf built this half-timbered house; in 1832 he is listed with an improved lot. Wolf sold it to Daniel Hollinger in 1834, who sold it to John Harlan in 1834. Harlan was a hatter by trade and had his shop on this property.

In 1837, Harlan was forced to declare bankruptcy. He had purchased this property and put up some buildings as well as added to the log house. Due to a death in the family and a long period when he was sick and couldn't work for a while, he was unable to pay the notes against him. Two of his creditors were Dan Krysher and Robert Sturgeon, both merchants to whom he owed $25 each. His inventory of personal effects listed one cow, 2 beds and bedding, a stove, a table, a bureau, 6 chairs, cupboard and kitchen furniture, and

1283 Boiling Springs Rd.

hatter's tools. Apparently, he was allowed to keep the property after selling some of his personal effects.

By 1853, Harlan had moved from Churchtown and in 1858, he was forced to assign this property to Robert Wilson and Jacob Bowman, who sold it to Sam Plank in 1859. This was the same time that Plank built his new house on Old Stone House Road, so this was a rental for him. (Or he may have lived here until his house was finished since he had sold his house at #338 Old Stone House Road.) In 1860, Plank sold this house to John Gensler, and in his will, made right after buying the house, he gave the house to his two daughters, Rebecca, widow of John David Zell and Elizabeth. He rented the house to his daughter Rebecca Zell, who had moved from High Street with her four children.

Her son John, Jr. was a hot-blooded lad. In 1868, he was one of the principal antagonists involved in that brawl with George Yohn, mentioned earlier in the description for #1279 Boiling Springs Road. In May 1877, he got into another fight with a local man. For some reason, there was bad blood between him and Harry Givler, and on May 1st, John struck him in the back of the head with his fist. He then told Givler to be out of town by the next morning, or he would break his head. Givler wasn't impressed and had Zell arrested by Sam Morrett, the town constable. Zell admitted his actions, and his mother had to put up the bail for him. For some reason, the court ignored the case, and Givler had to pay the costs.

After Rebecca's husband died, her father moved in with them. He was quite old and needed someone to care for him. John lived here until he died in 1875, and then Rebecca's brother, George, moved in with her. After

1285 Boiling Springs Rd.

Rebecca died in 1894, the house passed to her heirs, one of whom, Warren, who lived just a few houses away at #1279, was a blacksmith who reputedly made over 16,000 Plank plows. Warren was born in 1847 and was apprenticed as a blacksmith in 1861. After his term was over, he spent three years in Chicago and three in Lancaster before moving back to Churchtown. In 1890, he went into business for himself. Warren sold the house to his daughter-in-law Cora Zell in 1895, and John bought it in 1927. The house stayed in the Zell family until recently. John "Mugs" Zell lived here until he died in 1944. Mugs was quite a character. He was a blacksmith who worked in his shop, now torn down, at Old Stone House Road and Union Alley. With the advent of the automobile, blacksmiths became a dying breed, and he found work for the Harrisburg Transit Company. In his later years, after he retired, he would do a little smithing for some pocket money. John had a liking for moonshine and since he never drove a car, he must have obtained it from someone here in Churchtown. It seems to have been Nelson Lighter. Mugs and his dog "Spigot" were an institution in Churchtown in the late 1930s. Spigot was a little white dog with short legs that got his name because he was always lifting his leg to pee. Mugs and Spigot used to spend a lot of time at the baseball field on High Street, attending both games and practice sessions. Usually, he was under the weather. One day George "Boob" Peffer was taking batting practice when he hit a line drive down the third base line that hit Spigot in the head. Spigot rolled over with all four feet in the air, and Mugs bawled out, "You killed my dog." When he bent down to carry his body back home, Spigot got to his feet and took off. Mugs was also a staunch Democrat who would have voted for the Devil if he was a Democrat.

This single-family structure is a two-and-a-half-story, two-bay German-sided house with half-timbered construction. The wooden beams framework, joined together in mortise-and-tenon fashion, remains, but the bricks that originally filled the spaces between the posts and their diagonal bracings were discarded during an extensive renovation in 2003 and replaced with modern insulation. The gable roof is covered with metal. The windows prior to the renovation did not go up and down but rather pushed outward and were propped open. An alley runs along the western side of the house, and the yard contains two outbuildings—a wooden outhouse and a one-story stable covered with asbestos shingles.

This home is one of three known half-timbered buildings that have been discovered in Churchtown during remodeling. These buildings seem to have been classified as "log" in the early tax lists and other documents for lack of any more suitable category. At least two other houses of similar construction also stand in Churchtown—#1285 Boiling Springs Road, built in 1831, and #1289 High Street, built in 1842. Both of these houses were also extensively renovated, #1289 by the same man who purchased and renovated #1285, and like this house, their interstitial bricks were also removed, leaving the empty but sturdy mortise-and-tenon wood framework in place. On the other side of the Yellow Breeches Creek from Churchtown, a log house at #497 Criswell Dr. also seems to have a half-timbered addition, evidence of which can be seen exposed in the basement stairway. Perhaps this European building tradition, also seen in Lancaster County, was brought to Monroe Township by some of the German immigrants who settled in and around Churchtown.

1287 Boiling Springs Road

This now empty lot once contained a two-story log house. It was torn down sometime after 1940. This lot marks the northeast corner of a one-acre tract that Sam Hyer bought from Rudolph Krysher in 1823 for $200. Hyer sold this lot to Michael Stephens in 1829, and it may have had a log house on it even then. A house was definitely standing by 1831. Stephens sold it to John Lutz in 1834 and he to Solomon Diller in 1837. Diller already owned a house two lots down to the west (no longer standing); this was a rental. In 1843, he sold it to Peter Bricker, who owned several large farms in the township. Bricker lived in a stone house in Lutztown #1447 Lutztown Road and owned several houses in and around Churchtown that he rented out. In 1850, the tenant was Ross Anderson, a tailor and brother to Richard, just a few houses up.

Ross had been living with his family of a wife and three children, two boarders, a woman, aged 60, and a man, aged 65. Later that year, Ross bought a lot on High Street and in 1851, he moved there. Bricker then sold this house in 1851 to Susan Lehman (1792–1875), the widow of John Jacob, mentioned earlier. Susan moved in and lived by herself for a few years. In 1870, her daughter, Sarah Liggett, also lived here with her kids. Sarah owned the old tavern on Old Stone House Road, but she rented it out and lived here. In 1875, Susan's heirs sold this house to Sarah. Sarah bought another house and rented this one out. Her heirs sold it in 1896. In 1900, it was rented out to Daniel Walters, a carpenter. At one time, 1908–09, it was owned by the Brethren's Old Folks Home of Churchtown. After that, the Zells owned it until it was torn down in the 1940s.

A cinderblock garage with four-pane windows sits on this now vacant lot. However, the foundation and major joists of the ell-shaped log house can still be seen as an outline of earthen mounds over which the grass tends to die in dry weather because of the shallow soil. Like its neighbor, #1285, this house stood right up against the alley.

1289 Boiling Springs Road
This property forms an ell shape around 1287, being 46' in front but 87' in the back. Part of the one-acre lot bought by Hyer was sold to Michael Stephens in 1829. Stephens had bought these two lots (#1287 & #1289) together and immediately subdivided them, selling this half to Solomon Rider. Rider had this log house built prior to 1832. He sold it to John Lutz in 1834, who had also bought the log house at #1287. In 1837, he sold #1289 to Christian Richwine (1785–1871), whose brother-in-law Solomon Diller already owned the houses on either side. Christian owned a farm along Route 74 (the York Road) and used this as a rental. He sold it to his son Jacob in 1843. In 1853, Jacob sold it to Sarah and Margaret Young, two unmarried sisters. They were the daughters of Mathias Young, who had bought 113 acres of the Diller warrant near the intersection of Route 174 and Route 74. The sisters lived here until their deaths. Sarah's heirs sold it to Anna Spahr (nee Diller) and Henrietta Eslinger in 1884. Anna sold her half interest to Henrietta in 1888, and she sold the whole property to Maria Hollinger and her daughter Adaline in 1895. Maria also bought the property to the right. She sold both of these to Joseph Gates in 1906.

This two-and-a-half-story log home is truly constructed of logs rather than being half-timbered. A two-and-a-half-story rear frame extension, formerly with a side porch and balcony on its eastern elevation, forms an ell off the original log structure under a multiple gable roof. The original log portion has a three bay front façade, and another modern frame addition, also two-and-a-half stories, now extends from its eastern side wall. Fenestration is even, and molded casings surround windows. The roof is covered with seamed metal, and the cornice is of molded wood. This house has

1289 Boiling Springs Rd.

undergone extensive renovation. The centered front entrance has been converted into a window, and a new sliding glass door has been installed on a side wall. An L-shaped porch wraps around two sides of the house, and the exterior walls are covered with aluminum and vinyl siding. Outbuildings include a wooden outhouse and a large garage to the rear.

1291 Boiling Springs Road
This lot, now containing the driveway and garage of #1289, once had a two-story log house on it. This was part of a tract that Rudolph Krysher sold to Sam Hyer in 1823, Hyer to Michael Stephens in 1829 and Stephens to Solomon Diller (1807–1891). Diller, a cabinetmaker (as were two of his sons), was the son of Casper Diller III. His sister was Rachel Goodyear, who lived just across the road (#1288) and later built a house just down the road (#1316 Church Street) after her husband died in 1849. Another sister was Sarah, who married Christian Richwine. His brother, David, was a merchant for a few years in the square. The rest of the family lived along the York road. Solomon had a son, Sam, who was born here in 1844. In 1860 he was apprenticed to John Bricker, a master cabinet maker. Sam joined the army in 1863, enlisting with his neighbor and friend Henry Quigley into Company D, 20th Pennsylvania Cavalry. Like Henry, he re-enlisted in Company I, 195th, and then into Company B, 195th. Soon after returning to Churchtown in June 1865, he left his father's house for Ohio, where he lived the rest of his life.

By 1874, Solomon's eyesight was failing, and he was forced to retire. A few years later, he became an invalid and in 1883, Solomon had to sell the house to his daughter Ida. It was sold to George Ringwalt in December 1891 for $70. It became a vacant house that the local men used to slip over to at night to play cards. In February 1892, it burned to the ground; the fire may have been started by accident at one such card-playing gathering. In 1895, Maria Hollinger bought the lot to add to her house lot at #1289 and sold it with that house in 1906 to Joseph Gates.

1301 Church Street
At this end of the former Isaac Sheaffer lot extending back to and fronting High Street, Elmer Rank built the structure you now see as a barbershop about 1928. It is now a private residence.

This frame bungalow with a hipped roof is square in shape and one-story high. The roof is covered with seamed metal and its walls with asbestos siding. Inside, the floors are hardwood, and the walls are plaster. It currently serves as a single-family dwelling. The barbershop was in the front right room.

Along the alley here stood the Allen Knitting Company from 1902–1910. The company was incorporated in March 1902 with 200 shares of stock valued at $50 a share. Only $2,800 worth of stocks were sold, and the rest of the money needed to erect the mill was borrowed from several banks. The directors of the company were Dan Bowman, Theo Brandt and S. Bacastow. They erected three buildings along the alley, the mill itself being a one-story frame structure, 80' by 30'. Inside were 20 knitting machines and 5 Hepworth Loopers. There was a carpenter shed, 12' by 25', and a boiler house, 12' by 20'. The company also used the stone house that sat on the other end of the lot.

The Houses of Churchtown 135

1301 Church St. (2007)

The company made hosiery and for a few years did quite well, enough so that expansion was being planned. But the economy became sluggish, and by 1910, their debt was $7,000. Theo Brandt was the major stockholder with 19 shares and he was the one who felt the pinch the most. With creditors on all sides demanding their money, the directors went to court in June 1910 to try to fend them off. What the court did was put the company into receivership, allowing it to continue filling orders until the financial affairs were finalized. Brandt was made the receiver, and a bitter fight ensued as Bowman kept trying to buy more time for the company to land on its feet. Brandt began selling off the assets and equipment, and by 1911, the company was no more. Its creditors only got back 8 cents on the dollar. Bowman was forced to file for personal bankruptcy. The question becomes: what happened to the buildings? They were only eight years old. Hearsay makes the former mill now the apartment building on High Street. The dimensions are close but nobody in the village seems to really know. The tax records may shed some light on this. In 1913, Alfred Musselman, who had bought the lot, was still being taxed for a frame manufacturing building and stone house. In 1910, Frank McElroy opened a hosiery mill near Boiling Springs. Did he buy the machinery first and later the building? A picture of McElroy's mill shows a large brick building in front of the frame building, mostly obscured.

1288 Boiling Springs Road
Cross over Route 174 until you get to #1288 Boiling Springs Road This is a house that sits off the road a little ways. This house is on the old Goodyear homestead, and some of it may be part of the original home. It is impossible to date the house through tax records. The earliest mention of a house is the 1841 assessment when Fred Goodyear had 141 acres and a log house. In 1853, Dan Stees bought the 161-acre farm, and in 1856, he was assessed for a log house. Stees was a sometime preacher in his younger days. His sister married George Atticks, a wagon maker, and moved to Whorleystown further southeast along Route 74 in Monroe Township. Daniel moved there to learn the trade from him. He also became a master tinner as well. While there in Worleystown, he met Sarah Morrett, whom he married. He married into one of the most prominent local families, and therefore, money. Sarah was the daughter of Michael Morrett, Sr. and Catherine Young. Daniel's son, Francis, of Company D, 20th Pennsylvania Cavalry, later died at Andersonville on October 12, 1864. In 1856, Daniel sold 79 acres to John W. Leidig.

John had a son, John Jr., who lived with him here. In 1862, John joined Company F, 130th Pennsylvania Infantry. He was with the regiment at Bell Plain Landing, Virginia, in November 1862. While there, it rained non-stop for several days, and the men were forced to sleep in the water without tents. John developed an abscess in his right thigh and suffered from colic and cramps. For a day, he was unconscious, and messmates assumed that he would be dead by morning. He was sent to the hospital in Washington, D.C., and stayed there until the regiment mustered out in May 1863. In July 1864, he served a hundred-day enlistment in the 195th. In 1877, John married Rebecca Miller, and they moved out to Kansas, where he died in 1903.

John Leidig, Sr. sold this farm to Joseph Farenbaugh in 1863. Joseph died in 1877, and his widow, Katie, aka Catherine, lived here off and on from 1877 until she died. In 1880, George Landis, a carpenter, and John Wood pulled down the old hog pen for Mrs. Farenbaugh. Tearing up some old floorboards, they found a nest of 73 full-grown rats. Only one escaped; the rest were buried in a mass grave nearby. In 1882 Katie sold the property to her daughter Sarah Landis, wife of Harry. Harry farmed here until 1889, growing wheat, oats, and corn supplemented with an orchard. In 1889 his mother-in-law sued him for being in arrears in his mortgage to her. He owed $6,385 to her plus another $2,800 to other creditors. After they sold everything, everyone was paid off, Harry was left with $360, and Catherine Farenbaugh got the farm back.

After Catherine's death, her daughter, Katherine Plank, a widow and childless, lived here. In 1910, her boarder was Tura Landis, 28, the bookkeeper for the knitting mill.

To most residents, this is known as the Vance Enck place. He lived here during the 1930s. At one time, Vance owned a blue Chrysler, which he always kept nicely polished, so much so that you could see your reflection. One of Vance's sheep walked by and looked at the car and, seeing its reflection,

1288 Boiling Springs Rd.

became quite agitated. He began to butt the car until it became quite battered. Vance also grew corn on his land. His neighbor was Guy Rinehart, who lived at #1284. Every time Vance would go away Guy would come over and help himself to the corn, carrying away sacks filled with which to feed his chickens.

The main portion of this two-and-a-half-story four-bay farmhouse is entirely log. It was restored by the owner in the 1990s, a process which involved knocking all the plaster and lathe off the interior of the walls. This process revealed that numerous changes had occurred over time. Several randomly arranged openings in the western wall, the first story, had actually been "logged in" and sealed over, suggesting that perhaps the logs used to build that section of wall had been salvaged and reused from another structure that had different fenestration. The central switch-back stairway of the house also did not seem to be original, so the owner had it removed and replaced by a rebuilt corner stair on the site of an earlier one—the southwestern corner of the house. The home as it stands today has German-style double front doors and 6/6 windows with louvered shutters. A four-bay portico supported by round columns spans the front façade. Wood siding covers the exterior, though its style varies—German lap in the front, with some extremely wide (and presumably old), plain weatherboard strips on the western side. The gable roof is covered with seamed metal, and the cornice is ornamented by wood molding. A one-and-a-half-story kitchen extends from the rear of the house. Two of the original three interior chimneys still stand at the rear and west gable ends. Behind the house is a wooden outbuilding. In front of the house was once an orchard, where Route 174 now runs. The bank barn, which formerly stood to the northwest of the house, was razed in 1989.

1284 Boiling Springs Rd.

is covered with asphalt shingles. No outbuildings are present.

1284 Boiling Springs Road

This is part of the Fred Goodyear to Dan Stees sale of 1853. Stees sold this lot to Sam Darr in 1860. In 1860, Darr, a carpenter, lived here for just a few months before selling it and moving to Schuylkill County. He stayed away from this area until 1888, when he returned to Monroe Township. In 1860, Darr sold it to John Elliott Swanger (1835–1907) for $700. It would seem that the house was built 1853–1860. John was a day laborer by trade. It was from here that John joined the army in March 1865. He was in Co. F, 101st Pennsylvania Regiment. He stood 5'8" and weighed 140 pounds. John and his wife Nancy were childless and lived alone in this house until 1904, when he sold it to David Miller and moved to Mechanicsburg, where he died. Nancy died in 1903, and John remarried in 1906 but lived only another year.

This two-story, three-bay square frame house has a one-story extension in the rear. The front entrance is positioned on the east side of the façade and is framed by sidelights. Replacement windows are 1/1. The gable roof

1282 Boiling Springs Road

A modern brick and frame ranch house site on the site of a much older two-story frame house, long gone. Dan Stees sold this lot to John H. Bricker in 1860. Bricker was a 24-year-old master cabinet and chair maker who lived here with his wife and one apprentice. Their first child, Clare, was born here in 1861, but she died two years later.

In 1860, Bricker employed 3 people at $20 per month. His raw materials—walnut, poplar, pine and cherry—cost him $500. His employees produced 500 chairs valued at $960, 20 coffins at $160, 6 bureaus at $90, 20 tables at $120, 30 bedsteads at $300 and other furniture at $900. His net profit that year was $1,200, about double what his employees made. There must have been quite a shop here. Bricker sold the house and shop to Peter A. Diller in 1866. Diller was a tinner who employed two men at his shop, and he lived here with his wife, three sons (the eldest of whom worked for him), a minister and Ida Diller, daughter of Solomon, who lived across the street. After 1870 he bought another

1282 (& 1280B) Boiling Springs Rd.

324A North St.

house and rented this one out. Diller sold this house to Sam Burgard (1841–1892) in 1883, and his widow Lydia sold it to Warren Zell in 1893. He then sold it right back to Lydia. Lydia remarried William Enck, and they sold the house to Cornelius Smyser, a mason and Civil War veteran, in 1897. He had been living on High Street but moved here. In 1904, he sold the house to Elizabeth Nickey. One of their tenants here in the 1920s was Nelson Lighter. He was a pow-wower and a reputed bootlegger. Someone was making moonshine in the village, and the finger seemed to have pointed to him. The house later burned down.

324 North Street
Walk up North Street to the left of #1282. This first house on your left is part of the property now considered to be #324 North Street. This was part of the land that John Elliot Swanger bought in 1860. In 1864, he sold off a small lot to John Lutz, who in 1865 was assessed for one-story frame and one-and-a-half-story log. This is the frame house. In 1867, he sold it to Hannah Shupp (born 1801). She lived alone in this little house until she died, and in 1890, her heirs

sold it to Cyrus Brindle, who rented it out. In 1892, Cyrus sold it to Levi Enck, the butcher. Sometime between then and he died in 1922, the other house at the northern end of this property was built, as the deed in 1922 describes this as two lots. The smaller house has been vacant for about 10 years.

On this property are two small, irregularly shaped frame cottages, both vacant at the time of first publication. Shupp's cottage is ell-shaped with one-and-a-half stories and a multiple-gable, metal roof. Windows are 6/6 and 4/4, and the exterior is covered with German lap siding. The cottage to the north sits back from the road. This one-and-a-half-story saltbox structure has a side wing and

324B North St.

rear ell extension. Its façade is three bays wide with a centered front entrance sheltered by a portico. Windows are 6/6. The steeply pitched multiple gables of the roof are covered with seamed metal, and the walls are covered by German lap siding.

325 North Street
Cross the street to the house on your right. This is #325 North Street, currently occupied by a mid-twentieth-century Cape Cod home. To its right, there once stood a house until 1893. Part of the Goodyear land was sold to Dan Stees; it was sold to Sam Plank, the plowmaker, in 1853. The lot where the other house once stood went to David Darr in 1859. Darr was a carpenter and may have built a two-story frame house here that year. He and his family were living here in 1860. David would later enlist in Company B, 165th Pennsylvania Infantry, in 1862. He sold the house to John Lutz, Sr. in 1862. Lutz owned seven houses, six in the township and one in Churchtown. Lutz kept this house until 1880, when he willed it to his daughter, Henrietta, wife of Edmund Eslinger, a shoemaker.

On Monday, January 9, 1893, Henrietta was building a fresh fire in the stove. It was about 1 p.m. The stove pipe came apart, and the garret caught fire. The alarm went out, and the fire company raced here. But they were helpless. The last ones to use the pumper had not drained the water from the pipes, and the water froze. They stood around while the house burned to the ground. The contents of the house were saved, and Edmund and his wife moved to a vacant house that he owned on Boiling Springs Road. They sold the lot to David Kauffman in 1896 for $30.

325 North St.

The other house once standing at #325 North Street, on lot fourteen of Plank's addition, was the victim of another fire but once existed on the site now occupied by the modern Cape Cod. The lot was sold by Plank to Ben Shatto about 1859. Shatto, at the time was living over on the east part of High Street. He built a small frame house here. Shatto died in 1863, leaving a wife and young daughter. His administrator was Sam Plank, and at the public auction on October 3, 1863, Plank sold the house to Jacob Filler. Jacob was a returned soldier from Company A, 158th Drafted Militia, or so he always claimed in later years. In October 1862, he and David Westfall, another Churchtown lad, were at the Hummelstown corral tending the government horses. Jacob left there for Martinsburg but enlisted into the 158th along the way. However, Jacob's name does not appear on any muster rolls for the regiment, although his brother Lewis, who also served, does appear. Jacob, who stood 5'8" and 112 pounds and was illiterate, was denied his pension.

Filler lived here with his wife and one daughter until he sold it in 1879 to Adam Gensler, the shoemaker on High Street. Gensler rented it out, one of his tenants being Anna

Goodyear and her family (1880). Anna was the wife of Henry M. Goodyear. Henry was a Civil War veteran and had enlisted first in Capt. Zinn's company and later was in Company H, 36th Pennsylvania Regiment. He was captured at Gaines Mills in June 1862 and paroled two months later. He re-enlisted in November 1863 and was captured at the Wilderness on May 5th, 1864. He spent seven months in captivity, most of it at Andersonville, along with Taylor Miller and Francis Stees, both from Churchtown. While here, Henry contracted malarial fever, which haunted him for the rest of his life. When he returned to Churchtown in the summer of 1865, he was broken in health. After he and Anna moved in here he went to Arkansas in the summer of 1880, for reasons unknown. He hired out to a farmer to chop wood, but the fever returned with the usual chills. He died from malaria in October 1880. Anna and her family continued to live here for a couple of more years, but by 1883, she moved to Harrisburg.

In 1882, Adam Gensler sold the house to William Firestine, who sold it to Levi Goodyear in 1889. During the fire of 1893 next door, this house was saved, but with difficulty. It was not so lucky the second time. The house burned down in 1931. By 1928, Anna Nell was its owner. It was unoccupied on May 26, 1931, but was to have been sold and inhabited at the end of the week. Guy Rinehart lived next door, and at about 2 a.m., he was aroused by his pet terrier. He looked outside and noticed the house here on fire. He quickly dressed and roused about a dozen men. They summoned the Carlisle Fire Company and, in the meantime, went down to the fire station on High Street. Nobody could find a key, so they broke open the door and brought out the chemical fire truck. Although they were able to confine the fire to this house, it burned to the ground.

The chemical fire wagon was used for a short time in Churchtown. It held a 35-gallon tank and two hoses, one chemical and the other a two-and-a-half-inch water hose. When the wagon arrived at the fire, 72 ounces of sulphuric acid was turned into 96 ounces of a bicarbonate soda solution by a liberator. An agitator was turned that caused the acid and the soda to form a gas which produced a pressure of about 150 pounds. This pressure was then used to throw the water onto the fire.

323 North Street

Sam Plank sold this lot to Sam Lehman (1813–1896), the son of Jacob Lehman mentioned earlier, in 1862. This house was built between 1862 and 1864. Lehman lived here until after 1870 and then rented it out, John A. Wood being a tenant in 1880. John was a Civil War veteran who served two enlistments. In 1862/63, he was in Company F, 130th Pennsylvania Regiment, and in 1864/65 he was a corporal in Company C, 3rd Pennsylvania Heavy Artillery. A miller before the war, he was wounded at Antietam. The

323 North St.

ball went through his left hip, struck the bone and came out of his right hip. By the time he moved to Churchtown about 1875 he was having problems stooping or lifting. He gave up being a miller and became a laborer. He did get a pension for $2 a month in 1875, which was backdated to 1863, but it was hardly enough to live on. In 1891, John moved to Carlisle. He was married with several kids.

This ell-shaped frame house sits at the corner of West and North Streets. It has two-and-a-half stories and a five-bay front façade. The centered front entrance has a transom and is sheltered by a front porch, which runs the entire length of the façade. The multiple gable roof is covered with seamed metal, and twin brick chimneys protrude from the roof at either end of the front wing. Outbuildings include a wooden wagon shed and a chicken house. The original part of the house was just four rooms, two down and two above. The back addition was added in 1917.

276 Old Stone House Road
Turn right onto West Street and walk out to Old Stone House Road. Turn left onto Old Stone House Road and stroll up out of the village to the beautiful farmhouse on your left, where the walking tour will begin anew. Now known as the Drake farm, it was sold in 1991. This 22-acre farm is made of three tracts joined together. All three tracts were part of the Goodyear land that Daniel Stees bought. Eight acres were owned by Sam Plank when he died in 1880. His widow sold them to Albert Plank in 1883, and in 1901, Plank sold them to Adam Nell. Another eight acres were sold by Stees to Issac Mishler in 1856. Eight months later, he sold them to Moses Bricker

276 Old Stone House Rd.

for $983, who sold them to Michael G. Brandt in 1867 for $1,011. In 1869, Brandt sold them to William Menear for $1,200. The 1872 Beers Atlas has Menear shown as the owner of the house here. William lived in Warrington Township, York County, but rented the house to his brother Francis. Both were Civil War veterans. Francis was a sergeant in Company I, 200th Pennsylvania Infantry, in 1864/65. While in the trenches in front of Richmond, he caught malaria. He came home in May 1865 in broken health. His skin was a greenish-yellow color; he was very thin and hardly able to walk. He also had chills and a fever. A doctor from Dillsburg tried to treat him but could do nothing. When Francis moved here in April 1872, Dr. Hartzell took over. Francis used to have two severe chills a day. These soon increased to four, and he was unable to do any work at all. Francis died in Carlisle in 1875 from the effects of malaria. Henry Goodyear of North Street was the other malaria victim in Churchtown and died five years later. In 1875, after his brother's death, William Menear sold the land to Adam Nell.

The third tract of ten acres was sold by Stees to John Paul, the butcher, for $900. He did not sell the land to Nell until 1897, and in the tax records, he is never listed as having a house here.

Three lime kilns were on part of Adam's land, and here, he employed some men burning limestone to be used as fertilizer. Burnt during the spring, some years, he would produce as much as 14,000 bushels. Nell put up a new barn in June 1882. In 1885 John Day was the tenant farmer for Nell. That February, the new barn burned down; the one you see here postdates to 1885.

Adam farmed, burned lime and raised stock until 1892. He then became a blockman with McCormick Harvesting Machine Company and traveled for five years for them until 1897, when he went to work for the Johnson Harvester Company doing the same thing. Adam died in 1911, and his wife, Fianna, in 1929. Fianna was a Diller, her sister being Eliza Johnson, who lived at #348 Old Stone House Road. Fianna's heirs tried to sell the house a number of times, but there were some old lawsuits and liens against the house. One of the lawsuits was Fianna against her husband, Adam. Finally, in 1941, everything got settled, and the farm could be sold.

The dating of this house presents a sticky problem. It appears to have been built by 1860. The census of that year suggests that Sam Plank, the plow maker, was living here. Even though Plank owned a lot at #338 Old Stone House, the house may not have been built then. For years, that has been referred to as the Sam Plank house, but I doubt he ever lived there, though his son Albert most certainly did. The 1860 census put Plank living next to George Brindle, and Brindle's farm was just to the north. From this house Plank may have moved to #351 Old Stone House, where he was living in 1870.

This 22-acre farm on Locust Hill marks the northern boundary of historic Churchtown. The property includes a Civil War-era farmhouse with Victorian detailing, a bank barn and carriage house, the remains of an eighteenth-century lime kiln, and the best view in the town of South Mountain. The large four-bay farmhouse features side hall construction, a multiple gable roof with fish-scale slate shingles, and numerous Victorian detailing added between 1905 and 1907. The evenly spaced 1/1 windows are crowned by projecting lintels ornamented with dentils. The large first-floor window on the front façade is tripartite, with a stained glass transom above it. The front entrance has double doors and a two-pane transom. The covered front porch extends the entire width of the façade. The rear ell has a side porch with a balcony along its southern side. Interior features include some random pine plank floors, a double parlor with sliding doors, and a winding rear staircase. Although the remaining internal chimney appears centered in its gable from the outside, it is not centered from within the house and had to be slanted diagonally along the attic wall to achieve its outward appearance. The house is now covered with asbestos siding, and all the buildings on the property have been painted in a matching red and yellow color scheme. The barn was built around 1900, and the carriage house once served as an antique shop. At one point, the land was used exclusively as an asparagus farm.

300 Old Stone House Road
This lot was sold by Sam Plank to John Moul in 1878 for $120. Moul (1818–1900) had the house built that year. He sold it to Levi C.

300 Old Stone House Rd.

Goodyear in 1896. Levi died in 1901, aged 35, and it was then sold to his wife, Sara. Sara lived here until she sold it to Sylvester Trostle, who sold it to Daniel Lehman in 1927. Daniel and his family, who lived in the rooms above, ran a beer garden on the first floor. The first floor consists of two front rooms and a kitchen across the back. He put his tables in the two front rooms. The plaster walls still bear the damage from chairs being pushed into them. The bar was in the kitchen. Friday and Saturday nights, they served meals as well, and occasionally supplied music. Dan worked on the railroad and it was his wife who ran the place. She came down with tuberculosis and went to Hamburg for treatment. She got homesick, so Daniel closed the beer garden and brought her home. In 1934, they sold it to their son Irvin.

The five-bay, two-and-a-half-story ell-shaped house has a multiple gable roof. The centered entrance is topped with a transom, and the evenly spaced windows are 2/2. The wooden four-bay front porch has a tongue-in-groove floor, and its roof is supported by four carved wooden posts ornamented with corbels. The rear wing features a side porch with a balcony. The roof features slate shingles, although a small one-story addition on the north side has a metal roof. The exterior of the house is covered with aluminum siding.

304 Old Stone House Road

Sam Plank sold this lot to Solomon Byers in 1878 for $246. The house was built prior to 1878 and Byers was living here in 1880. Byers, a stone mason, was only 22 when he bought this house. For many years, he shared the house with this recently widowed father, Cornelius (1829–1904), also a stone mason, and his brother and two sisters. Byers sold it to Oliver Brownawell for $850 in 1891.

Oliver was a Civil War veteran from Company G, 84th Pennsylvania Infantry. He served from 1862 to 1865. He got through the war unscathed, but in 1866, while cutting wood on South Mountain, his axe slipped and went into his left kneecap, causing a deep gash. He was in bed for six weeks and on crutches for several months after that. The fluid never returned to the knee, and he had a dry joint. He moved to Monroe Township in 1873 and into Churchtown in 1891. By that time, he was in his late fifties; walking was difficult for him. Whenever Oliver walked down to the store on the square the people always knew it was him by the way he walked. He tended to drag his left leg, being unable to lift his foot, and often tripped over any obstruction on the sidewalk. Dr. Sam Smith was his family doctor, but there was nothing that could be done. He eventually got a veteran's pension for this disability. In 1910, it was $20 a month, and this was his main source of income. He died in 1911, and his heirs sold the house to Lydia Myers in 1914.

David and Ruth (Baish) Ilgenfritz lived here in the 1930s. On October 30, 1940,

304 Old Stone House Rd. (2007)

306 Old Stone House Rd.

Ruth committed suicide in the front room with a shotgun to the heart. She left three young children.

A two-and-a-half-story ell-shaped building with frame construction, this house has German lap wood siding. The house is five bays wide with a centered front entrance. The 2/2 windows are evenly spaced and topped with pediments. The cornice is ornamented with molded wood. The multiple gable roof is covered with seamed metal, and one large chimney remains at the north gable end. A frame summer kitchen is attached to the dwelling, and other outbuildings include wooden sheds and an outhouse. Several enclosed porches have been added onto the house, including a one-story, three-bay enclosure sheltering the front entrance and the windows flanking it. Also, some of the rear windows have been sided over or replaced with modern sashes.

306 Old Stone House Road
This property consists of two lots. They were sold by Sam Plank to Henry Knaub, the basket maker on Boiling Springs Road, in 1878. He sold them to Anna Spahr in 1883. She held onto them and never built on them until she sold them to the twins Emma and Mary Strickler for $150 in 1900. In 1900, they had this house built. Emma and Mary were the daughters of Abraham Strickler, a local Mennonite. Emma later moved out, and by 1910, Mary, 34, was here by herself.

This two-story rectangular frame house features a bungalow-type construction. Its five-bay first floor is covered by a gable roof, from which protrudes a wide, four-bay dormer. The evenly spaced windows are 2/2 and are crowned with projecting lintels. Some windows in the rear of the structure are bipartite. A transom crowns the non-centered entrance. Attic lights are centered, and no chimneys are present. The exterior of the house is German lap wood siding, and the roof is seamed metal. The cement front porch is sheltered by a hipped shed roof extending from the main roof but at a shallower pitch. The porch roof is supported by three fluted pillars, as is the roof of the side porch. A rear porch is also present. Behind the house is an old two-story frame stable or barn with sliding doors and a metal roof.

307 Old Stone House Road
This lot was part of the Strock lands. In 1912, Joseph Plough sold this lot to Emma

307 Old Stone House Rd.

308 Old Stone House Rd.

Engle for $225. She did not build here until 1914–1916. For many years Marcus Devinney lived here with Emma in between tenants at his house. In 1932 Emma was committed to the State Hospital. Lloyd Stone then rented the house at $12 a month until it was sold to Foster Arnold in 1933.

This is a two-and-a-half-story, ell-shaped frame house with multiple gable roofs. Its façade is four bays in width, and window panes are 1/1, crowned with projecting lintels. The front door with transom is also topped with projecting lintels and sheltered under the four-bay front porch. A side porch with a balcony extends along the side of the structure. Exterior walls are covered with aluminum siding, and the roof with seamed metal. Molded cornice returns are still exposed. This is one of the only two homes older than 50 years still standing north of the town square on this side of the street. The other is #313. Three other old homes, all farmhouses, were razed sometime after 1872.

308 Old Stone House Road
This lot was sold to Catherine Ellen Goodyear. She was a widow with two teenage kids and had the house built in 1879/80. Her son was Levi C. Goodyear, who bought the house at #300. In 1880, she lived here with her children and her aged parents, John and Elizabeth Seager. Her mother died the next year. John Seager died in 1893 at age 94. John lived quite a colorful life. He was born in Berks County but lived most of his life in Perry County. He was 6'2" and 200 pounds—quite large for his day. For years, he was in the local militia as both a captain and a musician. He participated in the "Buckshot War" and was a staunch Democrat. Prior to 1880, he moved to Churchtown and lived here for the rest of his life. After her children moved out, Catherine Goodyear lived here alone for a while. She sold the house in 1924.

The five-bay, two-and-a-half-story, ell-shaped frame house has evenly spaced 2/2 windows and a centered front entrance topped with a transom. The multiple gable roof is covered with seamed metal in front and corrugated metal in the rear. The exterior is covered with vinyl siding, and a wooden deck has been added. Outbuildings include a wooden shed.

310 Old Stone House Road
Sam Plank sold this lot, number fifteen in his town plans, to Elizabeth Pipher (1817–1884)

in November 1876 for $86. Elizabeth, who never married, was the daughter of John Pipher, who owned the house at #1320 Church Street. This house was completed in the summer of 1877. Elizabeth lived here for only a couple of years before renting it out. She went into the household of David Neisley as a servant, even though she was 63. This arrangement went sour after three years. They wanted her out, and she wanted out, so on December 21, 1883, she moved back to her house. Her health was poor and her brother Joseph came here to care for her. On February 24, 1884, she went to his house and lived there until she died on October 8, 1884. During her sickness, she was given a large room in the lower story of her brother's house. This was the room that her brother had used to carry on his business as a shoemaker. For a couple of months, she was okay, but then she took a turn for the worse, and from April 23 until she died, she was bedridden. During the last six weeks of her life, she was nearly blind, her mind was gone, and she suffered from diabetes and dropsy. She required constant care from members of her family and her neighbor, Elizabeth Wise. This care became a bone of contention when it came time to settle her estate. Apparently, poor Elizabeth had a problem with her bowel movements, which occurred many times during the day, often soiling her clothes, and the smell seemed to seep into the very walls of the house. Joseph sued the estate for his rendering of care.

Eventually an auditor agreed that $250 was enough for him. But Joseph wanted more, and he tried to bilk the estate out of another $100. He claimed that at her funeral, he served a meal to 200 mourners at 50 cents a meal.

310 Old Stone House Rd.

The auditor was not impressed and, in a very sarcastic comment, wrote that it was highly unlikely that an unmarried woman would know 200 people and that, furthermore, when she was alive, barely ten people would recognize her walking along the street and greet her. Joseph's claim was disallowed. In 1885, her brothers and sisters, heirs to the house, sold it to Elizabeth Arnold for $525. Elizabeth and Jacob Arnold lived here for 40 years.

This ell-shaped frame house has two-and-a-half stories and four bays. Windows are 2/2 above and 1/1 below. The front portion of the house has a gable roof covered with seamed metal, while the 2-story rear wing has a gently pitched shed roof. Attic lights are off-center. This house has undergone numerous renovations, including the addition of two wooden decks to the side and rear, replacement of wooden doors and windows, and covering with vinyl siding. Outbuildings include two wooden sheds.

311 Old Stone House Road
This house was built after 1947 by Graham Rupp. The lot goes back to the Strock lands and will be discussed later. Rupp was a member of the Gettys family, which built a number

311 Old Stone House Rd. (2007)

312 Old Stone House Rd.

of other homes on Old Stone House Road. This one-and-a-half-story, 3-bay rectangular house is constructed of cinderblock and covered with brickface. The front entrance is centered, and rows of vertical stretchers crown the evenly spaced 1/1 windows. The gable roof has asbestos shingles.

312 Old Stone House Road

This house sits on what was two lots, numbers thirteen and fourteen. Sam Plank sold the first one to Philip Beidle in March 1876, and Philip bought the second one two months later. He paid $80 for each lot. Beidle was the township constable in 1879. Charged with keeping the peace in a sometimes boisterous village, he often lacked the sense of humor required. In the fall of 1879, the village doctor, Philip Koons, got married. After the return from his honeymoon, the local "boys" got together to give him a calathumpian serenade. Beidle was on the scene before a single note was struck and sent them home. Not to be outdone, the boys secretly gathered the next night and gave Koons a serenade. Beidle never showed. Later in November, Daniel Bowman got married, and his serenaders had just finished the third "song" when Beidle came charging along Boiling Springs Road, chasing them away. The modern village carolers ought to be glad there is no Beidle today.

The house went up in 1876. Beidle, a laborer, lived here with his wife and five children. Philip always claimed that as a youth, he lived in Illinois, prior to the war, working on a farm. Abraham Lincoln used to visit the farm, and Philip made his acquaintance. When the war came, Philip enlisted in Battery B, 112th Pennsylvania Artillery. He sold this house to William Firestine (1820–1900) in 1882 for $875. Firestine sold it to Lavere Firestine in 1893. Lavere lived in Mechanicsburg, and after renting it for a year, he sold it to George W. Ringwalt in 1894. Ringwalt's heirs sold the house to Adam Hollinger in 1900.

This four-bay rectangular frame house still features wooden clapboard siding. Its evenly spaced windows are 2/2, and a two-pane transom crowns the front entrance. The two-and-a-half-story structure has a seamed metal gable roof, off-center attic lights, and external cinderblock chimneys. Extending from the rear wall is a one-and-a-half-story addition with a shingled gable roof. As does its neighbor at #314, this house has a covered, four-bay, cement-based front porch extending across its front façade, with its roof supported by wooden columns.

313 Old Stone House Road

Jacob Kenower (1762–1833), who married Maria (1767–1827), a daughter of Jacob Wise, patented this land in 1793. He named it "Union." In the 1790s, he sold it to Jost (Joseph) Strock. Joseph willed this farm to his son Jacob (1779–1852), and when Jacob died in 1852, his younger son, George (1807–1886), bought it from his brothers. In 1880, George had to assign his property to creditors to pay his bills. He had a farm of 130 acres, which occupied the lands north of the church. On that land, there stood a two-story brick house, probably #277 Old Stone House Road, a new wash house, a bank barn, a wagon shed, and a hog pen. There were fruit trees and a well near the kitchen door. On this lot, #313, which adjoined the 130 acres, there was a two-story brick house and a frame stable. His wife Margaret (1808–1888) bought the lot. In June 1886, George fell from a cherry tree in his yard and sustained internal injuries. He was 79 and never recovered from them. For a while, he could move around, but in the last ten weeks of 1886, he was unable to leave the house. On Christmas, he was bedridden for five days and died at the end of the month. Margaret died in 1888, and in 1893, her heirs sold the house to Joseph Plough.

Joseph was born in 1836 in York County but moved to Cumberland County when he was one year old. After his marriage in 1866 he located in Monroe Township and farmed north of here until buying this property. At that time, a two-story part-brick-part-frame house stood here. He demolished it and built the current one in the 1890s. Plough and his

313 Old Stone House Rd.

wife were Mennonites, and they attended the church at the end of Church Street. He was a Sunday school teacher there for over 25 years.

This five-bay, two-and-a-half-story house is constructed of common bond brick but has been covered with aluminum siding. The floor plan is Georgian in style, with a central staircase and double parlors on either side. The centered front entrance is hung with double doors set with four-pane window panels. An ell-shaped porch supported by eight columns stretches across the front façade and wraps around to the south. The original 6/6 windows have been replaced by 1/1s. The interior floors are pine, and the original wood molding around doors and windows remains intact. Formerly used as a farmhouse, this house has a two-story stable/carriage house with hand-hewn peg construction. The previous farmhouse, now demolished, sat just south of the current house.

314 Old Stone House Road

This house sits at the corner of the main road and Chestnut Alley. It was originally two lots, numbers eleven and twelve, in Sam Plank's subdivision. Plank had his new town lots surveyed in December 1858. He sold these lots

314 Old Stone House Rd.

to Lewis Filler (1829–1908) in March 1860 for $110. The house was built that summer. Filler had rented at #328 Old Stone House, so it was easy to supervise the building of it. Lewis was a tanner who worked at Diven's tannery. It went out of business about this time, and in 1862, he joined the army, joining Company A, 158th Pennsylvania Infantry. He was 33, a little old for army life, but times were bad. The bounty must have been an enticement, and at least he got paid, even if it was irregular. After the war, Lewis lived here with his wife and two daughters. Unable to return to tanning, he became a day laborer. By 1880, his eldest daughter had married, and she lived here with her son. In November 1907 Filler had contracted with John Starry to sell him his home, then occupied by Frank Hosler. Filler died prior to the sale, and Starry had to get a court order to buy the house at $500. Hosler was the man who murdered Sam Eckart in 1893. Frank lived here between 1900 and 1910 and perhaps later.

Originally just one-and-a-half stories, this two-and-a-half-story, four-bay frame house has two German-style front entrances topped with transoms and 2/2 windows crowned by projecting lintels. The structure is ell-shaped and currently covered by aluminum siding. The multiple gable roof is covered with corrugated metal, and the cornice is ornamented by molded wood. A four-bay porch with ornamented wood columns and a shingled roof extends along the front façade. Off-center attic lights suggest that centered internal chimneys were once present along the gable walls. The current chimneys are external structures made of cinderblock. Occupants relate that the rear kitchen wing was built first, and the front section of the house was added later. Behind the house is a frame outhouse.

316 Old Stone House Road

Sam Plank sold this lot, number ten, to Sarah Gross (1803–1883) in 1859. She had formerly lived on High Street but sold that place to her son-in-law, John Messinger, and had a house built here in the summer of 1859. She lived here alone for many years, though it would appear that in 1880, she was renting the house out, possibly to a Scott Miller. When Sarah died, her heirs sold the house to her son, George W. Leidich, for $386. Leidich sold it to the merchant, G.T.B. Herman, in 1884, and he to George Eberley in 1887 for $450. It was sold again in 1903 for $350 and in 1918 for $200. It would seem that this

316 Old Stone House Rd.

present house was built about 1920 on top of a previous house's foundation.

This two-story frame cottage has two bays and a gable roof covered with seamed metal. Original windows are 6/6, with some 1/1 replacements, and a nine-pane window is in the front door. The foundation of the front half of the building is random limestone, which suggests an earlier house. An ell-shaped porch wraps around two sides of the structure, and an external cinderblock chimney is attached to the wall. Outbuildings include a shed.

318 Old Stone House Road
Plank sold this lot, number nine, to Henry Long in 1859. The house was built by 1860, as Long was living here then with his family. Long was a wagon maker and may have worked for Sam Plank. There was a wagon shop then just down the street beyond #328. Long sold this house to Abraham Shearer in 1865 and he to John Swanger in 1867. Swanger already had a house, so he rented this one out. He sold it to Bassela Bonholzer in 1870. Bassela, then 67, was a laborer born in Germany. He lived here with his wife for three years before selling to Warren Zell, the blacksmith. In 1876, Zell sold it to G.T.B. Herman. Herman used it as a rental before selling it to Jacob Enck in 1885. In 1906, his heirs sold it to John Hertzler.

The rear kitchen section of this two-and-a-half-story, ell-shaped, side-hall frame house was reputedly built about 1825. This cannot be proved; tax records would indicate the opposite. In 1859, Sam Plank, the owner, was assessed for a brick house (#338 Old Stone House), a two-story frame (#340 Old Stone House) and a lot. The front section was supposed to have

318 Old Stone House Rd.

been added in 1850, but this is also doubtful. Most likely, the house was built in 1859/60.

The multiple gable roof is covered with seamed metal. Sheltered under it along the south wall is a side porch and balcony. Single windows are 2/2, while the two-story bay projecting from the front façade has tripartite 1/1 windows. The front entrance is surrounded by ornamented wood molding and crowned by a transom and a projecting lintel. Of the former three internal chimneys, one remains in the rear gable, while an external one is now attached to the southern gable.

320 Old Stone House Road
This house sits on two lots, numbers seven and eight. Sam Plank sold these to Catherine Weaver in March 1859. Catherine and her husband, Levi W. Weaver (1810–1885), a saddler, also bought the lot across the street at #319. Deeds for #319 have not been fully recorded, and none are on record for Levi Weaver. The house now at #319 is modern, the older one torn down. Levi was quite active in local politics. He was inspector of elections in 1850, a Justice of the Peace in 1855 and the township clerk in 1856 and 1859–60. At #320, the house now here was built after

320 Old Stone House Rd.

319 Old Stone House Rd.

1872, as it is not shown on the Beers Atlas map of Churchtown. In 1876, the lot was sold to Michael Landis, who also owned houses on High Street. Michael, a blacksmith, was born at Ephrata in 1820. He moved to Cumberland County in 1830 and, except for one year in Iowa, spent the rest of his life here. He was living in this house in 1880, so it was built about 1876. Doubtless, the shop in the rear was his blacksmith shop. In 1880 Michael employed four men at his shop. He paid his skilled workers $1.25 for a ten-hour day while those unskilled got 75 cents a day. Michael was another one of the protagonists who was involved in the beating of George Yohn in 1868, detailed in the description for #1279 Boiling Springs Road. Michael was a school director in 1860–1861, a constable in 1863, and an election judge in 1874. In 1894, he sold the house to Jacob Hoffer.

This imposing two-and-a-half-story brick house has five bays and a multiple gable roof. Its cornice is ornamented with double corbels. The double doors of the recessed front entrance are crowned by a projecting lintel supported by two corbels. Windows are 2/2 with projecting lintels and shutters that are each louvered (above) and solid (below). Attic lights are also 2/2. The foundation is limestone, the brickwork is common bond, and the basement windows are topped with arched brick lintels and covered by iron grillwork. The rear ell has a side porch and balcony under its gable roof, and a brick summer kitchen with a wooden extension is attached to the rear of the wing. Two interior chimneys remain. Outbuildings include a two-story frame structure, which was formerly a wagon shop, a frame barn with German lap siding, a shed, and an outhouse. This corner property was once the side yard of the older house, #318, next door.

322 Old Stone House Road
This property also consists of two lots, which were not combined into one until 1897, when Mary Eichelberger bought Sam Plank's lot six, on which sat a small frame shop to the rear. Lot six was sold by Plank to Henry Zinn, a teacher, in 1859. This was Colonel Zinn, of Civil War fame, who was living at the time on Boiling Springs Road. He sold it to Dr. L. H. Lenher in 1860. Lenher sold it to Joseph and Daniel Goodyear in 1861. They sold it to John Paul, the butcher, in 1864 and his heirs to John Herman in 1897. Herman then sold it

to Mary Eichelberger that same year. The shop was built prior to 1872 and perhaps as early as 1860. It was either Paul's butcher shop or slaughterhouse.

Lot five, on which the house stands, was sold by Plank to Conrad Drager. Drager (1824–1891) was a master tailor from Hanover, Germany. He learned the trade of tailoring in Germany and, after extensive travels throughout Germany, emigrated to America. He landed in Baltimore and lived there for two years before moving to Churchtown prior to 1858. He became a citizen while living in Churchtown in 1858. He lived in this house with his family until 1873, when he moved to Boiling Springs. Conrad had married Charlotte Zinn, whose brother was Henry Zinn who had bought lot six in 1859. It's possible that Zinn bought the lot for Conrad to use for his business, or he may have meant to build on it for himself. Most likely, Conrad, newly arrived, lacked the money to buy it for himself. Two of his daughters died here, one in 1863 and the other in 1869.

Drager sold the house to Levi Gross and he to Jesse Brindle in 1884. Brindle was head of a committee who were the guardians of Issac Eichelberger, a lunatic. Issac and his wife Mary (1849–1936) were renting this house by 1880. He was an illiterate laborer with a wife and three small children. When or how he went insane is not known. They rented here for a few years until Mary bought the place outright in 1892. In 1892, it was described as a one-and-a-half-story frame house with a kitchen. By 1936, when it was sold again, the two-story front portion had been added.

This two-story frame cottage sits back from the road and was built in two stages.

322 Old Stone House Rd.

The rear portion, a two-story structure with a flat roof and scalloped cornice, was built in 1859. The front portion, with a gable roof and front portico, was added prior to 1936. Windows are 1/1, arranged symmetrically. The house is now covered with aluminum siding. At the rear of the side yard is an old wooden structure, now used as a garage.

323 Old Stone House Road

This house was built after 1940 when the lot was set off from a larger tract. It sits on land formerly of the Strock farm. This two-story frame bungalow sits along the driveway of the Lutheran Church. It has three bays, with 3/1 windows, and a hipped gable roof with two

323 Old Stone House Rd.

gabled dormers. Front façade windows on the lower level are bipartite. The centered front entrance is crowned by a cleaved pediment and framed by pilasters. Over it is a canopy supported by square pillars. The side porch, facing the road, has wooden latticework supports; the house, covered by asbestos siding at the time of this writing, is now stone-faced. A small garage with a hipped roof also sits on the property.

324 and 326 Old Stone House Road
This double house sits on lots three and five of Sam Plank's subdivision. The lots were sold by Plank to Moses Bricker in 1859 for $100. Bricker had the house built and rented it to E. Kauffman in 1860. He was a blacksmith who worked at the blacksmith shop in the alley. Moses sold the new house to Barbara Bricker in 1863 for $1,000. Barbara, who lived in Carlisle, sold lot three to Rosana Lucas in 1866 for $700. The other half of the house, lot four, went back to Moses on Barbara's death. Moses was forced to assign lot four to his creditors, and they sold it to Mary Givler in 1878 for $442. She moved out to Kansas, and in 1884, she sold the house to Jacob Sierer. In 1870, Rosana, who always lived alone, lived at #326, while #324 was rented to Moses' brother, Sam Bricker.

Sam was another one involved in the many village fights. In July 1865, he, Peter Diller, Henry Goodyear, Sam Diller and John W. Leidig had a five-hour spree of causing trouble through the village. Most of these young men had just recently returned from the war and, in celebrating, had perhaps filled up on too much bug juice. William Devinney, a brother to David, happened to get in their way, and they beat him up. He

324 Old Stone House Rd. (with 326) (2007)

pressed charges and not until April 1866 did it finally go to trial. At that time, the only one who had been arrested was Leidig; the others were still at large. Several residents testified how they had been terrorized by these men that day. Leidig was found guilty and paid a $25 fine. The charges against the others were dropped.

In 1880, Rosana Lucas was still living alone, and George Seifert, a laborer with a wife and two small children, lived at #324.

This common bond brick duplex has a multiple gable metal roof and a cornice adorned with many corbels. The building as a whole is T-shaped and has six bays across its façade, including the centered double

326 Old Stone House Rd. (with 324) (2007)

front entrances (one for each unit). Windows are 6/6 above and 6/1 below, with louvered wooden blinds. Crowning the doors and windows are lintels ornamented with a zigzag design. The southern unit has a two-bay front stoop supported by carved wooden posts, and its front entrance has a transom. The transom of the other unit has been boarded up. Outbuildings behind the units include a frame garage and a two-seater outhouse.

325 Old Stone House Road: Mt. Zion Lutheran Church

In 1790, the Lutheran and German Reformed congregations united in building the original church that sat on this property. The adjoining cemetery lot, on one corner of the town square, was subdivided in 1795. Communion records show that the number of regular communicants increased steadily over the decades, from 39 in 1802 to 128 in 1833. In 1849, the trustees of both congregations, Michael Beltzhoover, Joseph Brandt and Enoch Young, bought an adjoining parcel of land from Jacob Strock and his wife on which to build a new, larger building—the present church. The original church was torn down. In 1853, the congregations changed the name of the church from "Christ's Church" to "Mt. Zion." The German Reformed congregation disbanded in 1932, leaving the Lutherans as sole owners of the property. For almost two hundred years, the congregation was served part-time by clergy from larger districts until, in 1978, they hired their first full-time pastor.

The church building is a two-and-a-half-story rectangular brick structure on a banked, cut field-stone foundation. It is three bays wide and four bays long, with its gable end serving as the front façade. A molded wood

325 Old Stone House Rd. (Mt. Zion, 2007)

cornice and frieze ornament the gable roof. The octagonal-shaped cupola beneath the steeple is open and supported by eight pairs of round and square columns. The second-floor sanctuary has tall, arched, stained glass windows. Two arches of headers cap those on the side of the church, while those windows on the front of the building have three, which are further ornamented with keystones and corner blocks of red sandstone. A circular attic light in front is also framed by a triple row of headers and ornamented by four keystones. The larger round window on the rear wall, illuminating the altar area, was added in the mid-twentieth century. Many changes have been made to the building and surrounding property in the last century and a half. In 1900, the front steps, balcony and galley of the church were removed, the cellar dug out for Sunday School rooms, and the front lawn graded. The large stained glass windows were also installed at this time. The cemetery by 1910 had become quite unkempt; few descendants remained in the area to care for the graves. The plot was, therefore, leveled and cleared of broken headstones, and the names of those buried were inscribed onto a central stone monument, which still stands. In 1933, the choir loft was raised, and in 1949, an altar was added, and the round window was placed above it in the rear wall. In 1964, a new wing was added to the west of the building to provide office and Sunday School space. The pews have been replaced several times, and the organ is fairly new.

328 Old Stone House Road
This lot was part of the land that Dan Stees bought from the Goodyear heirs. I believe that this house was built between 1856 and 1860. Stees is only recorded for a log house in 1856. The 1860 census indicates that a family may have been here. This was Lewis Filler, a tanner, and his wife Rebecca. Lewis, who later bought a house at #314 Old Stone House Road, joined the army in 1862. At any rate, Stees sold this house and lot to Nancy Moore in 1863 for $1,100. A house is mentioned in the deed. Nancy and her husband, William, then sold it to Henry Bonholtzer in 1866 for $1,800. The lot also included a wagon shed to your left, along Union Alley. Bonholtzer, who lived on Boiling Springs Road, rented this house out to John Neiman, who was a coach-maker and used the wagon shed as his place of business. In 1870, Neiman, aged 29, lived here with his wife and two apprentices. Neiman was still here in 1872, his rent being $150 per year. Bonholtzer was forced to assign this property and two others in 1871. When everything was liquidated his creditors only got back 9 cents on the dollar. They sold this house to George T. B. Herman in 1872, who then sold it to Jacob Goodyear. In 1871, this lot was described as being 90' by 190' with a two-story frame house, 24' by 27', and a two-story kitchen. At the rear of the lot stood a two-story coach shop, 36' by 47', a stable and other outbuildings.

328 Old Stone House Rd.

Jacob Goodyear was a laborer who was then living several houses north of here on Old Stone House Road. In 1879, he sold part of the lot with the wagon shop to George Plank. He kept the house and moved here. Plank wanted the wagon shop, which was quite large, for a new business. In April 1879, he converted it into a machine shop, and in early May, they opened for business. It was called the Churchtown Agricultural Works. He employed at least 8 other machinists; his foreman was George Heiges, age 53, who also boarded with him. Some of the things made here were corn planters, grain drills, threshing machines, and separators.

In 1880 a machinist's work day was 10 hours, normal for most trades. Plank paid his skilled workers $1.65 a day, and the unskilled ones got $1. That year, Plank paid out almost $2,000 in wages. His shop produced agricultural implements, and their major source of income came from the 18 threshers made that year.

In June 1880, Plank put up a windmill to force water into his workshop. One day that month, while working at it, he fell off the ladder and dislocated his elbow quite severely.

On March 3, 1882, a Friday morning, there was a stiff March breeze outside. Inside, Plank's boilers in the machine shop became overheated, and the building caught fire. The fire company came racing down Old Stone House Road. The townspeople gathered here, and together, the fire was put out. Satisfied with a good morning's work everyone went home congratulating themselves. But some embers remained alive, and in the stiff breeze, they were blown all over town. They cut a swath through the buildings along Old Stone House going up the hill. A.W. Plank's blacksmith shop next door, John Plank's stable, Mrs. Cocklin's and the Hotel's stable all burned to the ground. The houses of A.W. Plank, John Paul, Leah Diller, John Dill and Jacob Goodyear all caught fire but were saved. Herman's store on the square caught fire three times, and it, too, was saved with minor damage. This was the worst fire to hit Churchtown.

This two-story frame house has a virtually flat roof. Its centered front entrance is topped with a transom. Windows are 6/6 and unevenly spaced. The house is currently covered with aluminum siding. The shop has since been razed, and the house added on to it. Extensions include a carport with a half-story dormered gable roof above it and a sun porch to the rear.

332 Old Stone House Road
This was part of Nancy and William Moore's land that they bought in 1863. They sold it to Jacob Richwine. Up until the 1940s, the lot to the right of the house was occupied by the blacksmith shop of Sam Diven, which sat at the corner of Union Alley and Old Stone House. The shop sat on a lot 80' by 50'. Part of lot two in Diven's plan, it was sold by Richard Anderson, a blacksmith, to Henry Bonholtzer

332 Old Stone House Rd. (2007)

in 1862, along with other property. Bonholtzer lived on Boiling Springs Road and worked here. Forced into bankruptcy, the shop was sold to Daniel Harris in 1871. Harris also bought the house at #1279 Boiling Springs Road. Harris sold it to Christian Baker, who rented it out, and he sold it to Albert Plank in 1881. He built a new blacksmith shop here after the fire. It had three fires and employed three men. His foreman was Warren "Wall" Zell, who had been a smith for 15 years. Plank sold the shop to Annie Cooper in 1895. She and her husband, William, lived at #1278 Boiling Springs Road. William had to assign his property to George Sheaffer, and he sold it to Daniel Bentz, Cooper's father-in-law. Bentz died soon after, and it was sold to Warren Zell in 1899 for $700. Sometime between 1895 and 1899 a wagonshop was added to the structure.

The blacksmith shop was a brick building, 33' by 33'. There was a cistern nearby and some sheds attached to the shop. By the 1930s, the building had become dilapidated. The last one to work here was John "Mugs" Zell. Mugs had become one of the local characters who, in the 1930s, lost all the fingers on one of his hands. He kept asking Hobart Souders, a butcher, to let him work the meat grinder. Souders refused, as Mugs was often drunk. One day Mugs managed to get to the grinder when no one was around and cut off all his fingers on one hand.

Originally a one-story brick building, the shop was expanded with a frame second story with a sloping shed roof on the northern side. The building sat right up against Union Alley, and later, when the wagon shop was added, it joined the older shop at the back and came out to Old Stone House, creating an ell-shaped structure. The wagon shop was a two-story frame building with 6/6 windows. In 1920, Mugs's son Harper bought the building from Warren W. Zell. Simon Richwine, Jacob's brother, had been living in the rooms above the shop. How long he stayed here is not known. In the crook of the ell, Harper set up two quoit pits and above each pit, he had an electric light. On summer nights, the village men converged here to play quoits after dark. Harper charged 5 cents a game to help pay for the lights. Harper sold the building to Paul Baker in 1939. In the 1940s, the blacksmith shop was torn down.

The date of the house is difficult to ascertain. The 1870 census would put the Jeremiah Kreiner family here. Jeremiah was a blacksmith, and he worked at the shop next door, owned by his brother-in-law Henry Bonholtzer. Henry and Jeremiah had married sisters, Annie and Louisa Richwine, daughters of Henry Richwine of High Street. Likely this small house was a tenant house, then owned by Jacob Richwine, a brother to Louisa Kreiner. The problem with this is that the house does not appear on the 1872 Beers Atlas map. The only other place for Jeremiah would be in the rooms above the brick store at #334. Jeremiah's wife was Louisa; she was the daughter of Henry and Lydia Richwine of High Street and probably the niece of Jacob Richwine. Jeremiah and Louisa had four babies die between 1872 and 1877, possibly while they were living here. Jacob sold the house to his sister Christiann (born 1820) in 1884. She never married and lived here with her sister Margaret. In 1903, her heirs sold it to her nephew, Harry R. Richwine, for $400. During the early years of the twentieth century, it served as a store. At one time, it was a tin shop run by John Nunemaker; later, it housed a typewriter repair business. Not until about 1942 did it again become a private residence.

This two-story frame cottage has a metal gable roof and a two-bay front porch with wooden balustrade. Its eave wall serves as the two-bay front façade. A beaded clapboard covers its exterior. Windows are 6/6 on the first floor and 1/1 on the second and are crowned by pediments. Outbuildings include an outhouse and a modern garage.

334 Old Stone House Road

This house sits on one of the most historic sites in the village. For a full history of the early years of this site, refer back to the section on #1272 Boiling Springs Road, the home that is attached to the rear of this building.

There used to be a log house on this site. It had been built prior to 1812. In 1859, John Harlin, the owner, was assessed for a two-story frame and log house. By 1862, the new owner, Richard Anderson, had a brick house and blacksmith shop. This house was most likely built in 1860.

This house sits on lot two of Diven's addition. He sold this lot and the shops on it to John Brandt in 1850. Brandt sold it to John Harlan, a cooper, in 1852. Harlan owned it for six years; since he lived out of the village, he rented the house. He was forced to assign his property, and his assignees, Robert Wilson and Jacob Bowman, sold it to Richard Anderson, a blacksmith, in 1859. Anderson sold it to Daniel Stees, a tinner, in 1860. Living with Daniel was William Keesaman, a tinner from Mt. Holly and probably a nephew of George Keesaman of Churchtown. William worked for Stees, but later, he served two enlistments in the war. The first was for three months in 1861, and then in January 1864, he enlisted in Company E, 20th Pa. Cavalry. He served as a teamster.

Stees sold the property to Tobias Kaufman and John Nisley in 1866. They were the first ones to open a store here in 1866. They sold it to John N. Plank in 1869. Plank also bought the house at #1272 Boiling Springs Road as well as part of lot one, which adjoins this lot to the north. Plank (born 1836) was also a merchant. In 1871, John was mentioned as having a brick house and a tinner shop (the house at #1272 Boiling Springs Road) on a corner lot. He was listed as a merchant. John and Elizabeth had three sons, and they all helped in the store. His son George (1855–?) was later apprenticed out to a machinist, and he bought the wagon shed next to his father's property (see #328). In the summer of 1877, George got himself into trouble, getting a girl pregnant. She had him arrested and Sam Morrett went bail. George never showed up at his trial in September. By 1879, the store was being run by Frank Moist, 27. He boarded at the hotel up the hill while John Plank lived here in the back rooms and second floor. His assistant was Jacob M. Niesley, about 30. Jacob had to give up farming because of

334 Old Stone House Rd. (2007)

ill health. At first, he worked for his uncle George Brindle in Boiling Springs, but after 1880 he moved here. By 1884, F. G. Burtner took over Moist's store and Niesley stayed on as his employee. John Plank lived here through 1880 and perhaps as late as 1890 when he was forced to assign the house to Jacob M. Niesley. It was sold to Henry Bowman in 1891. Bowman then sold it to George Souders that same year, who sold it to Hattie Sheaffer in 1892 for $1,500. In April 1892, John Sheaffer opened a grocery store here. In later years (1930s), it was known as the Rank store.

This common bond brick house was built in 1860/61 and served as a general store and specialty shop for many years. The

334 Old Stone House Rd. (side view) (2007)

two-and-a-half-story, ell-shaped structure has six bays and a multiple gable roof covered with seamed metal. The lower half of its front façade features two large display windows, two entrances, and two 2/2 windows set in molded wood panels and separated by pilasters. Corbels support a narrow overhang above this storefront. Both front entrances have transoms and sidelights. The rest of the windows on the front portion are 2/2, while those on the rear wing are 6/6. The windows are capped by projecting lintels, and the cornice above them is ornamented by sawtooth soldiering. Behind the house was one of the first community wells dug in Churchtown.

1260 Boiling Springs Road: Churchtown School

Turn east onto Boiling Springs Road and walk towards the first building on your left. You'll be passing the old cemetery and the church off to your left. This landmarks the area where four farms were joined, those of Jacob Wise, Fred Goodyear, Jacob Strock and Hartman Morrett. By the 1880s, a stone wall stood around the graveyard. The graves were removed early this century.

The building, now at 1260 Boiling Springs Road, was formerly the Churchtown School. There has been a school here since 1779. In 1805, the local farmers subscribed for a new one to be built; that one lasted until about 1850, when the third one was built. The present building was built in the spring of 1880. The contractor was John Keeny of Boiling Springs. He started it about March, and by June, it was ready to be roofed. Unfortunately, construction came to a halt because they ran out of lumber for two weeks. By the first week of July, it had the roof on and soon,

1260 Boiling Springs Rd.

the plastering was finished. Churchtown once boasted two schools. The other one was where Gish Lane joins Route 174. One was the primary school and the other a high school. The second one was built at the same time this one was and was decommissioned between 1903 and 1905. In August 1880, the new teachers were examined and hired: Sam Byers for the high school and Harriet Enck for the primary. Until 1892 the school term was six months, for which teachers earned about $30 per month. Following the lead of other communities, the school term was increased in 1892 to eight months.

These buildings were used for other purposes. Churchtown, like so many other communities, had a Literary Society. It met on Friday nights in the 1880s and the 1890s on Saturday nights and was a forum for formal debates, much like our modern school debating clubs. A typical program would start with some music followed by some referred questions, such as: "Explain the formation of West Virginia," which Daniel Bowman had to do. Another was: "What was the first telegram in the world?" A formal debate between the two groups followed this. A judge then decided in favor of one team or the other. Another group to use the school building was the Monroe Township Temperance Alliance. They were organized in February 1880 after a lecture by Rev. Josephus. Among the Churchtown people involved, Dan Bowman was elected secretary, John Paul was the treasurer, and some of those on the executive committee were Dr. Koons, Henry Knaub, Carrie Quigley, Mrs. Ella Goodyear and Mrs. John Beidle. Temperance sermons were frequently being preached in both the Lutheran and United Brethren Churches at this time.

In December 1893 a meeting was held here to find out about the possibility that the newly proposed trolley could be extended from Mt. Holly to Mechanicsburg and pass through Churchtown. Work on the trolley began in March 1894 in Carlisle, and 1901, it finally made it to Churchtown.

On the grounds of the school lot was one of the earliest baseball diamonds in Churchtown. Baseball was organized here as early as 1880 and there was a field behind the school in the 1920s until being moved to a lot south of High Street. From there, it went to the northwest corner of Route 174 and Zimmerman Road.

Now serving as a single-family residence, this brick schoolhouse had two classrooms, each two bays long by two bays wide, flanking a central entrance hall. In the 1930s, students entered the building through the double front doors set at the end of a projecting front entry hall, hung their coats in the hallway, and separated into their respective classrooms—grades 1 through 4 in the east room, grades 5 through 8 in the west. When Boiling Springs Road was paved over, the front doors were closed off, and new doors were constructed out of windows on the sides of the entry wing.

1260 Boiling Springs Rd. (side view)

This was because the school sat right alongside the road, and children exiting the building by the front doors would have been walking out into the path of traffic.

After the trolley was discontinued in June 1930, Valley Transportation ran buses through here that connected the village with Carlisle and Mechanicsburg. This school only went to the 8th grade. After that, students had to catch the bus to school. But the ride was not free. It cost 10¢ a day for the round trip, and if the mother did not have the money, then the child was forced to stay home. Many Churchtown children missed a lot of school for that reason. There was only one bus stop for the whole village, and that was down at the square at #336 Old Stone House Road. The children would either bus to the High School at Boiling Springs or Mechanicsburg. What determined which school depended upon the parent. Boiling Springs was considered best for boys who were becoming farmers. The school at Mechanicsburg was five miles away, and there were a number of times that students missed the bus home and either had to hitch a ride or walk the five miles.

Today, most of the exterior openings in the schoolhouse have been altered. Many of the tall 6/6 windows have been shortened and replaced by 2/2 sashes. The original molded lintels, however, were lowered and retained. Several original windows remain on the side and rear walls of the eastern wing. Two picture windows have replaced the front double doors, although the twin side entrances remain. A wooden deck has been added to the rear of the building, and the interior has been extensively remodeled. Original features remaining include the multiple-gable roof covered with seamed metal, metal stove pipes protruding from each classroom wing, a small brick rear wing extension with plain lintels over its windows, the Gothic arched attic lights framed by headers, the molded wood cornice, and the common bond brick exterior. The school was decommissioned in 1957, and the building was sold in 1965.

324 Gish Lane
Continue up the same side of the street until you get to Gish Lane, which runs off on your left. Here, at #324 Gish Lane sits a house hidden from view somewhat from the main road. It sits on land that was formerly Jacob Strock's. In 1854, his son George sold a house and 57 perches of land to John Klinepeter. This is the earliest that the house can be dated, though it may be older by several years. Although Klinepeter owned it for a number of years, I don't think he often lived here. Instead, he rented it out. In 1860, the house was rented to a woman, H. Culbertson. Living with her were her daughter, Nancy Belle, a teacher; her son, Sam, a student of Dr. Lenher; and J. Weaver, a music teacher.

This family came to Churchtown in 1858. After moving from here in about 1861, they lived in a double house with the John

324 Gish Lane (along Boiling Springs Rd.)

W. Leidig family. These two young men, neighbors, joined the army together in 1862. They were in the 130th, Colonel Zinn's regiment. He was also their neighbor. They served at Antietam and Sam was wounded in the arm at Fredericksburg. When the boys returned home in May 1863, they were given a reception by the town. It was then noticed by everyone how much Sam had changed. People said he "looked sad and stupid," that he had a "depraved expression," he was "an old man in his movements," among other things. Sam also suffered from rheumatism and lung problems. For six months after coming home, he continued to read medicine at Dr. Lenher's. A fellow student at the time was E. J. Miller of Churchtown, who later became a doctor. Sam then went to Philadelphia and graduated in the class of 1866. That April, he moved to Illinois, where his brother William lived.

In 1870 Klinepeter was living here with his wife. In October 1882, it was sold at auction to John Webbert. It was described as being a one-and-a-half-story frame house with an attached washhouse. There was a cistern near the kitchen door, a frame stable and fruit trees on the property.

John H. Webbert was a Civil War veteran of Company I, 200th Pennsylvania Infantry. He stood 5'5" and 100 pounds. He had been wounded in the right hand at Fort Steadman in 1865, but this never bothered him in later years. He did develop heart problems and dyspepsia, and as a result, he was poorly nourished and was unable to do much physical work. He had moved to Churchtown from Mechanicsburg about 1877 and found odd jobs. Prior to coming here, he had been a brick-layer and had built up a small nest egg, and this he lived off of until 1884, when it was almost all gone. For a few years he worked for Albert Plank, doing such things as painting the plows and wagons built at the shop. One summer, he also tried to help with the haying in Plank's field, but he was too weakened by his heart problems to continue. About 1881, he worked for John O. Dill at #350 Old Stone House Road. Webbert had married his cousin so because he was family, Dill would pay Webbert for a full day's work, even though he was unable to work it. One summer day, after working in the fields, the crew sat down for supper at Dill's table. Webbert had a spell and was carried to the lounge. Dr. Koons was called and it was three hours until Webbert was able to leave. Dill had to drive him home in his carriage. This type of occurrence was frequent in Webbert's life. Eventually, he did get a pension. He needed testimony from the doctors in Churchtown who had treated him. Dr. Hartzell, his doctor in 1878/79, refused to give any testimony unless paid $20. Three times Webbert went to him but was refused each time. Dr. Koons eventually gave it. The only apparent income Webbert had while living here was his pension, whatever money he realized from the crops he grew here on his half an acre, and whatever his two daughters gave him from their jobs. By 1910, Mina, 27, was a stenographer at a steam fitting company and Mary, 21, was a saleslady at a department store. Both lived at home. In 1906 Webbert tried to get his pension increased. It was then about $17 a month. Seventeen times, the Board of Examiners examined him, and they thought he was getting too much. But he got his increase. He sold this house in 1921 and moved to Mechanicsburg, where he died.

This is a simple three-bay, ell-shaped frame house with side hall construction and multiple gable roof. Windows are 2/2 in front and 6/6 in the rear. The weatherboard is covered with aluminum siding, and the roof with seamed metal. Many outbuildings surround the house, including two large frame sheds or stables and two outhouses. Those on the east side of the lane, however, now belong to the adjoining farmland property.

Just on the other side of Gish Lane there once stood a house until about 1980. It was built after 1872 and was a two-story weatherboard with a wrap-around porch. It was the tenant house for the Peter S. Miller farm and usually housed two families. Squire Nickey owned it for a while. At one time in the 1930s Nickey decided to sell the field to the right into lots. The apple orchard that stood there was cleaned out and lots platted, but nothing ever happened. In the 1950s, the house lay abandoned, and about 1980, Paul Simmons tore it down and used the wood in his pole barn at #1251 Boiling Springs Road.

1251 Boiling Springs Road

Cross the street and walk up towards the farmhouse on your right. The address is #1251 Boiling Springs Road. This is currently a working farm of 40 acres. The land was part of the

George Michael Wise land, whose son Jacob sold 150 acres to Hartman Morrett in 1785. Hartman was from Lancaster County and had served in the Revolutionary War as a private in the county militia in 1780 and 1781. Shortly afterward, he moved here. Hartman (1744–1822) owned three plantations at the time of he died. He willed one to his widow Gertrude (1768–1836), one to his son John (1785–1837) and the other to his son Michael (1788–1840).

Michael got the lower farm of 100 acres, of which this farm is a part. Michael Morrett, Sr. died in 1840, and he willed the lower farm, where he was living, to sons Moses and Samuel; all except for two acres, which were to be set off and sold, which is where #1259 Boiling Springs Road is now located. There were other provisions to his will, which were very specific. His real estate was to be let out until the youngest daughter turned 18. Then, the land could be sold. His sons were to dig a well on the lower farm that year. The next year, 1841, they were expected to build a house and barn on the lower farm, the house to be not superfluous but common. When his widow Catherine (1791–1847) decided to give up farming, the executors were to build her a small house with a cellar under it and a stable. The house here is probably the one built in 1841. Across the fields in front of you, along Brandt Road, there is an old farmhouse, which may be the old Michael Morrett homestead.

In 1850, their youngest sister came of age, and her brothers began to piecemeal the farm and sell it. Forty acres went to John Leidig in 1850 for $3,216. In 1852, John was taxed for a two-story house, a new barn and 38 acres. John had married Lydia Morrett (1820–1855),

1251 Boiling Springs Rd.

a sister to Michael, Jr. In 1853, Leidig sold it to Adam Givler (1813–1867), and later Adam sold it to his wife. In 1868, Elizabeth Givler (1813–1890) sold it to Peter Brindle. Peter lived here until 1887, when he sold it to John Westfall.

This farm includes a house, barn, and numerous outbuildings. The house is a three-bay, two-and-a-half-story ell with a seamed metal, multiple gable roof. The centered entrance is protected by a three-bay front porch supported by four square columns on stone bases. Windows are 1/1 and have simple, slightly projecting lintels. The frame house, originally wood-sided, is now covered with asbestos shingles. End chimneys are internal. A one-and-a-half-story, one-room extension, also with a metal gable roof, is attached to the rear wing. Outbuildings, including the barn, are also frame structures with metal-covered roofs. This property marks the eastern boundary of the village.

Across the road is where the trolley tracks veered north on their way to Mechanicsburg. The old raised bed lays on the boundary between the timber and the open field, slanting diagonally behind the modern Monroe Elementary School.

1259 Boiling Springs Road

Turn back toward the square and walk to the last house on the tour: #1259 Boiling Springs Road. This two-acre farmette was set off as such by the will of Michael Morrett Sr. in 1840. He stated that the two acres be surveyed starting along the road that leads from Dr. Sawyer's to Livinger's corner and then eastward until it measured two acres. The road that he mentions here is the alley, aka Green Street, to the right of the house that goes back to High Street. He also mentioned that the western edge of this tract adjoined a brick building and shops. The purpose of Michael setting off these two acres is not made clear in his will unless it was to provide a house for his widow. In 1850, the house was rented to their brother-in-law, John Goodyear, who had married Elizabeth Morrett. They had eight children at the time. Her brother Moses was also living with them. He was a merchant in the corner dry goods store. When Moses and Sam sold these two acres to Andrew Singiser in 1850 it already had a house and two shops on it.

By 1841, Michael Jr. was being assessed for a brick house. This is about the only land that Michael apparently owned in the village so the tax record may refer to this house. In 1844, he was assessed for a two-story brick house, wagon maker shop and a smith shop. When this house was recently remodeled a piece of paper was found in a hole in the wall that apparently describes this property in 1864 for insurance purposes. It calls this a part brick/frame and weatherboard house, 38' in front and 26' wide. This house is currently 26' across the front, not including the summer kitchen. Perhaps the front of the house faced the alley at that time. It also mentioned porches on the front and back

1259 Boiling Springs Rd. (2007)

with two chimney pipes and two lightning rods. There was a bank barn 62' by 36' with a wagon shed, 15' by 36', attached. There was a frame weatherboard horse shed, 26' by 26', and a frame and weatherboard wash house, 24' by 16'. This gives an idea of what the various outbuildings listed on a property at that time were.

Andrew Singiser had married their sister, Caroline Morrett, and never lived here that I can tell. At the time, he also owned a flour mill, and in 1853, he was listed as a non-resident, so most likely, he rented the farm out. In 1855, he sold the farm to John Bowman and his son Henry. John sold his half-interest to Henry in 1859. Henry was born in 1817 in York County. In 1854, he married Barbara Goodyear, a daughter of Jacob. Henry was a butcher, and for fourteen years, he was in partnership with John Paul. In 1868, he bought another farm but never moved there; a tenant did the farming for him.

Roads in Henry's day were to be maintained by the road supervisors elected yearly by the township citizens. Being dirt, there were often long periods when they were rutted so deeply as to be impassable. That may be the reason for what Henry tried to demonstrate here in 1864. On April 1, Henry dug out a stretch of road in front of his house 150 feet long, 8 feet wide and one foot deep. Here, he put a stone pavement, and around the outside of it, he put four wooden posts. Nothing was done for apparently few complaints were lodged, but something spurred David Darr, one of the township road supervisors, to try and get Henry to remove the obstruction that winter. Henry refused, and in December, a warrant was filled out for Henry's arrest. As a countersuit, Henry's neighbor and friend, Peter Baker, sued David Darr and David Landis for non-maintenance of the township roads in January 1865. Henry was arrested in March and put up on bail. He pleaded not guilty at first but then later withdrew that plea and pleaded guilty.

Apparently, Henry also tried some peddling until he was caught doing so without having a license, a misdemeanor. In October 1874, Sam Baker accused Henry of huckstering without a license. Henry would buy or barter for eggs, butter, dried fruit, chickens, ducks, turkeys and geese. These he would then take them out of the county to sell. Adam Gensler went on bail for Henry. In the trial that ensued, Henry was found not guilty.

In later years he did a lot of livestock dealing and was quite successful. Henry was a director of the Dillsburg Bank, being one of the organizers. His son took over after he died. He was also a director of the Second National Bank of Mechanicsburg. In 1895, at the age of 78, a tree he was cutting fell on him while he was on South Mountain and killed him. His only son, Daniel, was born in 1854 and took over this property after the death of his father. In 1898 the Court awarded him the property which he gave to his mother.

D.G. became a teacher at age 16, one of the youngest ever to be given a certificate. He taught for 25 years. He married Elizabeth, daughter of George Strock, who lived on Old Stone House Road. It was his serenade that Beidel broke up. D.G. was also one of the organizers of the Allen Knitting Company in 1902. The company bought the Shaeffer property on High Street and built a factory there. At its peak, they employed about 28 people, but about 1910, business took a downturn and Daniel was forced to declare bankruptcy. In 1911, he put the company into receivership, and Theo Brandt was put in charge. Daniel was forced to sell his two remaining farms. Luckily, he had sold this one to his mother, and in her will she gave it to him. She died in 1913, and Daniel and his wife lived here until their deaths. He was the postmaster, and the office was here in his house. He died in 1924, Lizzie the following year, and in 1926, the estate sold the farm to George Ewing.

Henry's neighbor across the alley in the 1860s was Anna Enck and her family. One son, Levi, became a butcher, and it is possible that Henry was his master. Levi probably worked for Henry until he bought his own house at #336 Old Stone House Road.

This two-story painted brick house is currently in good condition. A single-family residence now, the building was partially used as a business in the past, with one room housing the town's post office. The three-bay building has a metal gable roof and a rectangular plan. The brick on the front of the structure displays Flemish bonding and soldiering along the cornice, i.e., bricks whose pointed corners slant outward, resembling a saw-tooth blade. The shuttered windows have wood lintels on the exterior. An attached summer kitchen sits behind the house, with brick arches and a straight line of headers over its windows. The back porch has been enclosed, and the front porch was added at a later date. Its columns were also used as posts. An iron fence runs around the front of the two-acre property, and the wooden outbuildings include an outhouse, a barn (garage), and one other structure. Little interior integrity remains. If you walk back Green Street a few feet to the last window, you can see where a door once stood but is now bricked over. Here was the entrance to the post office.

Churchtown's Streetscapes, Alleyways and Outbuildings

(Unless otherwise noted with a "(2007)", these photos were taken during the 1990s, around the same time as the first edition of this book was written.)

The square: the intersection of Boiling Springs and Old Stone House Rds., looking SW (2007)

The Houses of Churchtown 167

Looking up "the hill": the distinctive stepped rowhouses of Old Stone House Rd., with the Churchtown Church of God and parsonage at the top of the rise (2007)

The intersection of Old Stone House and Boiling Springs Rds., looking south up "the hill."

Boiling Springs Road, looking southeast from North St.

Old Stone House Rd., looking north towards the intersection with High St.

The Houses of Churchtown 169

Old Stone House Rd., looking north from the 320 block

The tour begins at Upper High St., looking east at the 1260 block.

High St., looking east at the 1290 block on a wintry day.

Outhouse, upper Old Stone House Rd.

"Dead Man's Curve": Paul's Alley, between High St. & Boiling Springs Rd., looking west.

The Houses of Churchtown 171

347–341 Old Stone House Rd. from the rear, looking northwest from Locust Alley & High St.

Outbuildings and alley behind 310–326 Old Stone House Rd., looking south

The intersection of West St. and the alley behind 320–310 Old Stone House, looking north.

Carriage house/shop of 1263 Boiling Sps. Rd.

Blacksmith shop of 320 Old Stone House Rd.

Summer kitchen at 1288 Boiling Springs Rd.

Summer kitchen, 346 Old Stone House (2007)

The Houses of Churchtown

Barns next to 324 Gish Lane (2007)

The stone barn originally of 352 Old Stone House

Barn at 313 Old Stone House Rd.

Barn at 1299 Brandt Rd. (2007)

Barn and outbuildings at 276 Old Stone House Rd., at the northern edge of the village, looking south.

Agricultural Life in Decades Past
(Photographs courtesy of Shirley Peffer)

Elizabeth Hertzler Brindle (1848–1913), William Brindle (1844–1929) and, in buggy, daughter Carrie Brindle Deitch (1887–1940) in front of house at 291 Locust Point Rd., 1863. Written on back of the original photo is the caption "William Brindle went by horseback to hear Lincoln dedicate Gettysburg Civil War Cemetery on this day.

Edgar W. Peffer, winning a living room sofa from Reichart's Fertilizer Co. for growing 400 bushels of potatoes per acre, 1937.

Jonas Brindle working in the fields with a cultivator, 1919.

4-H Baby Beef Club at Kline's Stockyard, 1933, including Harold Hertzler, Leon Miller, John J. Baish, Lawrence Shultz, Guy Shultz, Fred Myers Jr., Emmanuel Zeigler, George, Robert, and Clyde Strock, Sara Myers, Taylor Rays, and Mr. Miller's daughter. Also pictured are Jimmy Keim, State Club Leader, Mr. Elmer Brindle (far left), and Jacob Kline, Stockyard owner (far right).

Jonas and Paul Brindle flattening a field with a wooden cultipacker near the barns on the Brindle farm at 335 Brindle Rd., 1921.

Cumberland Co. 4-H members with steers, selecting the project for the year, Kline's Stockyard, Mechanicsburg, 1933.

Harvesting hay, 1920, Jonas Rupp is on the mule. Jonas Brindle is on the wagon, and little Jonas Rupp is standing.

Paul Brindle moving a new outhouse into position with a sledge, ca. 1920s.

Glenn Peffer, son of Edgar W. Peffer, winning showmanship award, Lancaster, 1948.

Barbara Hammaker, Gretchen Berkheimer and Shirley Brindle with Grandpa Harry Berkheimer on porch of house at 1360 W. Lisburn Rd., 1938.

CHAPTER 9

Colonel Henry Zinn and the 130th Pennsylvania Infantry

by Suzanne Sunday

Nineteenth-century historian Samuel Bates wrote of Colonel Zinn's death in battle, "Thus fell one of the truest and boldest spirits that went forth from the Keystone State to do battle for his country. It was not a reckless bravery—a daring without thought—but with appreciative heroism, he went with considered step to his death."[19]

Who was Henry I. Zinn? He was born on December 11, 1834, in Dover Township, York County, Pennsylvania, the son of John and Anna Mary (Beitzel) Zinn. He studied at the Cumberland Valley Institute in Mechanicsburg and became a local teacher at several rural schools, including Givler's School on Lisburn Road in Monroe Township and Plank's School on South Middlesex Road in South Middleton Township. Henry was by nature well endowed and by taste studious. He was fitted to have taken a commanding position among his fellow man in any walk or profession. Henry was by stature five feet ten inches, stout, robust, and healthy.[20]

Henry married Mary Ann Clarke on September 18, 1855. The Zinn family lived at 1265 Boiling Springs Road in Churchtown, boarding with Sam Kline and his wife Elizabeth. There is a record of Henry Zinn purchasing lot six (now part of 322 Old Stonehouse Road) in Churchtown in 1859, possibly for his sister, Charlotte Zinn.[21]

Mary and Henry had three children, but only one survived to adulthood. In March 1862, three-year-old James died from measles, and on Christmas Day, 1862, six-year-old Elsie died from diphtheria. George, born in 1861, graduated from West Point (first in his class) in 1883. He served several decades as an engineering officer, retiring as a Colonel, and died in 1946 at age 85. He married, but there are no descendants. Mary never remarried and lived on her $30-a-month widow's pension, for which she had to hire a lawyer from Washington, D.C. to get. Mary died in 1920 at the age of 85. Henry, Mary, Elsie and James are buried in Mount Zion Cemetery, as are his sister, Charlotte, and her husband, Conrad Drager.

Henry raised a company of men from the Churchtown area, and they entered the service of the United States for a three-month enlistment on April 3, 1861, as part of the Seventh Pennsylvania Reserve, 36th Regiment. He was named First Lieutenant on May 28, 1861, and was promoted to Captain on June 28, 1861. However, on November 30, 1861, Henry

---

19. Bates, Samuel P. *Martial Deeds of Pennsylvania*, 442.
20. Bates, Samuel P. *History of the Pennsylvania Volunteers 1861–65*, 427.

21. Vanderlodge, Kevin. *Churchtown: An Architectural and Historic Walking Tour*, 85.

resigned, stating, "feeling it due to myself to sever my connection to the regiment."[22]

Then, on August 16, 1862, Henry re-entered service as Captain in the 130th Pennsylvania Volunteers, part of the Army of the Potomac. This was a nine-month enlistment. The next day, he was promoted to Colonel. Private John D. Hemminger described Colonel Zinn in his address at the ceremony dedicating the monument to the 130th Pennsylvania Reserves on the Antietam battlefield, which includes a bas relief of Colonel Zinn: ". . . we think of Colonel Zinn as the man who made the One Hundred and Thirtieth Regiment what it was . . . Surely so noble an officer as he was, fearless in battle, a good disciplinarian, affable and courteous, and yet dignified, is worthy of this recognition in which you, my comrades, may take pride from the fact that in response to our secretary's appeal for funds with which to do it, you liberally contributed."[23]

Colonel Zinn was in a sphere fitted to his capabilities, and under his molding hand, the Regiment rapidly gained knowledge and skill in the practice of military duty.[24] Colonel (Retired) Tom Faley described Colonel Zinn as "the perfect citizen soldier . . . His men had only a few days of training . . . before being sent to war."[25]

At Antietam, the 130th Pennsylvania was a crucial part of the fighting at "Bloody Alley." As part of General William French's Third Division's Second Brigade, the 130th was in the center of the Union line as they crossed Antietam Creek. "Everyone finally got over in good order, and the column of our Regiment put into shape again. Colonel Henry I. Zinn led his Regiment calmly on, whilst Major John Lee, who was most of the time with the rear guard, was galloping about swearing his hardest at the men," recalled Corporal John B. Landis.[26] As the Union soldiers advanced on the Roulette farm, the 130th engaged in the fiercest fighting at the Sunken Road (also known as Bloody Alley).

Despite the continuous rain of fire poured upon them, the men of the 130th pressed on towards the Sunken Road to witness small white flags being hoisted along the Rebel lines. In wonderment and assuming that the Rebels were surrendering, the 130th ceased firing and began to advance. Allowing the Union to approach within mere yards, the Rebels dropped their white flags. "Suddenly, they poured a deadly volley into our ranks . . . with many falling about us," recalled Private James Hemminger.[27] The 130th was directly in the sights of the awaiting Rebel skirmishers. Corporal Landis wrote, "We finally drove the enemy from the cornfield and going forward over a clover field, we found him entrenched in a cut with piles of rails thrown up in front."[28] The arrival of additional Federal troops near the southern portion of the Sunken Road broke the Rebel line. The Regiment had suffered 178 casualties (46 dead, 132 wounded out of 650 soldiers), a casualty rate of 27 percent.[29] Colonel Zinn had his horse shot out from under him.

Recalling the ordeal years later, Edward Spangler wrote, "With the close of the day ended the bloodiest single day of the war. Night afforded to the unharmed needed slumber."[30]

---

22. *Find a Grave* website.
23. *One Hundred and Thirtieth Regiment Pennsylvania Volunteer Infantry: Ceremonies,* 13.
24. Bates, *Martial Deeds,* 441.
25. Miller, Matt. *Honoring Heroes.*
26. Beltz, Terrence. *The History of the Qne Hundred and Thirtieth,* 53.
27. Ibid., 66.
28. Ibid., 60.
29. Tracey, Jon. *The 139th Pennsylvania Infantry Regiment.*
30. Beltz, *History,* 71.

On September 19, 1862. Colonel Zinn wrote to his wife, "Dearest Mary: We have gone through our first fight, and I am safe, although many of our brave 130th have been sent to their long home. John Zinn and Emerson Zinn passed through untouched, but Rush Zinn was killed on the spot. A cannon shot took off his head while in the act of loading his gun. We have lost forty killed and one hundred and fifty to one hundred and sixty wounded. I hope it may never be our misfortune to get into another battle so terrible. My horse received two balls in the neck; one ball passed through the back part of the saddle and another through the blanket strapped behind the saddle. Lieutenant Givler of Company F was shot through the head at the beginning of the engagement and died soon after. He was insensible after being shot."

"Our Regiment is reduced to four hundred and fifty men. A number of the men disappeared before the fight. They are probably among the skedaddlers."[31]

Colonel Zinn had clearly demonstrated his leadership ability to both his men and his superiors. Although he had no prior formal military training, and his men were equally untrained and untested, they successfully overcame General Rodes' Alabamians, who were combat veterans in a superior protected defensive position. In his official report, Brigadier General French remarked, "The conduct of the new regiments must take a prominent place in the history of this great battle."[32]

On September 21, Colonel Zinn wrote to his wife," The 130th has been engaged three days in burying the dead. The destruction of life in Wednesday's battle was enormous. We buried 400 rebels and 48 Union soldiers. Dead horses are scattered around by scores. Thousands of arms of every description lie scattered in all directions. These are being collected by the government."[33]

After burying the dead at Antietam, the 130th went with the rest of the Second Corps to the heights overlooking Harper's Ferry on September 22. They numbered 583, reduced significantly from the original strength of 986, and the men were wearing the same clothing since their departure from Camp Marcy on September 7. On September 24, in a long letter to his wife Mary, Colonel Zinn shared the situation he and his men were enduring: "Dearest Mary: We left the battleground near Sharpsburg on Monday morning and arrived here the same evening. The rebels burned the railroad and pontoon bridge at this place so that we were obliged to wade the Potomac. The water is not deep, but the river bottom is rough, making the wading difficult. Harper's Ferry is a dilapidated-looking place, all the government buildings, which were the only important ones, having been destroyed . . . Our encampment is on Bolivar Heights, about a mile from the town. The scenery is beautiful and, if not marred by the ravages of war, would be the finest I ever saw."

"A great many people from Cumberland County visited us during our stay on the battlefield, among them Isaac Enck, who promised me that he would go to see you upon his return home. I was informed that Bros. Alexander and Edward were on the way to see us but were obliged to turn back on account of the great number of troops that were passing over the Cumberland Valley Railroad."

---

31. *One Hundred and Thirtieth Regiment Pennsylvania Volunteer Infantry: Ceremonies*, 62.

32. Beltz, *History*, 77–78.

33. *One Hundred and Thirtieth Regiment Pennsylvania Volunteer Infantry: Ceremonies*, 62–63.

"The Regiment is still without the desired appointments, in consequence of which considerable dissatisfaction exists among the men. We have but sixteen commissioned officers left for duty, some having left after the battle who were not wounded but sick . . ."

"You have never heard of as poor a place as this. Not enough can be had here for man or beast to live on. There is no corn, oats or hay for horses. The man who takes care of my horses was obliged to go to a cornfield in the neighborhood and cut off the green cornstalks for feed . . ."

"The following is a list of the killed and wounded of Company F: Killed: Second Lieutenant John A. Givler: shot through the head; Private Thomas English: struck in the right side and on the right leg by a shell. His whole side was torn out, and yet he lived until Thursday morning; Private T. Rush Zinn: whole head torn off by a shell or cannon ball; also his left hand torn off by the same shot; "Private Samuel May shot through head by musket ball; Private Levi Bender: shot through head."

"Wounded: "First Sergeant Levi M. Haverstick: right arm; Ira D. Braugher: right arm, amputated; Wm. Ebersole: shot through hand; D. D. Landis: shot through hand; Samuel A. Miller: shot through both legs; John Snavely: shot through the chest, may recover; John Wood: shot in both hips."

"It is now nearly three weeks since we left camp at Fort Marcy, and as few of us brought along a change of clothing, you can imagine how dirty we are by this time. Yesterday I wore no shirt as mine was being washed. I have often heard of such things but never thought I would be reduced to such straights. It is impossible to get any clothing where the rebel army has been. If you get an opportunity, send me a shirt or two and a few pairs of stockings. All of our camp equipage and officers' baggage was stored in Washington, where I presume it is safe. An effort is being made to have it all sent here, when we will select from it what we need and send the balance home. I sent to Washington for the box you sent me, but presume part of the contents will be spoiled by the time it arrives."

"Some men of one of the Carlisle companies have just sung the doxology, which implies that the soldier's day is ended, so I will close my letter by sending my love to all."[34]

The Regiment's camp equipment, officers' baggage, and men's personal belongings were still in storage in Washington. Officers' commissions had not yet arrived from Governor Curtin, nor had advance pay and promised government bounties been paid.[35] On October 5 Colonel Zinn related his increasing concerns to his wife, "All is well with me. This cannot be said of many of the poor fellows of the Regiment who have been suffering for want of proper medical attendance since the battle. All our medical stores were left behind with the exception of a small lot brought along by one of our surgeons, most of which was expended during and after the battle . . . By borrowing a few medicines we have managed to shift along, though lacking in drugs for special cases. Harper's Ferry is situated at confluence of Potomac and Shenandoah rivers. A heavy fog rises from the river during the night, which, with a chilly atmosphere, makes the place unhealthy. Water is poor and scarce, and produces diarrhoea and dysentery, the prevailing diseases among the men."[36]

---

34. Ibid., 63–65.
35. Beltz, *History*, 80.
36. *One Hundred and Thirtieth Regiment Pennsylvania Volunteer Infantry: Ceremonies*, 65–67.

The Regiment was finally adequately supplied by early October. Colonel Zinn wrote to his wife, "We have ample supplies of good living now. The good old days of Camp Curtain . . . have returned, but how long they will last I cannot tell."[37] In early October, the Regiment's long-awaited officer appointments finally arrived. Colonel Zinn wrote Mary, "The organization of the Regiment is completed . . . there is no danger we will lose our pay . . . we expect to get money enough to pay our debts and to keep our families besides."[38]

The Regiment, with improved living conditions and supplies, slowly regained the strength it had prior to the losses sustained at Antietam. As October came to an end, the weather turned rainy and colder. Colonel Zinn expressed his concern to his wife, "The cold winds of winter are fast coming, and I must have clothing for myself and blankets for my horses and boys."[39]

At the end of October, Colonel Zinn wrote home, "From present indications, I presume it is intended that we shall remain here this winter, but as movements of the army are uncertain, a week hence may find us far from here."[40] Colonel Zinn was correct. Within days, the Regiment was on the move, marching across the Shenandoah River, following the retreating Confederate troops deeper into Virginia.

Camped just outside Warrenton, Virginia, the overall health of the Regiment was improving, with the number of men available for duty increasing by the day. In spite of the general improvement, cases of jaundice were taking a toll among the regiments. On November 9, Colonel Zinn wrote Mary, "My skin and the whites of my eyes are as yellow as saffron. I have the jaundice. You can imagine how I feel camping in this cold, snowy weather . . . There are quite a number of cases of jaundice in the Regiment."[41]

Union General George McClellan, Commander of the Army of the Potomac, was replaced by General Ambrose Burnside, whose plan for engaging the Confederates involved deception. Burnside planned to fool them into thinking he was planning to attack either Culpepper or Gordonsville. Instead, Burnside intended to make a rapid drive into Fredericksburg. Once Fredericksburg fell, he would set his sights on Richmond.[42]

On November 19, the 130th arrived at Belle Plain Landing after marching nine miles in pouring rain. The first tasks given to the 130th were repair work and loading and unloading supplies from federal transports and canal boats. The men of the 130th were enduring soaking rains and chilly mornings with little protection. Private Spangler later recounted, "The weather was cold, and it rained a great deal, often mingled with snow. As we had no tents or shelter of any kind, and the plain being low, flat and impervious, causing water to stand inches deep, we suffered intensely."[43]

In a November 20 letter to his wife, Colonel Zinn had a somewhat different point of view. "It has been raining nearly all the time since we came here, which makes it very unpleasant for the men, as they are without any shelter except their gum blankets (rubberized canvas, similar to today's tarps). The government furnishes the men no shelter save that

---

37. Ibid., 68.
38. Ibid., 69.
39. Ibid., 70.
40. Ibid.

41. Ibid., 72–73.
42. Beltz, *History*, 97.
43. Ibid., 100–3.

of the shelter tents, consisting of three pieces, carried by them and affording shelter for two men. Poles for the tents are procured by the men on arriving in the new camp. Up until within a few days, the men have demanded "A" tents, refusing the shelter tents; and now that they have consented to accept them, they should not murmur at delay as there may not be opportunity to get them immediately."[44]

On December 12, General Burnside received intelligence that there was a deep trench running through the town that would be an obstacle to troops assaulting the hills occupied by the Confederates. Burnside assessed the information as mistaken and decided that no such trench existed. In effect, Burnside had directed that 5,000 to 10,000 advance on 40,000 veteran Confederate troops entrenched on high ground overlooking a large plain.[45]

On December 13, Major General William French's Corps, including the 130th, were among the first to attempt the assault on Marye's Heights. On that foggy morning, the Regiment was given the order to charge.[46]

Pushing forward and emerging into the open plain, the 130th came under deadly artillery fire as it reached the canal Burnside had refused to acknowledge existed. The men slipped and clawed their way out of the murky wastewater canal and moved forward under fire. Colonel Zinn shouted, "Stand up to it, boys!" Pouring rifle fire into the enemy as the Regiment moved forward, the 130th came under a terrific storm of bullets from the veteran Confederates. The 130th returned fire while crossing the ground, stopping halfway.[47]

Gunsmoke shrouded everything, and soldiers relied on their color-bearers, who held the regimental flags above the smoke, to guide them.[48]

As the Regiment's color bearer fell, Colonel Zinn, waving his sword in his right hand, grasped the falling regimental colors in his left and lifted them in the air, shouting, "Stick to your standard, boys! The One Hundred and Thirtieth never abandons its colors; give them another volley!" These were the beloved Colonel's final words.[49] Zinn was almost immediately killed. The remnants of the Regiment withdrew to the edge of the fairgrounds. With no hope for success and dwindling ammunition, General French ordered his own division, the 130th Pennsylvania included, off the field. This was the end of the Regiment's battle.[50]

In his after-battle report on Fredericksburg, dated December 18, 1862, General William H. French said, "I call to the special notice of the commanding the gallant conduct of Colonel H. I. Zinn, One hundred thirtieth Pennsylvania Volunteers. This officer, conspicuous for his valor at Antietam, was killed while carrying the colors of his Regiment to the front, after the standard-bearer had fallen."[51]

One of Zinn's officers, Lieutenant John Hays, shortly after the battle, wrote, "The greatest loss in our Regt. is Colonel Zinn. There is not a man in the Regt. for whom the men would fight so well. He was brave, energetic and a good tactician. The men knew it and had confidence in him."[52]

Most fallen soldiers were buried on the battlefield, but Zinn, who apparently was

---

44. *One Hundred and Thirtieth Regiment Pennsylvania Volunteer Infantry: Ceremonies*, 76.
45. Beltz, *History*, 110–11.
46. Tracey, Jon, *In the Footsteps of the 130th*.
47. Beltz, *History*, 114–17.

48. Miller, *Honoring Heroes*.
49. Beltz, *History*, 117.
50. Tracey, *In the Footsteps of the 130th*.
51. Antietam on the Web, *Henry I. Zinn*.
52. Faley, Colonel (Retired) Thomas. *Remarks: Monroe Township*.

adored by his men, was an exception.[53] In an unusual act of compassion shortly after the battle, Colonel Zinn's remains were delivered by his devoted friend, Chaplain Chalfont, by train to Mary Zinn, then residing in Churchtown. His body arrived in his dress uniform with long-legged boots, and in the casket at his side lay his sword. He was buried December 15, 1862, in Mount Zion Cemetery.[54]

In March of 1864, the Monroe Teachers' Institute met at Givler's School. The national flag was hoisted over the schoolhouse with much enthusiasm, betokening patriotic regards for our country's cause, and in commemoration of the noble, lamented Colonel Zinn, our late fellow laborer in the cause of education, whose teaching in that School house (Givler's) is a theme of grateful remembrance by many friends of the departed patriot."[55]

During his remarks at the dedication of the 130th monument at Antietam, Dr. Samuel E. Whistler recounted, "You all recall Colonel Zinn's apparent cheerfulness, his words of encouragement, his fearlessness to get at the foe. He left his horse in the rear and mingled with the men on foot . . . calling in a firm, clear voice, 'Forward men!' Terrific was the crash of artillery from the heights and deadly the effect of the fire of the infantry from the sunken street, at the foot of the heights, protected by a heavy stone wall . . ."

"Color bearer after color bearer to the last fell when the intrepid, noble Zinn sprang out to the colors, and seizing them, lifted them aloft and shouted: 'Stick to your standard, boys! Forward!' That was your brave leader's final word."[56]

So, who was Henry Zinn? He was a husband, a father, a teacher, a soldier, a Churchtown resident, a brave hero and a beloved leader who led by example. He stepped forward when he was needed and used his talents and abilities for the benefit of others and in service to his country. He is Monroe Township's Civil War hero.

Sources:

Bates, Samuel P. *History of the Pennsylvania Volunteers 1861–5*, Harrisburg, Pennsylvania: B. Singerly, State Publisher, 1869.

Bates, Samuel P. *Martial Deeds of Pennsylvania*. Philadelphia, Pennsylvania: T. H. Davis and Co., 1876.

Beltz, Terrence W., The History of the One Hundred and Thirtieth Regiment, Pennsylvania Volunteer Infantry, University of Richmond Masters Theses, 2004.

_____. *One Hundred and Thirtieth Regiment Pennsylvania Volunteer Infantry: Ceremonies and Addresses at Dedication of Monument at Bloody Lane, Antietam Battlefield*, September 17, 1904. N. p. 1904.

Vanderlodge, Kevin. Churchtown: An Architectural and Historical Walking Tour, Johnson Imaging Systems, Inc. 2007.

Tracey, Jon. *The 130th Pennsylvania Infantry Regiment*, emergingcivilwar.org, Internet Article, October 17, 2023.

Tracey, Jon. *In the Footsteps of the 130th Pennsylvania at Fredericksburg and Chancellorsville*, battlefields.org, Internet article, May 7, 2021.

Antietam on the Web, Antietam.aotw.com, *Henry I. Zinn*, September 2024

Find a Grave, www,findagrave.com, *Henry I. Zinn*, August 1, 2007.

Faley, Colonel (Retired) Thomas. Remarks: Monroe Township Memorial Day Ceremony, May 30, 2016.

Miller, Matt. *The Patriot-News: Honoring Heroes*, Harrisburg, Pennsylvania, May 26, 2007.

Cumberland Valley Journal: Monroe Teachers' Institute, March 24, 1864.

---

53. Miller, *Honoring Heroes*.
54. Faley, *Remarks: Monroe Township*.
55. *Cumberland Valley Journal*.
56. *One Hundred and Thirtieth Regiment Pennsylvania Volunteer Infantry: Ceremonies*, 27.

Colonel Henry Zinn

130th flag

130th Regiment at Antietam

130th Regiment Statue at Antietam

Henry Zinn gravesite

Form MAGO-41—200M—6-35 Commonwealth of Pennsylvania Department of Military Affairs	RECORD OF BURIAL PLACE OF VETERAN	Cumberland County
NAME Zinn H. I.	DATE OF BIRTH	DATE OF DEATH
VETERAN OF Civil WAR	SERVED IN ARMY (x) NAVY ( ) MARINE CORPS ( )	
DATES OF SERVICE 8/16/62-12/13/62	ORGANIZATION(S) 130th Regt.	RANK Col.
CEMETERY OR PLACE OF INTERMENT	NAME Mt. Zion Cemetery LOCATION Churchtown, Pa.	
LOCATION OF GRAVE IN CEMETERY SECTION LOT No. 106 RANGE GRAVE No.	HEADSTONE High Sq. Sandstone GOVERNMENT ( ) COUNTY ( ) FAMILY ( )	
INFORMATION GIVEN BY DATE 12/31/34 Bush MNP	REMARKS	

After being Recorded in the County Veterans' Grave Registration Record This card is to be sent to THE ADJUTANT GENERAL'S OFFICE, Harrisburg, Pennsylvania, for final Record.

Henry Zinn's burial card

Givler's school

Plank's school

APPENDIX A

Alphabetical Index to Early Settlers' Names

(Numbers refer to tracts on Patent Tract Overlay Map, detailed in Appendix B)

Abernathy/Abernethy, William, 1, 2, 18, 26, 27, 50
Adams, Elizabeth L., 35
Allen, Robert, 94
Barnes/Barns, David, 24
Barton, Thomas, 18
Barton, William/Mr., 43, 52
Bauermaster, Frederick, 30
Beelman, Christian, 5
Beelman/Peelman, Jacob, 43, 52
Beelman, Peter, 11
Beetem, William M. & Co., 35, 86, 91
Bigbie/Rigby, John, 35
Blackford, Joseph, 37
Boar/Boor, Michael, 37
Boar/Boor/Boore, William, 37, 43, 52, 54
Bobb, John, 37
Bollinger, Abraham, 15
Bollinger/Pollinger, Christopher, 15
Boor/Boar, Michael, 37
Boor, Nicholas, 37
Boor/Boore/Boar, William, 37, 43, 52, 54
Boyl, William, 19, 43
Brandon, James, 19, 51
Brandt, Adam, 27
Brandt, Martin, 4, 79
Bricker/Breeker, Jacob, 22, 36, 47, 48, 69, 84, 94
Bricker, Peter, 12, 68, 72, 95
Brown, James, 8
Brownlee, John, 45

Bryermaster, Stophel, 26
Campbell, John, 5
Carl, George F., 89
Carothers, John, 90
Cauff/Kauff/Couff/Couf/Canff, Phillip/Philip, 17, 19, 51
Clark, John, 3, 83
Clark, William, 3
Clime, Frederick, 50, 56
Cocklin/Cockley, David, 11, 38, 56
Cocklin, Deitrich/Deitrick, 11
Cocklin/Cockley, Jacob, 11, 38, 56
Cockley, John, 55
Coebright (no first name), 55
Comfort/Comfert, Daniel, 37
Cook, Hugh, 50
Cook, Robert, 4
Cook, Roger, 15
Coover, George, 54
Coover, Dietrich, 11
Couff/Couf/Canff/Cauff/Kauff, Phillip/Philip, 17, 19, 51
Crisher/Kreisner, Jacob, 27
Crockett, Alexander, 65
Crockett/Crocket/Crocket, Andrew, 31, 33, 65, 67, 73, 75
Crockett/Crocket/Crocket, George, 31, 33, 34, 66, 65, 67, 73, 76
Crockett/Crocket/Crocket, James, 34, 49, 55, 66, 67, 73, 75, 76
Crockett, James Jr., 34

Crocket/Crocket, William, 34, 76
Culbertson, Samuel, 25
Culbertson, William, 25
Dickey, John, 23
Dickey, Robert, 23, 91
Diller, Casper, 25
Diller, David, 76
Diviny, Hugh, 93
Donley, Barney, 93
Dorn (no first name given), 18, 27
Dorn, Jacob, 43
Dorun, Thomas, 43
Douglas/Douglass, James, 22, 36, 48, 82
Duffield, George, 22, 48, 69
Duncan, John, 89
Duncan, Thomas, 45, 88, 89
Dunlap/Dunlop, William, 44
Dullebahn, John, 37
Eberly (no other name given), 45
Eberly, Henry, 39
Eberly, Joseph, 39
Ege/Eagy/Edge, Michael, 23, 35, 44, 83, 86, 87, 88, 89, 90, 91, 92, 95
Ege, Michael Jr., 45
Eichatz, John, 15
Erwin/Irwin, Samuel, 24
Ewig, Jacob, 20
Faree, Henry, 4
Fleming, John, 24
Fleming, Morgan, 37
Frazier, Alexander, 7
Frees/Freze/Fuze, Michael, 43, 52
Gaert/Gaerte, Jacob, 43
Gantz, Frederick, 61, 62
Gerhart/Gerhard/Garret/Garrett, Frederick, 43, 52
Gibler, Henry, 27
Gibson, Hugh, 71, 80
Giles, John, 27
Gill, John, 55

Glenn, Thomas, 15
Goodyear, Abrm., 78
Goodyear, Daniel, 71
Goodyear, Frederick, 71
Goodyear, Godfrid, 71
Goodyear, J., 78
Graff/Greaff/Graeff, John, 50
Gregor/Greegor/Greer, John, 19, 51, 53, 57, 61
Greiger/Gregor, Adam, 44, 62
Green, Joseph, 3
Gregory, James, 14, 28, 38, 50, 56
Gregory, Walter, 2, 14, 28
Guyer/Guyar, George, 20
Hamersly, Robert, 70
Hammersly/Hammersley/Hamersley/Hamerly, Thomas, 12, 21, 48, 70
Hammersly/Hamersley/Hamersly, William, 12, 21, 87
Hamilton, Alexander, 8
Hartman (no other name given), 27
Hassen, Catherine, 73
Heald, Thomas, 3
Heibler, Benjamin, 21
Heibler, Samuel, 21
Henderson, William M., 21, 55
Henry, Margaret (aka Indian Peg?), 94
Hertzel/Hartzler, Abraham, 39
Hide, Abraham, 44
Hoge, David, 26
Holmes/Holoms, Andrew, 53
Hoover, David, 53, 57
Hoover, Michael, 57, 61
Hopple, John, 76
Houser, John, 43
Huber, Michael, 51
Hudson, Jane, 16
Hudson, William, 16
Hunter, John, 25
Imhoff, Charles, 50

Iron Works Company, 45
Irwin/Erwin, Samuel, 24
Jacobs, Robert W., 21, 55
Johnston, Thomas, 22, 48
Kauff/Cauff/Couff/Couf/Canff, Phillip/Philip, 17, 19, 51
Keller, Henry, 30
Kennedy, John, 61, 62
Kissinger, Peter, 44
Kitch, John, 18, 27
Knawer/Kenower/Knorr, Jacob, 20, 49
Kreisner/Crisher, Jacob, 27
Krill, Jacob, 30
Lamb, John, 10, 57, 59, 60
Lamb, Samuel, 17, 39, 57
Lamb, William, 81
Lee, Timothy, 43
Lewis/Lowe, Robert, 6
Long, James, 49, 55
Long, James Jr., 55
Long, Martha, 49, 55
Lowe/Lewis, Robert, 6
Lutz, John, 34, 94
Lyon/Lyons, William, 18, 26, 41, 50
Martin, Samuel, 40, 46, 78
Martin, Samuel Jr., 46
Martin, Thomas, 78
Marks, Henry, 43
McCalley, Samuel, 24
McCoskrey, William, 43
Mccurdy, John, 54
Mccurdy, Robert, 54
McGawen/McGauan, David, 67
McNeal, Daniel, 20
McNeal/McNeall, John, 20, 21
Meyers/Myers/Moyer, George, 55, 58, 63
Miers/Myers/Meris/Maris, Joshua, 10, 41, 42
Miller, Andrew, 5, 11, 13, 38, 56
Miller, Andrew Jr., 5, 11, 13
Miller, Philip, 67

Miller/Millar, Rudolph, 18, 26, 27, 43, 52, 71, 80
Moore, William, 23
Marrett, Hartman (?), 27
Morris, John Jr., 35
Morris, Samuel, 35
Moyer/Myers/Meyers, George, 55, 58, 63
Muchmore/Mushmore, Shadrach/Shadrick: 37, 49
Musselman, Jacob, 5, 11
Myers/Miers/Meris/Maris, Joshua, 10, 41, 42
Myers/Meyers/Moyer, George, 55, 58, 63
Neagly/Neagley/Nagely, Daniel, 10, 64
Orbison, Thomas, 69
Ore Bank, 76
Parker, Andrew, 17, 21, 29
Parker, James, 29
Parker, Richard, 17
Peelman/Beelman, Jacob, 43, 52
Peters, Richard, 1, 4, 7, 16, 23, 24, 27
Pippin, Charles, 5
Pollinger/Bollinger, Christopher, 15
Proprietaries, 32
Quigley, Elias, 27
Rankin, John, 9
Rankin, Richard, 74, 77
Rankin, Thomas, 68, 72
Reed, David, 23
Rigby/Bigbie, John & Co.: 35
Rosbro (no first name given), 26
Roseberry, Robert, 5, 9
Roseborough, Eleanor, 9
Rutledge, Isaac, 42, 57, 58, 60, 63
Rutledge/Rutlidge, Matthew, 9
Sailor, Mathias, 37
Sailor, John, 37
Sanderson, Francis, 35
Schultz, Charles, 50
Scott, Hetty, 74
Scott, John, 74, 77

Scott, William, 74, 77
Seely, Jonas/Jona, 50
Seidel/Sidle, Henry, 89
Sewell, Richard, 4, 18, 27
Sidle/Seidel, Henry, 89
Shoemaker (?), 8
Smith, Dr./Mr., 43, 52
Smith, Abraham, 20
Smith, Samuel, 16, 36
Sollenberger, Jo., 45
Starrett/Starett, John, 17, 39
Steel, Adam, 12
Steel, Richard, 27
Steel, Widow, 82
Stear, John, 64
Sterrett, Robert, 17, 39
Stoddart (no first name given), 43
Stotler, Henry, 52
Strock, Jacob, 12
Strock/Stroke/Strike, Joseph, 49, 80
Swisher, Cristopher, 54
Thompson, Robert, 23
Thornburgh, Joseph, 81
Trent, William, 17
Trindle/Trendle, Alexander, 42, 54, 58, 60
Trindle/Trundle, John, 59, 63, 64
Trindle/Trendle/Trundle, William, 10, 30, 42, 58, 59, 63, 64
Trindle, William Jr., 42
Urie, Thomas, 39
Vance, Patrick, 30, 44, 55

Vanier, Christopher, 32
Wallace, Ruth, 53
Wallace, William, 53
Weaver, John, 20
Weiss/Wise/Wire, Jacob, 12, 68, 70, 72
Weiss, John, 70
Weist, Jacob, 50
White, David, 21
White, Richard, 52
Whiteside, William, 20
Whitmore, Abraham, 50
Wilderidge/Wildridge, Susanna, 8
Wilkin/Wilkins, Robert, 5
Wilkin/Wilkins, Rachel, 6
Williams, David, 21
Williams, James, 6, 7
Williams, John, 6, 7, 13, 21
Williamson, Samuel, 17
Williamson, Thomas, 17
Wilson, David, 4
Wilson, James, 47
Wingler/Winkeler, George, 26
Wise/Weiss/Wire, Jacob, 12, 68, 70, 72
Wolf, Jacob, 82
Wolf, Joseph, 89
Wolf, Leonard, 82
Wolf, Peter, 85
Wolford, Peter, 47
Zeigler/Ziegle, John, 15, 43
Zerra, Adam, 50
Zuck, Jacob, 27

APPENDIX B

Patent Tract Information for Early Settlers

KEY:

1.) ed. 11/1/1752
316 acres
Peters, Richard: warrant, 9/30/1749 (Lanc. P212)
Peters, Richard, Esq.: survey, 11/1/1752 (C-155-220)
Abernathy, William: patent, 12/11/1754 (A-20-98)
additional names:
Vacant: 11/1/1735 (from C-84-63)
Peters, Richard?: 9/20/1750 (from C-146-177)
Abernathy, William, other land of: March, 1761 to
   3/14/1771 (from C-146-176 & 178, B-2-74, A-70-42)
tract number from map: ed. – earliest date shown by records consulted acreage shown on most recent survey
warrantee: warrant date (warrant county and number)
surveyee: survey date (survey number)
patentee: patent date (patent number)
additional names:
names of neighbors: date(s) and number(s) of survey(s) from which the information was taken

NOTES:

- Sometimes, patent acreage differs from that of the survey(s) due to combinations, subdivisions and record-keeping discrepancies. Known differences are noted. The acreage shown underlined at the top of the data block is generally that of the latest accepted survey for the portion of the land question.

- Names are usually given as they appear on each document cited. Abbreviations, qualifiers, etc., may differ from document to document.

- If seeking copies of any of these original documents at the Pennsylvania Historical and Museum Commission's State Archives, you will find them filed by the official document numbers cited in the parentheses, not the tract numbers from the map. County copies of the surveys may or may not exist in the Recorder of Deeds Office. If they do, they are arranged alphabetically by the name of the surveyee and do not bear the state survey numbers.

1.) ed. 11/1/1752
316 acres
Peters, Richard: warrant, 9/30/1749 (Lanc. P212)
Peters, Richard, Esq.: survey, 11/1/1752 (C-155-220)
Abernathy, William: patent, 12/11/1754 (A-20-98)
additional names:
Vacant: 11/1/1735 (from C-84-63)
Peters, Richard?: 9/20/1750 (from C-146-177)
Abernathy, William, other land of: March 1761 to
   3/14/1771 (from C-146-176 & 178, B-2-74, A-70-42)

2.) ed. 11/1/1752
"Aberdeen," 48 acres, 61 perches
Abernathy, William: warrant, 1/18/1753 (Cumb. A19)
Abernathy, William: survey, 3/14/1771 (A-70-42)
Abernathy, William: patent, 2/24/1774 (AA-14-322)
additional names:
Gregory, (first name obliterated): 11/1/1752
   (from C-155-220)

Gregory, Walter: 11/1/1766 (from A-11-66)

3.) ed. 4/30/1735
"Claremont," 300 acres
Heald, Thomas: Blunston license, 4/30/1735 (p.14)
Heald, Thomas: warrant, 11/1/1735 (Lanc. H66)
Heald, Thomas: survey, 11/11/1735 (C-84-63)
Clark, John: patent, 6/14/1785 (P-3-399)
additional names:
Green, Joseph: 9/1/1747–11/1/1752
  (from C-155-220, C-58-166)
Heald, Thomas: 11/13/1735 (from C-224-120)
Green, Joseph: transferred from Thomas Heald on
  9/25/1738 (from patent text, P-3-399)
Clark, John: transferred from Joseph Green on
  8/29/1760 (from patent text, P-3-399)
Clark, John: March 1761 through at least 3/14/1771
  (from C-146-176, A-70-42)
Clark, William: from at least 12/16/1811 through
  5/17/1827 (from C-161-274, D-13-81)

4.) ed. 6/19/1750
564 acres
Sewel, Richard: warrant, 6/19/1750 (Cumb. S4)
Peters, Richard: survey, March 1761 (C-146-176)
Peters, Richard, who promptly surrendered the land to
  David Wilson: patent, 7/25/1765 (AA-6-351)
additional names:
Peters, Richard, Esq., other land of: 11/1/1752
  (from C-155-220)
Vacant: 11/1/1735 (from C-84-63)
Faree, Henry: 9/29/1750–6/16/1764
  (from B-2-74, C-146-178)
Brandt, Martin, other land of: 4/27/1773
  (from C-5-248)
Cook, Robert: 5/17/1827 (from D-13-81)

5.) ed. 11/1/1735
249 acres
Wilkins, Robert: 1st warrant, 11/1/1735 (Lanc. W28)

Miller, Andrew Jr.: 2nd warrant, 11/8/1742
  (Lanc. M259)
Miller, Andrew, formerly surveyed to Robt. Wilkin, now
  divided among Andrew Miller, Charles Pippin and John
  Campbell, purchasers: 12/9/1742 (C-121-155)
Wilkin, Robert: patent, 1/5/1749 (A-1-303)
additional names:
Miller, Andrew: 5/7/1767 (C-149-86)
Roseberry, Robert, heirs of: 6/5/1776 (from B-12-31)
Miller, Andrew, other land of: 2/20/1798 to 2/15/1813
  (from A-53-207, C140-54, C-140-55)
Beelman, Christian: 6/13/1810 (from C-151-253)
Miller, Andrew, land formerly of: 8/25/1812
  (from C-149-87)
Musselman, Jacob, formerly Andrew Miller: 8/18/1815
  (from C-149-88)

6.) ed. 11/11/1735
300 acres
Lewis, Robert: possible warrant, 1735 (from C-224-120)
Wilkin, Rachel: warrant, 10/26/1742 (Lanc. W175)
Lewis, Robert: survey, 11/13/1735 (C-224-120)
Wilkin or Wilkins, Rachel: patent, 11/3/1742 (A-10-42)
additional names:
Lowe, Robt: 11/11/1735 (from C-84-63)
Lewis, R.: 11/12/1735 (from C-48-89)
Williams, John?: 6/5/1776 (from B-12-31)
Williams, James, other land of, formerly Rachael Wilkins:
  12/16–17/1811 (from C-161-274)

7.) ed 11/13/1735
114 acres, 84 perches
Peters, Richard: warrant, 9/30/1749 (York P3)
Peters, Richard: resurvey, 12/16–17/1811 (C-161-274)
Williams, James: patent, 12/28/1814 (H-9-688)
additional names:
Vacant: 11/11/1735 (from C-84-35)
Frazier, Alexand.: 11/13/1735 (from C-224-120)
Williams, John: sometime between 6/4/1764 and
  6/29/1827 (from D-18-230)

Williams, James: 5/17/1827 (from D-13-81)

8.) ed. 1/4/1737
"Hamilton Town," 236 acres, 114 perches
(indices claim 266 acres, 114 perches, contrary to survey)
Brown, James (Shoemaker) [*sic*]: 1st warrant (for 8a), 1/4/1737 (Lanc. B120)
Hamilton, Alexander: 2nd warrant (for 8a&b), 4/19/1776 (Cumb. H283)
Brown, James: 1st survey (for 8b, 120 acres), 4/15/1738 (B-12-32)
Hamilton, Alexander, in right of Susanna Wilderidge & James Brown: resurvey (for 8a&b), 6/5/1776 (B-12-31)
Hamilton, Alexander: patent, 7/19/1776 (AA-15-805)

8a.) 74 acres, 154 perches
additional names:
Wildridge, Widow: 11/1/1766 (from A-11-66)
Wilderidge, Susanna: pre 6/5/1776 (from B-12-31)
Hamilton, Alexander: 2/20–21/1798 (from C-140-54, C-137-119 & 121)
Williams, John: 6/13/1810 (from C-67-21)

8b.) 161 acres, 120 perches
additional names:
Brown, James: pre 6/5/1776 (from B-12-31)
Wildridge, Widow: 11/1/1766 (from A-11-66)
Hamilton, Alexander: 2/20/54 (from C-140-54)

9.) ed. 7/21/1738
"Rose-garden," 206 acres
Rankin, John: 1st warrant (vacated), 8/21/1738 (Lanc. R75)
Rutlidge, Matthew: 2nd warrant, 8/31/1747 (Lanc. R205)
Rankin, John: survey, May 1743 (C-170-197)
Rutledge, Matthew: survey return, 4/12/1803 (from survey C-170-197)

"Roseborugh, Eleanor, single woman": patent, 4/12/1803 (P-51-9)
additional names:
Roseberry, Robert, heirs of: 6/5/1776 (from B-21-31)
Roseberry, Robert: 2/20/1798 (from C-140-54)

10.) ed. 1/4/1742
167 acres, 100 perches
Trindle, William: warrant, 1/4/1742 (Lanc. T82)
Trindle, William: survey, 3/27/1743 (A-75-203)
Trindle, William: survey, undated (A-75-204)
Trindle, William: patent, 3/25/1745 (A-12-188)
additional names:
Trindle, William: 12/17/1766 to 7/3/1767 (from D-18-168, A-31-183, C-123-188)
Joshua Myers, formerly William Trindle: 9/10/1795 to 2/9/1807 (from C-139-86, 87, 88 & 89, A-31-181 & 182, C-134-200)
Neagly/Nagely, Daniel, in right of William Trindle: 4/24/1810 (from C-145-232, D-18-167)
Lamb, John, Esq., in right of William Trindle: 4/24/1810 (from C-123-189)

11.) ed. 11/8/1742
127 acres, 46 perches
Miller, Andrew Jr.: warrant, 11/8/1742 (Lanc. M258)
Miller, Andrew Jr.: survey, 2/20/1798 (A-53-207)

11a.) 23 acres, 150 perches
Miller, Andrew Jr.: resurvey, 6/13/1810 (C-137-118)
Cocklin, David: patent, 6/1/1818 (H-15-474)
additional names:
Miller, Andrew, other land of: 12/9/1742–1/18/1808 (from: C-121-155, C-149-86, A-7-40, C-137-121, C-41-56)
Miller, Andrew, "sold to Dutchmen": 6/5/1776 (from B-12-31)
Cocklin, David, in right of Andrew Miller: 6/13/1810–6/12/1812 (from C-137-117, C-41-36)
Beelman, Peter: 6/13/1810 (from C-151-253)

Miller, Andrew, land formerly of: 8/25/1812 (from C-149-87)
Musselman, Jacob, formerly Andrew Miller: 8/18/1815 (from C-149-88)
Cockley, David: 12/11/1821 (from C-43-185)

11b.) 26 acres, 120 perches
Miller, Andrew Jur.: resurvey, 6/13/1810 (C-151-253)
Musselman, Jacob: patent, 7/16/1822 (H-20-265)
additional names:
Miller, Andrew, other land of: 12/9/1742–5/7/1767 (from C-121-155, C-149-86)
Miller, Andrew, land formerly of: 8/25/1812 (from C-149-87)
Musselman, Jacob, formerly Andrew Miller: 8/18/1815 (from C-149-88)

11c.) 53 acres, 124 perches
Miller, Andrew Jr.: survey, 6/13/1810 (A-48-133)
Cocklin, Jacob: patent, 3/12/1811 (H-4-549)
additional names:
Miller, Andrew, other land of: 2/9/1742–2/21/1798 (from C-121-155, C-137-121)

11d.) 13 acres, 49 perches
Miller, Andrew: survey, 2/15/1813 (C-140-55)
Cocklin, Deitrich: patent, 2/24/1813 (H-9-65)
additional names:
Miller, Andrew, other land of: 12/9/1742 to 2/20/1798 (from C-121-155, B-12-31, C-140-54)
Coover, Dietrich: 6/13/1810 (from A-48-133)

12.) ed. 5/9/1746
192 acres, 119 perches
Steel, Adam: warrant, 5/9/1746 (Lanc. S482)
Steel, Adam: resurvey, 4/20/1802 (C-213-47)

12a.) 45 acres, 110 perches
Bricker, Peter, in right of Adam Steel: survey, 4/20/1802 (C-213-46)

Strock, Jacob: patent, 11/12/1822 (H-20-365)
additional names:
Hamersley, Thomas: 2/15/1769 (fromC-220-236)
Hamersley, William: 10/19/1774 (from C-220-235)
Wire, Jacob: 12/27/1785 (from C-233-64)
Bricker, Peter, in right of Adam Steel: 4/20/1802 (from C-199-295, A-14-85)
Weiss, Jacob, in right of Adam Steel: 4/20/1802 (from A-14-87)

12b.) 147 acres, 9 perches
Weiss, Jacob, in right of Adam Steel: survey, 4/20/1802 (C-199-295)
Wise, Jacob: patent, 5/15/1813 (H-9-42)
additional names:
Wire, Jacob: 12/27/1785 (from C-23-64)
Wise, Jacob, in right of Hammersly [sic]: 5/6/1792 (from A-47-80)
Wise, Jacob: 5/28/1795 (from D-488)
Weiss, Jacob, in right of Adam Steel: 4/20/1802 (from A-14-87, C-213-46)

13.) ed. 5/13/1746
90 acres, 120 perches
Miller, Andrew Jr.: warrant, 5/13/1746 (Lanc. M491)
Miller, Andrew Jr.: survey, 2/20/1798 (C-140-54)
Cocklin, Deitrick: patent, 2/24/1813 (H-9-65)
additional names:
Vacant: 12/9/1742 (from C-121-155)
Miller, Andrew, "sold to Dutchmen": 6/5/1776 (from B-12-31)
Miller, Andrew Jr.: 2/20/1798 to 6/13/1810 (from A-53-207, C-137-121 & 117)
Williams, John: 6/13/1810 (from C-67-21)
Cocklin, Deitrick, in right of Andrew Miller: 2/15/1813 (from C-140-55)

14.) ed. 9/23/1746
"Gregory's Pleasure," 156 acres, 80 perches
Gregory, Walter: warrant, 9/23/1746 (Lanc. G200)

Gregory, Walter: survey, 9/1/1747 (C-58-166)
Gregory, James: patent, 5/9/1774 (M-14-397)
additional names:
Gregory, Walter: 11/1/1766 to 3/14/1771
 (from A-11-66, A-70-42)

15.) ed.1/29/1749
314 acres, 27 perches
(Note: This corner of land is now primarily a part of Upper Allen Township rather than Monroe due to a development project several decades ago. It is included in this listing since it was part of Monroe, and thus Monroe's history, until recently.)
Cook, Roger: warrant, 1/29/1749 (Cumb. C1)
Bollinger, Abraham, in right of Roger Cook: survey, 9/21–22/1803 (C-31-211)

15a.) 47 acres, 28 perches
Cook, Roger: resurvey, 9/22/1803 (C-46-43)
Zeigler, John: patent, 3/25/1814 (H-10-486)
additional names:
Glenn, Thos.: 12/6/1766 to 1/18/1808
 (from C-29-263, C-41-56)
Pollinger, Christopher, in right of Thomas Glen: 9/10/1795 (from C-29-264)
Ziegle, John: 6/12/1812 (from C-41-117)
Eichhatz, Jno: 11/2/1822 (from C-29-256)

16.) ed. 9/30/1749
"Smithfield," 230 acres, 120 perches
Peters, Richard: warrant, 9/30/1749 (York [*sic*] P2)
Peters, Richard: survey, 6/20/1750 (survey text, C-146-178)
Peters, Richard: resurvey, 5/6/1762 (C-146-178)
Smith, Sarni.: patent, 4/26/1774 (M-14-289)
additional names:
Hudson, William: March 1761 (from C-146-176)
Hudson, Wm. & Jane, conveyed to by Richard Peters: 4/21/1763 (from patent text, AA-14-289)
Smith, Sarni., conveyed to by Hudsons: 5/14/1772
 (from patent text, AA-14-289)
Smith, Sarni., other land of: sometime between 5/24/1773 and 4/15/1774 (from C-183-143)

17.) ed 2/13/1750
389 acres, 130 perches
Trent, William: warrant, 2/13/1750 (Cumb. T4)
Trent, William: survey, 10/31–11/1/1822 (B.-4-60)

17a.) 181 acres, 98 perches
Trent, William: survey, 11/1/1822 (C-215-295)
Sterrett, Robert: patent, 5/6/1829 (H-22-231)
additional names:
Williamson, Samuel: 2/27/1764 to 4/9/1773
 (from A-48-189, A-71-249, C-166-90)
Lamb, Sarni.?: 4/8/1774 (from C-212-2)
Williamson, Samuel, land late of: 7/13/1809
 (from C-123-59)
Williamson, Thomas: 12/8/1812 (from C-124-18)
Starett/Starrett, Jno., heirs of, in right of Sarni. Lamb and Wm. Trent: 10/31–11/1/1822
 (from C-215-294 & 296)

17b.) 163 acres, 150 perches
Trent, William: survey, 8/31/1822 (C-215-296)
Williamson, Thomas: patent, 1/20/1824 (H-22-7)
additional names:
Williamson, Samuel: 4/5/1765 to 4/10/1772
 (from C-146-300, M-253 & 254)
Couff, Phillip?: 8/21/1767 (from A-18-271)
Williamson, Thomas: 11/1/1822 to 12/15/1822
 (from C-215-295, B-4-73)

17c.) 44 acres, 38 perches
Trent, William: survey, 12/15/1822 (B-4-73)
Parker, Richard: patent, 5/22/1829 (H-26-415)
additional names:
Williamson, Samuel: 4/5/1765 to 4/20/1767 (from C-146-300, C-159-198, C-36-21)
Parker, Andw.: 10/31/1822 (C-215-296)

PATENT TRACT INFORMATION FOR EARLY SETTLERS 197

18.) ed. 6/19/1750
"Kitchen Garden," 30 acres, 40 perches
(Note: This tract is completely overlapped by no. 27a, a survey that was never patented. See 27a for additional names.)
Kitch, John: warrant, 6/29/1810 (Cumb. K147)
Kitch, John: survey, 6/10/1810 (C-123-6)
Kitch, John: patent, 7/24/1810 (H-4-263)
additional names:
Sewell, Richard: 6/19–9/20/1750 (from overlapping survey C-146-177, warrant Cumb. S4)
Abernathy, Wm. & Willm. Lyons: sometime between 9/27/1750 and 6/16/1764 (from 8-2-74)
Barton, Revd. Thos. & Abernethy [*sic*] in dispute: 12/10/1766 (from B-12-69)
Dorn [*sic*]: 12/11/1767 (from C-79-163)
Miller, Rudolph, in right of John Kitch: May 1829 (from B-12-68)

19.) ed. 4/20/1751
"Brandonburg," 90 acres, 115 perches
Brandon, James: warrant, 4/20 or 25/1751 (Cumb. B11)
Brandon, James: survey, 5/24/1766 (C-3-8)
Kauff, alias Cauff, Philip: patent, 6/6/1768 (M-10-386)
additional names:
Boyl, William: purchased from Brandon sometime after 4/1751, deeded to Receiver General in 5/5/1760 (from patent text, AA-10-386)
Brandon, James: 4/20/1767 (from C-36-21)
Couff, Philip: 8/21/1767 to 8/9/1797 (from A-18-271, C-116-211)
Greeger, John: 4/3/1787 to 2/25/1788 (from C-189-281 & 285)

20.) ed. 4/24/1750
245 acres, 143 perches
Whiteside, William: warrant, 4/24/1750 (Cumb. W1)
Whiteside, William: resurvey, 12/28/1803 (A-14-4)

20a.) 101 acres, 76 perches
Kenower, Jacob, in right of William Whiteside: survey, southern half, 12/19/1803 (A-14-1)
Weaver, John, in right of William Whiteside: survey, northern half, 12/29/1803 (A-14-2)
Whiteside, William: survey, whole, 10/16/1812 (D-33-39)
Weaver, John: patent, 11/3/1812 (H-7-582)
additional names:
McNeal/McNeall, John: 8/21/1767 to 8/9/1791 (from A-18-271, M-254, C-115-39, C-116-211)
Weaver, John, in right of Wm. Whiteside: 6/28/1810 (from D-33-38)

20b.) "St. Georges," 124 acres, 110 perches
McNeal, Daniel, in right of William Whiteside: survey, 12/29/1803 (A-14-3)
Guyer/Guyar, George: patent, 6/28/1804 (P-54-339)
additional names:
McNeal/McNeall, John: from as early as 9/27/1750 to 8/9/1791 (from B-4-74, B-12-69, C-115-39, C-116-211)
McNeal, Daniel: 12/29/1803 (from A-14-1 & 2)
Guyer, Geo.: 8/24/1809 (from C-85-51)

20c.) 12 acres, 69 perches
Kenower, Jacob, in right of William Whiteside: survey, 12/19/1803 (A-14-1)
Whiteside, William: survey, 6/28/1810 (D-33-38)
Smith, Abraham: patent, 11/25/1812 (H-7-574)
additional names:
McNeal, John: 5/19/1785 (from C-115-39)

20d.) 7 acres, 77 perches
Kenower, Jacob, in right of William Whiteside: survey, 12/19/1803 (A-14-1)
Whiteside, William: survey, 5/24/1810 (D-9-5)
Ewig, Jacob: patent, 7/8/1817 (H-15-46)
additional names:
McNeal, John: 5/19/1795 (from C-115-39)

21.) ed. 4/24/1750
218 acres, 141 perches
Hamersly, William: warrant, 4/24/1750 (Cumb. H1)
Hammersly, William: survey, 12/10/1766 (B-12-69)

21a.) 56 acres, 51 perches
Hammersly, William: survey, 8/24/1809 (C-85-51)
Heibler, Benjamin & Samuel: patent, 6/9/1812 (H-7-251)
additional names:
Hamerly, Thomas: from 9/10/1750 as late as 6/16/1764 (from C-146-177, B-2-74)
Williams, Jno., heirs of: 12/29/1803 (from A-14-3 & 4)

21b.) 167 acres, 108 perches
Hammersly, William: survey, May 1829 (B-12-68)
Henderson, William M.: patent, 3/31/1830 (H28-112)
additional names:
McNeal, John: 8/21/1767 (from A-18-271)
Williams, David: 12/11/1767 (from C-79-163)
White, David: 8/9/1791 (from C-116-211)
Williams, John, heirs of: 12/29/1803 (from A-14-3 & 4)
Parker, Andrew, heirs of: 8/24/1809 to 6/10/1810 (from A-82-203, C-123-6)
Williams, John: 9/1/1809 (from C-41-47)
Henderson, Wm. M. & Robt. W. Jacobs, in right of William Hammersley: 3/13/1830 (from B-12-70)

21c.) 3 acres, 70 perches
Henderson, William M.: warrant, 3/4/1830 (Cumb. H479)
Henderson, William M.: survey, 3/13/1830 (B-12-70)
Henderson, Wm. M., et al.: patent, 3/31/1830 (H-28-112)
additional names:
Hamersley, William: sometime between 9/27/1750 and 6/16/1764 (from B-2-74)
McNeal, John: 8/21/1767 (from A-18-271)
White, David: 8/9/1791 (from C-116-211)
Williams, John, heirs of: 12/29/1803 (from A-14-3 & 4)

Parker, Andrew, heirs of: 8/24/1809 to 6/10/1810 (from C-85-51, C-123-6)
Williams, John: 9/1/1809 (from C-41-47)

22.) ed. 4/26/1750
"Ouffield'sFancy," 244 acres, 40 perches
Douglas, James: warrant, 4/26/1750 (Cumb. D1)
Douglass, James: resurvey, 6/9/1790 (Y-151)
Duffield, George, admr.: patent (for both this tract and tract #69, Y-150), 6/15/1790 (P-16-311)
additional names:
Douglas/Douglass, James: sometime between 9/27/1750 and 6/16/1764 (from B-2-74, C-146-178)
Duffield, the Rev. George: 11/7/1785 (from Y-150)
Johnston, Thomas, in right of Revd. George Duffield: 12/27/1785 (from C-233-64)
Bricker, Jacob: 5/28/1795 (D-488)

23.) ed. 5/15/1750
"The Boiling Spring," 398 acres, 132 perches
Thompson, Robert: 1st warrant. 5/15/1750 (Cumb. T4)
Peters, Richard, Esq.: 2nd warrant, 10/12/1762 (Cumb.P80-1)
Thompson, Robert: survey for 368 acres at a place called "the Boyling Springs," 5/29/1750 (C-234-80)
Peters, Richard, Esq.: resurvey, 11/10/1761 (C-155-281)
Peters, Richard, Esq.: patent, 10/13/1762 (AA-3-445)
additional names:
Reed, David: 6/27/1770 (from C-25-204)
Dickey, John, heirs of: January 1775 (from B-6-116)
Eagy, Michael & Moore, Willm.: 12/23/1785 (from C-25-276)
Dickey, Robert: 6/9/1792 to 4/23/1811 (from C-26-161, 170 & 173)
Ege, Michael: 11/7/1811 (from A-8-288)

24.) ed. 6/12/1750
"Dirty Springs," 316 acres, 40 perches
Barns/Barnes, David: warrant, 6/12/1750 (Cumb. B3)

Barnes, David: survey, 6/19/1750 (A-88-71)
Irwin, Samuel: patent, 4/2/1795 (P-25-24)
additional names:
Fleming, John, in right of Richard Peters, decd.:
   5/7/1753 (from C-25-142)
Peters, Richard: 2/14/1769 to 5/20/1784
   (from C-55-290, C-220-236, C-141-96)
McCalley, Samuel: 4/9/1773 to 4/8/1774
   (from C-166-90, C-212-2)
Erwin, Samuel, Esq.: 6/10/1791 (from A-28-217)

25.) ed. 6/19/1750
"Brickerstown Tract," 313 acres, 80 perches
Culbertson, William: warrant, 8/3/1750 (Cumb.C4)
Culbertson, William: survey, 5/7/1753 (C-25-142)
Culbertson, Sarni. & Wm.: patent, 6/25/1785 (P-3-426)
additional names:
Hunter, John: 6/19/1750 (from A-88-71)
Culbertson, William: 2/15/1769 to 10/19/1774
   (from C-220-235 & 236, C-25-223)
Diller, Casper, formerly Sam Culbertson: 6/10/1791
   (from A-28-217)
Diller, Casper, in right of Wm. Culbertson: 9/27/1793
   (from C-185-56)

26.) ed.9/20/1750
"Hickory Bottom," 90 acres, 111 perches
(Note: This tract is partially overlapped by no. 27a., a survey that was never patented. See 27a for additional names.)
Winkeler, George: west side application, 3/31/1767
   (#3285)
Hoge, David: warrant, 4/19/1796 (Cumb. H413)
Wingler, George: survey, 12/11/1767 (C-79-163)
Hoge, David: patent, 4/22/1796 (P-28-110)
additional names:
Rosbro, (no other name given): 9/20/1750
   (from C-146-177)
Abernathy, Wm. & Wm. Lyons: sometime between
   9/27/1750 and 6/16/1764 (from B-2-74)
Vacant land: 6/30/1766 (from D-18-207)
Wingler, George, claim of: 12/10/1766 to 5/29/1798
   (from B-12-69, C-72-251)
Hoge, David: 5/28/1790 (A-13-256 & 257)
Byermaster, Stophel: 6/10/1810 (C-123-6)
Miller, Rudolph, in right of George Wingler: May 1829
   (from B-12-68)

27.) ed 9/20/1750
797 acres, 40 perches
Giles, John: warrant, 9/27/1750 (Cumb. G5)
Peters, Rev. Richard: survey, undated (B-2-74)
Peters, Richard: patent, 4/18/1774 (AA-14-475)
additional names:
Vacant Land No. 119: 11/1/1752 (from C-155-220)
Sewell, Richard: 9/20/1750 (from C-146-177)
Peters, Richard, Esq.: 11/1/1766 to 5/19/1785
   (from C-146-178, A-11-66, B-12-69, C-115-39)
Abernathy, Wiliam: 12/11/1767 (from C-79-163)
Quigley, Elias: 5/28/1790 (from A-13-256 & 257)
Steel, Richd., in right of Revd. Richd. Peters: sometime
   between 4/26/1750 and 6/9/1790 (from Y-151)
Hartman [*sic*] (probably **Morrett, Hartman?**):
   4/20/1802 (from A-14-86)
Crisher, Jacob: 12/29/1803 (from A-14-3 & 4)
Kitch, John: 6/10/1810 (from C-123-6)
Zuck, Jacob: 6/10/1810 (from C-123-6)

27a.) 332 acres, 80 perches
(Note: This survey, never patented as such, not only overlaps tract no. 27 proper but also tracts 18 and 26. See nos. 18 and 26 for additional names.)
Sewell, Richard: warrant?, 6/19/1750 (Cumb. S4)
Sewell, Richard: survey, 9/20/1750 (C-146-177)
No patent issued. Survey marked "Void. Says Richard
   Peters, Esqr."
additional names:
Vacant Land No. 119: 11/1/1752 (from C-155-220)
Peters, Revd. Richard: as early as 9/27/1750 to
   12/10/1766 (from B-2-74, A-11-66, B-12-69)

Abernathy, William: 12/11/1767 (from C-79-163)
Dorn [*sic*]: 12/11/1767 (from C-79-163)
Quigley, Elias: 5/28/1790 (A-13-256 & 257)
Brandt, Adam: 8/24/1809 (from C-85-51)
Gibler, Henry: 8/24/1809 (from C-85-51)
Kitch, John: 8/24/1809 to 6/10/1810 (from C-85-51, C-123-6)
Kreisner, Jacob: 8/24/1809 (from C-85-51)
Zuck, Jacob: 6/10/1810 (from C-123-6)
Miller, Rudolph, in right of John Kitch: May 1829 (from B-12-68)

28.) ed. 5/13/1751
"Gregory's Prospect," 255 acres, 151 perches
Gregory, Walter: warrant, 5/30/1751 (Cumb. G9)
Gregory, Walter: resurvey, 11/1/1766 (A-11-66)
Gregory, James: patent, 5/9/1774 (AA-14-397)
additional names:
Gregory, Walter: 9/20/1750 to 3/14/1771 (from C-146-177, B-2-74, A-70-42)
Gregory, James: 6/5/1776 to 6/13/1810 (from B-12-31, A-13-256 & 257, C-137-119 & 120, C-67-20)

29.) ed. 1/22/1753
"Jamestown," 445 acres, 78 perches
Parker, James: warrant, 1/22/1753 (Cumb. P35)
Parker, James: survey, 4/5/1765 (C-146-300)
Parker, James: patent, 4/18/1774 (AA-14-301)
additional names:
Parker, James, other land of: 4/5/1765 (from C-159-198)
Parker, Andrew, heirs of: 10/31–11/1/1822 (from B-4-60, C-215-296)

30.) ed. 5/7/1753
"Krill-hall," 137 acres, 80 perches
Trindle, William: warrant, 5/7/1753 (Cumb. T13)
Trindle, William: survey, 7/1/1809 (A-82-203)
Krill, Jacob: patent, 6/29/1810 (H-3-652)
additional names:

Vance, Patrick: 12/6/1766 to 12/11/1767 (from C-123-36, B-12-69, C-79-163)
Vance, Patrick, land formerly of: 8/15/1809 (from C-123-56)
Trindle, William: 9/1/1809 (from C-41-47)
Keller, Henry & Bauermaster, Fred, in right of William Trindle: May 1829 (from B-12-68)

31.) ed. 11/10/1761
"Dalebrook," 102 acres, 80 perches
Crockett, Andrew: west side application, 2/23/1765 (#2843)
Crockett, Andrew: warrant, 6/16/1786 (Cumb. C377)
Crocket, Andrew: survey, 6/27/1770 (C-25-204)
Crockett, Andrew: patent, 6/22/1796 (P-6-329)
additional names:
Croket/Crocket, Andrew & George: 11/10/1761 to January 1775 (from C-155-281, B-6-116)
Crocket, Andrew, other land of: 6/27/1770 to 12/23/1785 (from C-25-224, C-25-276)

32.) ed 6/27/1770
3,345 acres, 93 perches
Honorable Proprietaries: order, 12/21/1774 (survey text, B-6-116)
Surveyed and divided into lots: survey, January 1775 (B-6-116)
Patents for individual tracts not yet found.
additional names:
Proprietary tract/land: 11/10/1761 to 6/27/1770 (from C-155-281, C-25-204 & 224)
Vanier, Christopher, heirs of: 3/31/1791 (from A-76-5)
Late the Proprietaries: 6/10/1791 (from A-28-217)

33.) ed. 11/10/1761
"Springfield," 80 acres, 80 perches
Crocket, Andrew: warrant, 9/9/1785 (Cumb. C356)
Crocket, Andrew: survey, 12/23/1785 (C-25-276)
Crockett, Andrew: patent, 10/5/1786 (P-8-24)
additional names:

Crockett, George & Andrew, claim of: 11/10/1761 (from C-151-281)
Crocket, Andrew, improved land of: 6/27/1770 to 6/9/1792 (from C-25-204, C-53-29, C-26-170)

34.) ed. 11/10/1761
249 acres, 100 perches
Crockett, James Jr., in trust for himself and the heirs of his late father William Crockett: warrant, 10/5/1786 (Cumb. C382)
Crockett, James: survey, 6/9/1792 (C-26-170)

34a.) 130 acres, 20 perches
James Crocket: survey, 4/23/1811 (C-26-173)
Crockett, James: patent, 2/26/1812 (H-6-662)
additional names:
Croket, Willm.: 11/10/1761 (from C-155-281)
Crockett, James: 11/7/1811 (from A-8-288)
Lutz, John: 5/10/1860 (from D-21-193)

34b.) 119 acres, 80 perches
Crockett, James, in trust: survey, 4/23/1811 (C-26-161)
Crockett, George: patent, 2/26/1812 (H-7-42)
additional names:
Crocket, William: 6/28/1770 (from C-152-254)
Crockett, Willm, decd., heirs of: 12/21–24/1785 (from C-26-270, C-24-159)
Crocket, George: 4/23/1811 (from C-26-169, 268 & 269)
Lutz, John: 5/10/1860 (from D-21-193)

35.) ed. 11/10/1761
350 acres
Rigby, John, Samuel Morris, Francis Sanderson & John Morris Jr.: warrant, 5/31/1762 (Cumb. R28)
Beetem, William M. & Co.: survey, 5/10/1860 (D-21-193)
Adams, Elizabeth L.: patent, 4/16/1930 (H-79-124)
additional names:
Barren pine land, South Mountain: 10/12/1761 (D-9-188)
Bigbie, Jno. & Compy.: 11/10/1761 (C-155-281)

Ege, Michael: 12/21/1785 to 11/17/1811 (from C-26-170, 161, 173, 270, 169, 268, 269, D-21-168)

36.) ed. 6/20/1750 to 5/6/1762
"Youghall," 96 acres, 98 perches
Smith, Samuel: warrant, 5/24/1773 (Cumb. S310)
Smith, Samuel: survey, undated (C-183-143)
Smith, Samuel: patent, 4/25/1774 (AA-14-290)
additional names:
Douglas, James?: sometime between 6/20/1750 and 5/6/1762 (from C-146-178)
Smith, Samuel: 4/27/1773 (from C-5-248)
Breeker/Bricker, Jacob, other land of: 11/7/1785 to 10/18/1794 (from Y-150, A-28-225)

37.) ed. 6/2/1762
251 acres, 28 perches
Mushmore, Shadrick: warrant, 6/12/1762 (Cumb. M135)
Mushmore, Shadrick: resurvey, 2/16/1803 (C-141-252)

37a.) 131 acres, 8 perches
Boor, William: survey, 2/16/1803 (C-156-37)
Sailor, John & Nicholas Boor, exrs. in trust: patent, 3/11/1823 (H-19-275)
additional names:
Blackford, Josh. (Joseph): 4/20/1767 (from C-36-21)
Boar, William and Michael: 4/3/1787 to 2/25/1788 (from C-189-285 & 251)
Boor, William: 2/16/1803 (from C-141-251, C-119-276)
Boor, Wm., heirs of, in right of Shadrach Muchmore: 3/20/1824 (from C-207-181)

37b.) 20 acres, 20 perches
Mushmore, Shadrick: survey, 2/16/1803 (C-119-276)
Fleming, Morgan: patent, 2/10/1804 (P-53-282)
additional names:
Blackford, Joseph: 7/3/1767 (from C-123-188)
Boor, William & Michael: 4/3/1787 to 2/25/1788 (from C-189-285 & 281)

Fleming, Morgan: 2/16/1803 (from C-141-251, C-156-37)
Dullebahn, John: 4/24/1810 (from C-123-189)

37c.) 100 acres
Sailor, Mathias, in right of Shadrick Mushmore: survey, 2/16/1803 (C-141-251)
Comfort, Daniel & John Bobb: patent, 6/5/1851 (H-48-210)
additional names:
Blackford, Joseph: 7/3/1767 (from C-123-188)
Sailor, Mathias: 2/16/1803 to 4/24/1810 (from C-119-276, C-156-37, C-123-189)
Daniel Comfert & John Bobb, formerly Mathias Sailor: 5/30/1850 (from C-141-253)

38.) ed. 6/4/1762
63 acres, 90 perches
Gregory, James: 6/4/1762 (Cumb. G41)
Gregory, James: 2/21/1798 (C-137-119)

38a.) 23 acres, 119 perches
Gregory, James: survey, 6/13/1810 (C-137-120)
Cocklin, David: patent, 6/1/1818 (H-15-474)
additional names:
Miller, Andrew, in right of James Gregory: 11/1/1766 (from A-11-66)
Miller, Andrew, land sold to Dutchmen: 6/5/1776 (from 8-12-31)
Cockley, Jacob: 5/28/1790 (from A-13-256)
Gregory, James: 2/21/1798 (from C-137-121)
Cocklin, David, in right of James Gregory: 2/21/1798 to 6/13/1810 (from C-137-121 & 117, C-67-20 & 21)

38b.) 40 acres, 33 perches
Gregory, James: survey, 6/13/1810 (C-67-20)
Cocklin, Jacob: patent, 3/12/1811 (H-4-549)
additional names:
Miller, Andrew, in right of James Gregory: 11/1/1766 (from A-11-66)
Miller, Andrew, land sold to Dutchmen: 6/5/1776 (8-12-31)

Miller, Andrew: 2/21/1798 to 6/13/1810 (from C-137-119, 120 & 121, C-67-21)

39.) ed. 6/10/1762
394 acres, 145 perches
Lamb, Samuel: warrant, 6/10/1762 (Cumb. L55)
Lamb, Samuel: survey, 2/27/1764 (A-48-189)

39a.) "Abraham's Wish," 193 acres, 92 perches
Lamb, Samuel: survey, 7/13/1809 (C-123-59)
Hertzel, Abraham: patent, 3/9/1810 (H-3-276)
additional names:
Lamb, Samuel, heirs of: 6/10/1791 (from A-28-217)
Hartzler, Abrm., in right of Sarni. Lamb: 10/31–11/1/1822 (from B-4-60, C-215-295)

39b.) 186 acres, 151 perches
Lamb, Samuel: survey, 12/8/1812 (C-124-18)
Urie, Thomas, executor of Henry Eberly, decd., in trust for Eberly's heirs: patent, 1/26/1813 (H-7-719)
additional names:
Lamb, Sarni.: 4/8/1774 (from C-212-2)
Lamb, Samuel, heirs of: 6/10/1791(from A-28-217)
Eberly, Henry, part of larger tract: 7/13/1809 (from C-123-59)
Eberly, Joseph, in right of Sarni. Lamb: 10/31–11/1/1822 (from B-4-60, C-215-294 & 295)

39c.) 24 acres, 5 perches
Lamb, Sarni.: survey, 11/1/1822 (C-215-294)
Sterrett, Robert (guardian to): patent, 5/6/1829 (from H-22-231)
additional names:
Lamb, Sarni.: 4/8/1774 (from C-212-2)
Starett, Jno., heirs of, in right of Samuel Lamb: 10/31–11/1/1822 (from B-4-60, C-215-295)

40.) ed. 2/9/1763 (correction: now 7/10/1752)
"Denmark," 382 acres
Martin, Samuel: patent, 6/19/1793 (P-19-353)

additional names:
Martin, Samuel: 8/21/1767 to 10/31/1822
(from A-18-271, C-166-90, C-115-39, A-14-1 & 2, C-215-296, B-4-60)

40a.) 181 acres, 67 or 80 perches
Martin, Samuel: warrant, 7/10/1752 (Cumb. M47)
Martin, Samuel: resurvey, 4/10/1772 (M-253 & 254)

40b.) 200 acres, 99 or 80 perches
Martin, Samuel: warrant, 2/9/1763 (Cumb. M225)
Martin, Samuel: survey, 4/10/1772 (M-254)

41.) ed. 4/30/1763
"Rural Grove," 126 acres, 80 perches
Lyon, William: warrant, 4/28 or 30/1763 (Cumb. L84)
Lyon, William: survey, 5/10/1763 (C-109-146)
Miers/Meris/Maris, Joshua: patent, 4/15/1796 (P-28-83)
additional names:
Lyon, William, Esq.: 12/6/1766 to 1/18/1808
(from C-29-263, A-31-182 & 183, C-41-56)
Myers, Joshua, in right of William Lyon: 9/10/1795 to 11/2/1822 (from C-29-264, C-31-183 & 211, C-134-200)

42.) ed. 5/10/1763
168 acres, 66 perches
Rutledge, Isaac, transferred to William Trindle Jr.: west side application, 9/27/1766 (#1372)
Myers, Joshua: warrant, 2/26/1806 (Cumb. M353)
Rutledge, Isaac: survey for 298 acres, 103 perches, 1/24/1767 (A-31-183)
Rutledge, Isaac: survey for 166 acres, 138 perches, 9/10/1795 (A-31-182)
Rutledge, Isaac: survey for 168 acres, 66 perches, 12/28/1803 (C-134-200)
Myers, Joshua: patent, 2/18/1806 (P-57-258)
additional names:
Vacant: 2/27/1743 to 12/17/1766
(from A-75-203 & 204, D-18-168)
Trindle, Alexander: 5/10/1763 (from C-109-146)
Trundle/Trendle, William: 12/6/1766 to 1/18/1808
(from C-29-263, C-68-183, C-41-56)
Rutledge, Isaac: 1/24/1767 to 12/28/1803
(from A-31-181 & 183, C-134-200)
Trendle, Wm., heirs of, in right of Isaac Rutledge: 9/10/1795 (from C-29-264)
Myers, Joshua, in right of William Trindle: 9/10–11/1795 to 4/24/1810 (from C-139-86, C-145-232, D-18-167)

43.) ed. 5/10/1763
305 acres, 150 perches
Dorn, Jacob: warrant, 8/7/1765 (Cumb. D85)
Dorn, Jacob: survey, 12/6/1766 (C-29-263)

43a.) 146 acres, 35 perches
Dorn, Jacob: survey for 142 acres, 141 perches, 9/10/1795 (C-29-264)
Dorn, Jacob: resurvey for 146 acres, 35 perches, 11/2/1822 (C-29-256)
Houser, John: patent, 1/17/1823 (H-19-259)
additional names:
Dorn, Jacob: 5/10/1763 to 9/11/1795
(from C-109-146, A-31-181 & 182)
Smith & Barton, Messrs.: 12/6/1766 (from C-123-36)
Merks, Henry, formerly Jacob Dorn: possibly as early as 1/20/1767 to 9/11/1795 (from C-139-86 & 89)
Dorun, Thos.: 1/24/1767 (from A-31-183)
Peelman, Jacob & - - - Stoddart [sic]: 9/21–22/1803 (from C-31-211)
Smith & Barton, land formerly of: 8/15/1809 (from C-123-56)

43b.) 124 acres, 52 perches
Dorn, Jacob: survey, 12/11/1821 (C-43-188)
Beelman, Jacob: patent, 3/7/1822 (H-19-151)
additional names:
Vacant: 6/30/1766 (from D-18-207)
Dorn, Jacob: 5/7/1767 (from C-149-86)

Peelman, Jacob & - - - Stoddart [sic]: 9/21–22/1803 (from C-31-211)
Lee, Timothy & heirs of Henry Marks, in right of Jacob Dorn: sometime between 1/18/1800 and 11/17/1812 (from C-41-55)
Garret, Frederick, formerly Jacob Dorn: 3/9/1815 (from C-43-181)
Peelman/Beelman, Jacob: 8/18/1815 to 12/11/1821 (from C-149-88, C-43-185, D-9-75)

43c.) 1 acre, 34 perches
Dorn, Jacob: survey, 1/18/1808 (C-41-56)
Boor, William: patent, 11/18/1812 (H-7-630)
additional names:
Vacant: 6/30/1766 (from D-18-207)
Lee, Timothy & heirs of Henry Marks, in right of Jacob Dorn: sometime between 1/18/1800 and 11/17/1812 (from C-41-55)
Garret, Frederick, formerly Jacob Dorn: 3/9/1815 (C-43-181)

43d.) 13 acres, 3 perches
Dorn, Jacob: survey, 3/9/1815 (C-43-182)
Gerhart, Frederick: patent, 9/17/1821 (H-18-288)
additional names:
Vacant: 6/30/1766 (from D-18-207)
Dorn, Jacob: 5/7/1767 (from C-149-86)
Peelman, Jacob & - - - Stoddart [sic]: 9/21–22/1803 (from C-31-211)
Lee, Timothy & heirs of Henry Marks, in right of Jacob Dorn: sometime between 1/18/1800 and 1812 (from C-41-55)
Garret, Frederick, formerly Jacob Dorn: 3/9/1815 (from C-43-181)
Miller, Rudolph: 12/11/1821 (from C-43-188)

43e.) 9 acres, 108 perches
Dorn, Jacob: survey, 6/12/1812 (C-41-117)
Zeigler, John: patent, 3/25/1814 (H-10-478)
additional names:
Vacant: 6/30/1766

Stotler, Henry: 9/10/1795 (from C-29-264)
Peelman, Jacob & - - - Stoddart [sic]: 9/21–22/1803 (from C-31-211)
Lee, Timothy & heirs of Henry Marks: sometime between 1/18/1800 and 11/17/1812 (from C-41-55)
Garret, Frederick, formerly Jacob Dorn: 3/9/1815 (from C-43-181)

43f.) 16 acres, 96 perches
Dorn, Jacob: survey, 12/6/1812 (C-41-36)
Boor, William: patent, 11/18/1812 (H-7-630)
additional names:
Vacant: 6/30/1766 (from D-18-207)
Smith & Barton: 2/21/1798 (from C-137-121)
Lee, Timothy & heirs of Henry Marks: sometime between 1/18/1800 and 11/17/1812 (from C-41-55)
Frees, Michael: 6/13/1810 (from C-137-117)
Dorn, Jacob: 6/12/1812 (C-41-59)
Garret, Frederick, formerly Jacob Dorn: 3/9/1815 (C-43-181)
Miller, Rudolph: 12/11/1821 (C-43-185 & 188)

43g.) 5 acres, 136 perches
Dorn, Jacob: survey, 12/11/1821 (C-43-185)
Gaert/Gaerte, Jacob: patent, 1/26/1822 (H-18-446)
additional names:
Dorn, Jacob: 5/7/1767 (from C-149-86)
McCoskrey, William, late: 2/20/1798 (from A-53-207)
Frees, Michael: 6/13/1810 (from C-137-118)
Beelman, Jacob, formerly Jacob Dorn: 8/18/1815 (from C-149-88)

44.) ed. 6/17/1763
85 acres, 158 perches
(Note: This tract appears to overlap no.54. See no. 54 for possible additional names.)
Dunlap, William: warrant, 6/17/1763 (Cumb. D81)
Dunlop, William: survey, 9/1/1809 (C-41-47)
Reiger, Adam: patent, 7/2/1812 (H-7-284)
additional names:

Vance, Patrick: 12/10/1766 to 8/9/1791
(from B-12-69, C-116-211)
Hide, Abraham: 4/3/1787 to 2/25/1788
(from C-189-281 & 285)
Dunlop, William: 9/1/1809 (from A-82-203)
Kissinger, Peter, in right of Wm. Dunlop: 3/13/1830
(from B-12-70)

45.) ed. 2/27/1764
"LargeSpring," 401 acres, 141 perches
Ege, Michael: warrant, 3/31/1791 (Cumb. E96)
Ege, Michael: survey, 6/10/1791 (A-28-217)
Ege, Michael Jr.: patent, 1/19/1792 (P-18-328)
additional names:
Vacant: 6/19/1750 (from A-88-71)
Edge/Ege, Michael: 5/7/1753 to 6/11/1791
(from C-25-142, A-76-5)
Brownlee, John, claim of: 2/27/1764 (from A-48-189)
Iron Works Co. Land: 6/27–28/1770 to January 1775
(from C-25-223 & 224, C-212-2, B-6-116)
Duncan, Thomas, Esq.: 7/13/1809 (from C-123-59)
Eberly's heirs: 12/8/1812 (from C-124-18)
Sollenberger, Jo.: 12/8/1812 (from C-124-18)

46.) ed. 2/27/1764
"Swallow," 76 acres, 51 perches
Martin, Samuel Jr.: warrant, 12/24/1771 (Cumb. M395)
Martin, Sarni.: survey, 4/8/1774 (C-212-2)
Martin, Samuel Jr.: patent, 3/29/1774 (AA-14-211)
additional names:
Vacant: 6/19/1750 (from A-88-71)
Martin, Samuel: 2/27/1764 to 12/8/1812
(from A-48-189, 6/10/1791, C-124-18)
Martin, Sarni. Junr.: 4/9/1773 (from C-166-90)

47.) ed. 6/4/1764
181 acres, 60 perches
(Note: the dotted line at the northwest corner of this survey indicates the difference between Wilson and Walford's versions.)

Wilson, James: 1st warrant, 6/4/1764 (Cumb. W59)
Wolford, Peter, Esq., guardian of Moses Bricker: 2nd warrant, 5/2/1827 (York W341)
Wilson, James: survey for 166 acres, 120 perches, undated (D-18-230)
Wolford, Peter, Esq.: survey for 181 acres, 60 perches, 5/17/1827 (D-13-81)
Wolford, Peter, in trust: patent, 8/6/1827 (H-24-498)
additional names:
Wilson, James: March 1761 to 4/12/1796
(from C-146-176, C-51-209)
Vacant: 12/2/1788 (from C-35-294)
Bricker, Jacob, formerly James Wilson and South Mountain: 12/16–17/1811 (from C-161-274)

48.) ed. 1750–1764
"Hope," 49 acres, 100 perches
Bricker, Jacob: warrant, 4/27/1792 (Cumb. B-449)
Bricker, Jacob: survey, 5/28/1795 (D-488)
Bricker, Jacob: patent, 6/28/1804 (P-54-341)
additional names:
Hammersly, Thomas?: sometime between 4/26/1750 and 6/16/1764 (from B-2-74)
Hammersly, Thomas, heirs of: between 1750 and 1790
(from Y-151)
Johnston, Thomas, in right of Revd. George Duffield: 12/27/1785 (from C-233-64)
Bricker, Jacob, formerly James Douglas: 4/20/1802
(from A-14-86 & 87, C-199-295, C-213-46 & 47)

49.) ed. 5/4/1765
"Union," 241 acres, 90 perches
Long, Martha & James Croket, executors of James Long, deceased, in trust for his heirs: warrant, 5/4/1765 (Cumb. L90)
Long, Martha & James Crocket: survey, 5/19/1785
(C-115-39)
Knawer, Jacob, et al.: patent, 8/10/1793 (P-20-129)
additional names:
Muchmore, Shadrach, formerly James Long: sometime

between 9/27/1750 and 6/16/1764 (from B-2-74)
Strike/Stroke/Strock, Joseph: 2/14/1769 to 4/20/1802
(from C-55-290, M-254(?), C-166-90, A-14-87)
Kenower, Jacob: 12/20/1803 (from A-14-1, 2, 3 & 4)

50.) ed. 9/13/1765
"Union of Claims," 194 acres, 21 perches
Seely, Jonas, Esq.: warrant, 9/13/1765 (Cumb. S208)
Graff/Greaff/Graeff, John: patent, 5/10/1791
(P-18-122)

50a.) 98 acres, 166 perches [sic]
Whitmore, Abraham & John Graff, in right of Jonas
Seely: resurvey, 5/28/1790 (A-13-257)
(Note on survey: "For Jas. Gregory & Charles Imhoff in dispute - Gregory claiming by a location in his own name #1376 and Imhoff by virtue of an improvt. - Imhoff obtained a judgment of 13d. day in his favor rejecting the location and survey of Gregory - Imhoff by deed of 20th Oct. 1768 conveyd. his impt. & land held thereby to Hugh Cook, who also by virtue of a deed from Jonas Seely dated 19th March 1770, became vested in the right to a 300 a. warrant, the location of which includes this survey with the adjoining one and Hugh Cook's right by virtue sundry conveyances became vested in John Graff (who applies for a patent this survey with the approbation of the Surv. General and Secretary").
additional names:
Abernathy, Wm. & Wm. Lyon?: sometime between
9/27/1750 & 6/16/1764 (from B-2-74)
Charles Imhoff, settled by: 6/30/1766 (from D-18-207)
Imhoff & Gregory, dispute: 11/1/1766 (from A-11-66)
Gregory, James: 12/11/1767 (from C-79-163)
Cook, Hugh: 10/20/1768 to sometime before
5/10/1791 (from A-13-257 note)
Whitmore & Graff: 5/28/1790 (from A-13-256)
Clime, Frederick & Jacob Weist: sometime between
1/18/1800 and 11/17/1812 (from C-41-55)
Zerra, Adam: 6/12/1812 (from C-41-59)
Clime, Frederick: 3/9/1815 (from C-43-181)

50b.) 95 acres, 21 perches
Seely, Jonas, Esq.: resurvey, 5/28/1790 (A-13-256)
additional names:
Schultz, Charles, settled by 6/30/1766 (from D-18-207)
Seeley, Jona: 11/1/1766 (from A-11-66)
Gregory, James: 12/11/1767 (from C-79-163)
Whitmore & Graff: 5/28/1790 (from A-13-257)
Cook, Hugh: 2/21/1798 (from C-137-119 & 121)
Clime, Federick & Jacob Weist: sometime between
1/18/1800 & 11/17/1812 (from C-41-55)
Clime, Frederick: 6/13/1810 to 3/9/1815
(from C-137-117 & 120, C-43-181)
Zerra, Adam: 6/12/1812 (from C-41-59)

51.) ed. 4/5/1765
"Cauff'sRight," 179 acres, 76 perches
Couff/Canff, Philip: west side application, 1/22/1767
(#2525)
Couff, Philip: warrant, 6/2/1768 (Cumb. C220)
Couff, Phillip: survey, 4/20/1767 (C-36-21)
Kauff, Phillip: patent, 6/6/1768 (AA-10-385)
additional names:
Brandon, James: 4/5/1765 (from C-159-198)
Couf/Couff, Phillip: 5/24/1766 to 8/21/1767
(C-3-8, A-18-271)
Greeger/Greer, John: 4/3/1787 to 11/1/1822
(from C-189-281 & 285, B-4-60 & 73, C-215-296)
Huber, Michael: 3/20/1824 (from C-207-181)

52.) ed. 7/20/1765
330 acres
White, Richard: warrant, 7/20/1765 (Cumb. W-126)
White, Richard: survey, 6/30/1766 (D-18-207)

52a.) 121 acres, 159 perches
White, Richard: survey, sometime between 1/18/1800
& 11/17/1812 (C-41-55)
Boor, William: patent, 11/8/1812 (H-7-630)
additional names:
Smith, Doer. and Wm. Barton: 12/6/1766 to 8/15/1809

(from C-29-263, C-123-36 & 56, C-79-163, C-72-251)
Peelman, Jacob: 5/28/1790 (from A-13-256 & 257)
Stotler, Henry: 9/10/1795 (from C-29-264)
White, Richard: 1/18/1808 to 6/12/1812
  (from C-41-36 & 56)
Gerhard/Garrett, Fred.: 6/12/1812 to 12/11/1821
  (from C-41-117, C-43-182 & 188)

52b.) 99 acres, 2 perches
White, Richard: survey, 3/9/1815 (C-43-181)
Gerhart, Frederick: patent, 9/17/1821 (H-18-288)
additional names:
Smith, Doer. and Wm. Barton: 12/6/1766 to
  9/10/1795 (from C-29-263 & 264)
Peelman, Jacob: 5/28/1790 (from A-13-256 & 257)
Stotler, Henry: 9/10/1795 (from C-29-264)
White, Richard: 1/18/1808 to 6/12/1812
  (from C-41-36 & 56)
Gerhard/Garrett, Fred.: 6/12/1812 to 12/11/1821
  (from C-41-117, C-43-182 & 188, D-9-75)

52c.) 31 acres, 23 perches
White, Richd.: survey, 6/12/1812 (C-41-59)
Freze/Fuze, Michael: patent, 12/5/1812 (H-7-637)
additional names:
Smith, Doer. and Wm. Barton: 12/6/1766 to
  2/21/1798 (from C-29-263, C-137-121)
Peelman, Jacob: 5/28/1790 (from A-13-256 & 257)
White, Richard: 1/18/1808 to 6/12/1812
  (from C-41-36 & 56)
Frees, Michael: 6/13/1810 (from C-137-117)
Miller/Millar, Rudolph: 12/11/1821
  (from C-43-188, D-9-75)

52d.) 74 acres, 15 perches
White, Richard: survey, 12/11/1821 (D-9-75)
Beelman, Jacob: patent, 3/7/1822 (H-19-151)
additional names:
Smith, Doer. and Wm. Barton: 12/6/1766 to
  9/10/1795 (from C-29-263 & 264)

White, Richard: 1/18/1808 to 12/11/1821
  (from C-41-36 & 56, C-43-188)
Gerhard/Garret, Fredr.: 6/12/1812 to 3/9/1815
  (C-41-117, C-43-182)

53.) ed. 5/24/1766
"Holmes's Tract," 111 acres, 31 perches
Wallace, Ruth: west side application, 5/8/1767
  (#3629)
Holmes, Andrew: warrant, 4/13/1772 (Cumb. H236)
Wallace, Ruth: survey, 8/21/1767 (A-18-271)
Holmes, Andrew: patent, 4/15/1772 (AA-13-88)
additional names:
Wallace, William: 5/24/1766 to 8/9/1791
  (from C-3-8, C-36-21, C-116-211)
Holoms, Andrew: 4/10/1772 (from M-254)
Hoover, David: 12/29/1803 (from A-14-2 & 4)
Greer, John, heirs of: 10/31–11/1/1822
  (from B-4-60 & 73, C-215-296)

54.) ed. 5/24/1766
"Spotsylvania," 246 acres, 147 perches
(Note: This tract appears to partially overlap no. 44. See tract no. 44 for more possible names.)
Swisher, Christopher: warrant, 3/11/1785
  (Cumb. #S383)
Mccurdy, Robert, in trust for the several children of John
  Mccurdy, deceased, in right of Christopher Swisher:
  resurvey, 2/25/1788 (C-189-281)
Mccurdy, Robert, etc. as above: patent, 5/20/1788
  (P-13-145)
additional names:
Mccurdy, John's heirs, claim of: 5/24/1766 to
  2/16/1803 (from C-3-8, D-45-246 & 260, C-36-21,
  C-141-252, C-156-37, C-119-276)
Trindle, Alexander?: 7/3/1767 (from C-123-188)
Mccurdy, John's heirs' improvement: 4/3/1787
  (from C-189-285)
Coover, George: 9/1/1809 (from C-41-47, A-82-203)
Boore, William: 4/24/1810 (from C-123-189)

54a.) 157 acres, 37 perches
Swisher, Christopher: survey, 4/3/1787 (C-189-285)
additional names: see no. 54 above

55.) ed.5/24/1766
"Georgia," 290 acres, 49 perches
Long, James: 1st warrant, 2/3/1755 (Cumb. L32)
Long, Martha & James Crocket, et al.: 2nd warrant, 9/3/1770 (Cumb. L118)
Long, Martha & James Crocket: resurvey, 8/9/1791 (C-116-211)
Myers, George: patent, 3/8/1792 (P-18-374)
additional names:
Long, Widw.: 5/24/1766 to 12/10/1766 (from C-3-8, B-12-69)
Vance, Patrick: 12/10/1766 (from B-12-69)
Long, James Jr., heirs of: 8/21/1767 (from A-18-271)
Gill, John: 12/19/1803 (from A-14-1)
Moyer/Meyers, George: 12/29/1803 (from A-14-2, 3 & 4, C-41-47)
Cockley, John: 3/13/1830 (from B-12-70)
Coebright (no additional name) heirs of: 3/13/1830 (from B-12-70)
Henderson, Wm. & Robt. Jacobs: 3/13/1830 (from B-12-70)

56.) ed. 6/5/1766
110 acres, 96 perches
Miller, Andrew: warrant, 4/25/1770 (Cumb. M361)
Miller, Andrew: survey, 2/21/1798 (C-137-121)

56a.) 57 acres, 45 perches
Miller, Andrew: survey, 6/13/1810 (C-137-117)
Cocklin, David: patent, 6/1/1818 (H-15-474)
additional names:
Miller, Andrew, land sold to Dutchmen: 6/5/1776 (from B-12-31)
Miller, Andrew, other land of: 6/30/1766 to 1/8/1808 (from D-18-207, C-29-263, A-53-207, C-137-117, C-41-55 & 56)
Cockley, Jacob: 5/28/1790 (from A-13-256)

Cocklin/Cockley, David, in right of Andrew Miller: 6/13/1810 to 12/11/1821 (from C-137-118 & 120, C-67-21, C-41-36 & 59, C-43-185)
Clime, Frederick: 3/9/1815 (from C-43-181)

56b.) 64 acres, 34 perches
Miller, Andrew: survey, 6/13/1810 (C-67-21)
Cocklin, Jacob: patent, 3/12/1811 (H-4-549)
additional names:
Miller, Andrew, land sold to Dutchmen: 6/5/1776 (B-12-31)
Miller, Andrew, in right of Jas. Gregory: 11/1/1766 to 6/13/1810 (from A-11-66, A-48-133)
Miller, Andrew, land formerly of: 2/15/1813 (from C-140-55)

57.) ed. 9/27/766
"Lamb's Pasture," 354 acres, 145 perches
Rutledge, Isaac: west side application, 9/27/1766 (#1371)
Lamb, John: warrant, 12/2/1809 (Cumb. L289)
Rutledge, Isaac: survey for 350 acres, 162 perches, 12/6/1766 (C-123-36)
Rutledge, Isaac: resurvey for 354 acres, 145 perches, 8/15/1809 (C-123-56)
Lamb, John: patent, 12/29/1809 (H-2-107)
additional names:
Vacant: 6/30/1766 (from D-18-207)
Rutledge, Isaac, other land of: 9/27/1766 to 9/12/1795 (from D-45-246 & 260, C-29-263, C-139-87 & 89, A-31-181 & 183, C-41-56)
Lamb, John, Esq., formerly Isaac Rutledge: 9/10/1795 to 9/1/1809 (from C-139-86, C-72-251, A-82-203)
Hoover, Michael, in right of Isaac Rutledge: 9/10/1795 to 11/2/1822 (from C-29-256 & 264)
Gregor, John & Michael Hoover: 1/18/1812? (from C-41-55)

58.) ed.9/27/1766
"Allindale," 134 acres, 98 perches

Rutledge, Isaac, then Alex. Trindle: west side application, 9/27/1766 (#1372)
Myers, George: warrant, 2/9/1807 (Cumb. M955)
Rutledge, Isaac: survey for 298 acres, 103 perches, 1/24/1767 (A-31-183)
Rutledge, Isaac: survey for 134 acres, 98 perches, 9/11/1795 (A-31-181)
Rutledge, Isaac: survey for 134 acres, 98 perches, 9/10–11/1795 (C-139-86)
Myers, George: patent for this tract and no. 63, 2/10/1807 (P-59-257)
additional names:
Trundle, Wm.: 12/6/1766 (from C-29-263)
Rutledge, Isaac: 12/6/1766 to 9/12/1795 (from C-123-36 & 188, C-139-87 & 89, A-31-182 & 183)
Myers (no additional name), formerly Isaac Rutledge: 9/10–11/1795 (from C-139-88)
Trendle, Alexander, heirs of, in right of Isaac Rutledge: 9/10/1795 (from C-29-264)
Rutledge, Isaac, formerly: 8/15/1809 (from C-123-56)
Trindle, Wm.: 11/2/1822 (C-29-256)

59.) ed. 9/27/1766
"Lamb's Rest," 134 acres, 63 perches
Trindle, John: west side application, 1/20/1767 (#2487)
Lamb, John: warrant, 5/5/1810 (Cumb. L291)
Trindle, John: survey for 214 acres, 69 perches, 1/20/1767 (C-123-188)
Trindle, John: survey for 134 acres, 63 perches, 4/24/1810 (C-123-189)
Lamb, John: patent, 5/7/1810 (H-2-456)
additional names:
Vacant: 3/27/1743 (from A-75-203 & 204)
Trindle, William: 9/27/1766 (from D-45-246 & 260)
Trindle, John: 7/3/1767 (from C-123-188)
Trindle, John, decd., heirs of: 3/7/1785 (from A-40-48, A-82-202)
Lamb, John, formerly John Trindle: 2/16/1803 (from C-141-251 & 252, C-119-276)

60.) ed. 9/27/1766
"Andalusia," 65 acres, 10 perches
Trindle, Alexander: west side application, 9/27/1766 (#1377)
Lamb, John: warrant, 10/30/1809 (Cumb. L288)
Trindle, Alexr.: survey, 12/6/1766 (D-45-246)
Trindle, Alexander: survey, 12/17/1766 (D-45-260)
Lamb, John: patent (for 84 acres, 44 perches), 12/29/1809 (H-2-108)
additional names:
Trundle/Trendle/Trindle, Alexander: 12/6/1766 to 8/15/1809 (from C-123-36, 56 & 188)
Rutledge/Rutlidge, Isaac: 1/24/1767 to 9/12/1795 (from A-31-181 & 183, C-139-87, 88 & 89)
Lamb, John, Esq., in right of Alexr. Trindle: 4/3/1787 to 2/25/1788 (from C-189-281 & 285, C-123-189)

61.) ed. 12/6/1766
30 acres, 68 perches
Kennedy, John: west side application, 2/5/1767 (#2699)
Gantz, Frederick: warrant, 1/8/1833 (G298)
Kennedy, John: survey, 5/29/1798 (C-72-251)
Gantz, Frederick: patent, 1/9/1833 (H-32-219)
additional names:
Vacant: 6/30/1766 (from D-18-207)
Kennedy, John: 12/6/1766 to 12/11/1767 (from C-123-36, C-79-163)
Kennedy, John, land formerly of: 8/15/1809 (from C-123-56)
Gregor, John & Michael Hoover: 1/18/1812? (from C-41-55)

62.) ed. 12/6/1766
approximately 100 acres
Warrant not found.
Survey not found.
Patent not found.
additional names:
Kennedy, John, other land of: 12/6/1766 to 5/29/1798 (from C-123-36, C-79-63, C-72-251)

Kennedy, John, land formerly of: 8/15/1809 (from C-123-56)
Gregor, Adam: 9/1/1809 (from A-82-203)
Gantz, Frederick: 1838–4/1/1862 (from Cumberland County Historic Resources Survey citation of tax records and 1862 will)

63.) ed. 1/20/1767
"Allindale," 88 acres, 7 perches
Trindle, John: west side application, 1/20/1767 (#2487)
Myers, George: warrant, 2/9/1807 (Cumb. M955)
Trindle, John: surveys, 9/12/1795 (C-139-87 & 88)
Rutledge, Isaac and Jno. Trindle: survey, undated (C-139-89)
Myers, George: patent for this tract and no. 58, 2/10/1807 (P-59-257)
additional names:
Vacant: 3/27/1743 (from A-75-203 & 204)
Trindle, William: 9/27/1766 to 12/28/1803 (from D-45-246 & 260, C-134-200)
Trindle, John: 1/24/1767 to 9/10–11/1795 (from C-139-86 & 89, A-31-181 & 183)

64.) ed. 1/24/1767
Apparently, 2 warrants, 3 surveys and 2 patents were issued for more or less the same tract of land.

64a.) "Danbury," 52 acres, 88 perches
Neagly, Daniel: warrant, 6/29/1810 (Cumb. N83)
Neagly, Daniel: survey, 4/24/1810 (C-145-232)
Neagley/Nagley, Daniel: patent, 7/20/1810 (H-4-248)
additional names:
Vacant: 3/27/1743 (from A-75-203 & 204)
Trindle/Trundle, John: 1/24/1767 to 12/28/1803 (from A-31-182 & 183, C-68-183, C-134-200)
Trindle, John, decd.: 3/7/1785 (from A-40-48)
Trindle, William: 4/24/1810 (from C-145-210)

64b.) "Stearington," 52 acres, 88 perches
Trindle, William: warrant, 5/7/1753 (Cumb. T12)

Trindle, William: survey for 51 acres, 91 perches, 12/27/1766 (D-18-168)
Trindle, William: resurvey for 52 acres, 88 perches, 4/24/1810 (D-18-167)
Stear, John: patent (for 50 acres), 6/25/1785 (P-3-425)
(Note: This despite a note on both surveys: "no patent should issue on this survey. There is another patent returned for patenting on the same warrant and all monies that were due the Commonwealth on said warrt. is [sic] of course paid.")
additional names: see 63a.

65.) ed. 2/3/1767
"Ringsend," 101 acres, 120 perches
Crockett, George: west side application, 2/3/1767 (#2842)
Crocket, George: warrant, 6/6/1786 (Cumb. C376)
Crocket, George: survey, 6/27/1770 (C-25-224)
Crockett, George: patent, 6/21/1786 (P-6-327)
additional names:
Crocket, George: 6/27-28/1770 (from C-25-204 & 223)
Crocket, George & Andrew: January 1775 (from B-6-116)
Crocket/Crockett, George, heirs of: 12/23/1785 to 6/10/1791 (from C-53-29, A-28-217)

66.) ed. 2/23/1767
"Allenbury," 107 acres, 140 perches
Crockett, James: west side application, 2/23/1767 (#2841)
Crockett, James: warrant, 6/16/1786 (Cumb. C375)
Crocket, James: survey, 6/28/1770 (C-25-223)
Crockett, James: patent (for 107 acres, 140 perches), 6/22/1786 (P-6-328)
additional names:
Crocket, James, formerly Alexr. Crocket: as early as 5/7/1753 to 9/27/1793 (from C-25-142, C-25-224, C-24-159, C-185-56)
Crocket, George, heirs of: 12/13/1785 (C-53-29)
Crockett, James, heirs of: 6/10/1791 (A-28-217)

67.) ed. 2/23/1767
15 acres, 69 perches
Crocket, George: west side application, 2/23/1767 (#2845)
Miller, Philip: warrant, 7/21/1829 (Cumb. M1045)
Crocket, George: survey, 6/28/1770 (C-152-254)
Miller, Philip: patent, 7/20/1829 (H-26-494)
additional names:
Crocket, James & Andrew: 5/6/1792 (from A-47-80)
Crockett, George: 6/9/1792 (from C-26-170)
McGauan/McGawen, David: 4/23/1811 (from C-26-169, 268 & 269)

68.) ed. 2/23/1767
"Weissenfeld," 120 acres, 80 perches
Rankin, Thomas: west side application, 2/23/1767 (#2837)
Rankin, Thomas: warrant, 2/23/1787 (Cumb. W283)
Rankin, Thomas: survey, 2/15/1769 (C-220-236)
Weiss (alias Wise), Jacob: patent, 11/25/1774 (AA-14-774)
additional names:
Bricker, Peter, in right of Thos. Rankin: 5/7/1753 to 4/20/1802 (from C-25-142, A-14-85, 86 & 87)
Rankin, Thomas: 2/14/1769 to 4/20/1802 (from C-55-290, C-213-46 & 47)
Wise, Jacob, other land of: 10/19/1774 (from C-220-234)

69.) ed. 4/10/1767
"Outfield's Delight," 180 acres, 40 perches
Orbison, Thos.: west side application, 4/10/1767 (#3412)
Duffield, George, in trust: warrant, 5/5/1790 (Cumb. D237)
Orbison, Thomas: survey, 11/7/1785 (Y-150)
Duffield, George, adm.: patent (for both this tract as well as no. 22), 6/15/1790 (P-16-311)
additional names:
Orbison, Thomas: as early as 4/26/1750 to 10/18/1794 (from Y-151, A-28-225)

Duffield, Rev. George: as early as 5/4/1773 to 12/27/1785 (from C-183-143, C-233-64 & 65)
Bricker, Jacob?: 10/21/1794 (from A-26-29)

70.) ed. 2/14/1769
58 acres, 74 perches
Weiss, John: warrant, 3/11/1776 (Cumb. W297)
Weiss, John: survey, 4/20/1802 (A-14-87)
Weiss, Jacob: patent, 2/12/1814 (H-10-288)

70a.) 51 acres, 32 perches
Weiss, John: survey, 4/20/1802 (A-14-86)
additional names:
Hammersley/Hamersly, Thomas: as early as 9/27/1750 to 2/14/1769 (from B-2-74, C-55-290)
Hamersly, Robt.: 5/19/1785 (C-115-39)
Wise, Jacob: 5/28/1795 (from D-488)
Weiss, John: 4/20/1802 (from A-14-85, C-213-46 & 47, C-199-295)

70b.) 7 acres, 42 perches
Weiss, John: survey, 4/20/1802 (A-14-85)
additional names:
Weiss, John: 4/20/1802 (from C-199-295, C-213-46 & 47)

71.) ed. 2/15/1769
144 acres, 120 perches
Gibson, Hugh: west side application. 2/14/1769 (# 2874)
Goodyear, Daniel & Frederick Goodyear: warrant, 1/1/1817 (Cumb. G290)
Gibson, Hugh: survey, 2/14/1769 (C-55-290)
Goodyear, Daniel & Frederick: patent, 1/7/1817 (H-13-4)
additional names:
Vacant: 6/19/1750 (from A-88-71)
Gibson, Hugh: 2/15/1769 to 5/19/1785 (from C-220-236, C-115-39)
Miller. Rudoph, other land of: 5/20/1784 (from C-141-96)
Goodyear, Godfrid, formerly Hugh Gibson: 4/20/1802 (from A-14-85, 86 & 87)

72.) ed. 2/15/1769
"Pond Tract," 124 acres, 40 perches
Wise, Jacob: warrant, 6/10/1773 (Cumb. W253)
Wise, Jacob: survey, 10/19/1774 (C-220-235)
Wise, Jacob: patent, 4/10/1776 (AA-14-775)
additional names:
Bricker/Breeker, Peter, in right of Thos. Rankin:
    5/7/1753 to 4/20/1802 (from C-25-142, C-220-236,
    A-47-80, C-185-56, C-199-295, C-213-46 & 47)

73.) ed. 6/27/1770
"Hopewell," 71 acres, 103 perches
Crocket, James, Andrew Crocket & Cathrine Hassen, in
    trust. exrs.: warrant, 9/9/1785 (Cumb. C354)
Crocket, James, Andrew Crocket & Cathrine Hassen, in
    trust, exrs.: survey, 12/23/1785 (C-53-29)
Crockett, James & Andrew: patent, 1/18/1791
    (P-15-426)
additional names:
Crocket/Crockett, George, improved land of:
    6/27–28/1770 (from C-25-223 & 24)
Crocket, George, decd., heirs of: 12/23/1785 to
    6/9/1792 (from C-25-276, C-24-159, C-26-170)

74.) ed/ 6/28/1770
311 acres, 147 perches
Rankin, Richard: warrant, 6/8/1776 (Cumb. R154)
Rankin, Richard: resurvey, 5/6/1792 (A-47-80)
Scott, Hetty: patent, 1/15/1823 (H-20-429)
additional names:
Rankin, Richard: 6/28/1770 to 10/19/1774
    (from C-152-254, C-220-235)
Scott, John & William: 12/21/1785 to 4/23/1811
    (from C-2-270, C-233-64, C-26-169 & 268)
Scott, William: 10/18/1794 to 4/20/1802
    (from C-60-181, C-213-47, C-199-295)
Scott, William, heirs of: 4/23/1811 (C-26-169 & 268)

75.) ed. 6/28/1770
"Fairfield," 129 acres

Crocket, James, et al., exrs.: warrant, 9/9/1785
    (Cumb. C355)
Crocket, James: survey, 12/24/1785 (C-24-159)
Crocket, Margaret, et al.: patent, 4/19/1798
    (P-33-614)
additional names:
Crocket, James, improved land of: 6/28/1770 to
    9/27/1793 (from C-152-259, C-25-233, C-53-29,
    C-185-56)
Crocket, James & Andrew: 5/6/1792 (from A-47-80)
Crockett, James, heirs of: 6/9/1792 (C-26-170)

76.) ed. 6/28/1770
65 acres, 99 perches
Crockett, James & George: warrant. 6/20/1785
    (Cumb. C347)
Crockett, James & George: survey, 12/21/1785
    (C-26-270)

76a.) 32 acres, 150 perches
Crockett, James & George: surveys, 4/23/1811
    (C-26-268 & 269)
Hopple, John: patent, 5/7/1813 (H-9-22)
additional names:
Crocket, William: 6/28/1770 (from C-152-254)
Crockett, James & George: 6/9/1792 to 4/23/1811
    (from C-26-170, 4/23/1811)
Ore Bank: 10/18/1794 (from C-60-182)
Diller, David: 5/10/1860 (from D-21-163)

76b.) 36 acres, 153 perches
Crockett, James & George: survey, 4/23/1811 (C-26-169)
Crocket, George: patent, 2/26/1812 (H-6-656)
additional names:
Crocket, William: 6/28/1770 (from C-152-254)
Crocket, Willm., decd., heirs of: 12/21/1785 to
    5/6/1792 (from C-26-270, A-47-80)
Ore Bank: 10/18/1794 (from C-60-182)
Crockett, George: 4/23/1811
    (from C-26-161, 268 & 269)

77.) ed. 6/28/1770
"Springhill," 140 acres, 55 perches
Rankin, Richard: warrant, 6/8/1776 (Cumb. R155)
Rankin, Richard: survey, 9/27/1793 (C-185-56)
Scott, William: patent, 4/27/1807 (P-59-482)
additional names:
Scott, John, in right of Richard Rankin: 5/17/1753
   (from C25-142)
Rankin, Richard: 6/28/1770 to 10/19/1774
   (from C-25-223, C-220-235)
Scott, John: 12/24/1785 (C-24-159)

78.) ed. 4/10/1772
"Carlisle," 350 acres
Martin, Thomas: west side application, 5/17/1769 (#5476)
Martin, Thomas: warrant, 4/12/1774 (Cumb. M441)
Martin, Thomas: survey, 4/9/1773 (C-166-90)
Martin, Thomas: patent, 4/12/1774 (AA-14-436)
additional names:
Vacant: 6/19/1750 (from A-88-71)
Martin, Thomas: 4/10/1772 to 4/8/1774
   (from M-253 & 254, C-212-2)
Martin, Samuel: 5/20/1784 to 5/19/1785
   (from C-141-96, C-115-39)
Goodyear, Abrm. and J.: 10/13/1822 to 11/1/1822
   (from B-4-60, C-215-295 & 296)

79.) ed. 8/7/1772
"Shorts," 100 acres, 80 perches
Brandt, Martin: warrant, 8/7/1772 (Cumb. B232)
Brandt, Martin: survey, 4/27/1773 (C-5-248)
Brandt, Martin: patent, 9/12/1786 (P-6-476)
additional names:
Vacant pine land at the foot of South Mountain: March
   1761 (C-146-176 & 177)
Brandt, Martin: 5/4/1773 to 5/22/1816
   (from C-183-143, C-35-294, C-91-193)

80.) ed. 4/9/1773
"Mt. Hope," 47 acres, 120 perches

Miller, Rudolph: warrant, 5/24/1774 (Cumb. M451)
Miller, Rudolph: survey, 5/20/1784 (C-141-96)
Strock, Joseph: patent, 4/30/1793 (P-19-394)
additional names:
Vacant: 6/19/1750 to 2/14/1769 (from A-88-71, C-55-290)
Gibson, Hugh: 4/9/1773 (C-166-90)

81.) ed. 1/1775
"Wood-land," 181 acres, 120 perches
Thornburgh, Joseph: warrant, 3/31/1791 (Cumb. T126)
Thornburgh, Joseph: survey, 6/11/1791 (A-76-5)
Thornburgh, Joseph: patent, 1/19/1792 (P-18-328)
additional names:
Lamb, William: January 1775 (from B-6-116)
Thornburgh, Joseph: 6/10/1791 (from A-28-217)

82.) ed 2/21/1785
"Junction," 348 acres, 140 perches
Wolf, Leonard: warrant, 2/21/1785 (Cumb. W343)
Wolf, Leonard: patent, 6/19/1786 (P-6-353)

82a.) 235 acres, 20 perches
Wolf, Leonard: survey, 12/27/1785 (C-233-64)
additional names:
Steel, Widow, in right of James Douglas: Sometime
   between 4/26/1750 and 6/9/1790 (from Y-151)
Wolf, Leonard, other land of: 12/27/1785 to 5/6/1792
   (from C-233-65, A-47-80)
Wolf, Jacob: 10/18/1794 to 5/28/1795
   (from C-60-181, D-488)
Wolf, Leonard, formerly James Douglas: 4/20/1802
   (from C-213-47, C-199-295)

82b.) 113 acres, 120 perches
Wolf, Leonard: survey, 12/27/1785 (C-233-64 and 65)
additional names:
Wolf, Leonard: 11/7/1785 to 10/18/1794
   (from Y-150, A-28-225)
Wolf, Jacob: 10/18/1794 to 5/26/1818?
   (from C-60-181, C-43-141)

83.) ed. 6/14/1785
"Clarksburg," 300 acres, 92 perches
(Note: This tract may be overlapped on its western edge by no.89b. See tract 89b for more possible names.)
Clark, John: warrant, 6/14/1785 (Cumb. C346)
Clark, John: survey, 12/2/1788 (C-35-294)
Clark, John: patent, 5/29/1790 (P-16-297)
additional names:
South Mountain: 4/27/1773 (from C-5-248)
Clark, John, land/claim of: 10/21/1794 to 2/20/1841
   (from A-26-229, C-51-209, C-205-234)
Ege, Michael, other land of: 4/12/1796 (from C-51-209)

84.) ed. 2/7/1785
"Bricker'sHall," 110 acres
Bricker, Jacob: warrant, 12/12/1792 (Cumb. B461)
Bricker, Jacob: survey, 10/18/1794 (A-28-225)
Bricker, Jacob: patent, 6/28/1804 (P-54-340)
additional names:
South Mountain: 5/24/1773–4/15/1774 (from C-183-143)
Breeker, Jacob, by a mountain: 11/7/1785 (from Y-150)
Bricker, Jacob: 10/21/1794 to 5/22/1816
   (from A-26-229, C-91-193)

85.) ed. 12/13/1785
402 acres, 13 perches
Wolf, Peter: warrant, 12/13/1785 (Cumb. W359)
Wolf, Peter: survey, 10/25/1786 (D-18-219)
Wolf, Peter: patent, 10/25/1794 (D-18-220)
Patent not found.
additional names:
Wolf, Peter: 10/18–21/1794 (from C-60-180, 181 & 182)

86.) ed.12/21/1785
431 acres, 11 perches
Ege, Michael: warrant, 1/19/1793 (Cumb. E102)
Ege, Michael: survey, 10/18/1794 (C-60-182)
Ege, Michael: patent, 8/6/1813 (H-8-642)
additional names:
Barren pine land: 10/12/1761 (from D-9-188)
Ege, Michael: 12/21/1785 to 4/23/1811
   (from C-26-169, 268, 269 & 270, D-18-219 & 220, C-60-181)
Beetem, William M. & Co.: 5/10/1860 (from D-21-193)

87.) ed. 1/23/1794
430 acres, 103 perches
Ege, Michael, Esq.: warrant, 1/23/1794 (Cumb. E107)
Ege, Michael, Esq.: survey, 10/18/1794 (C-60-181)
Ege, Michael: patent, 8/3/1813 (H-9-437)
additional names:
Hamersly, William, claim of: 12/27/1785
   (from C-233-64 & 65)
Ege, Michael: 10/25/1786 (from D-18-219 & 220)
South Mountain: 5/6/1792 (from A-47-80)
Ege, Michael: 10/18/1794 to 5/26/1818?
   (from C-60-182, A-26-229 & 230, C-43-141)

88.) ed. 10/25/1786
409 acres, 25 perches
(Note: This tract appears to overlap two others - no. 89c and no.95. See those tracts for possible additional names.)
Duncan, Thomas: warrant, 1/23/1794 (Cumb. D246)
Duncan, Thomas: survey, 10/21/1794 (A-26-230)
Patent not found.
additional names:
Duncan, Thomas: 10/18/1794 to 10/25/1786
   (from C-60-180 & 181, A-26-229, D-18-219 & 220)
Ege, Michael: 6/20/1814 (from C-15-150)

89.) ed. 12/2/1788
3 overlapping claims

89a.) 438 acres, 77 perches
Duncan, John: warrant, 1/19/1793 (Cumb. D245)
Duncan, John: survey, 10/21/1794 (A-26-229)
No patent issued. See 89b overlap.
additional names:
South Mountain: 4/27/1773 (from C-5-248)

By the foot of South Mountain: 12/27/1785
   (from C-233-64 & 65)
Vacant (northern half of tract): 12/2/1788 (from C-35-294)
Ege, Michael (southern half of tract): 12/2/1788
   (from C-35-294)
Ege, Michael: 10/18/1794–4/12/1796
   (from A-28-225, C-51-209)
Duncan, John: 10/18–21/1794 (from C-60-181,
   A-26-230)
Wolf, Joseph: 5/26/1818? (from C-43-141)
Ege, Michael, claim of: 2/20/1841 (from C-205-234)

89b.) 220 acres
(Note: This tract appears to overlap no. 83. See tract 83 for more possible names.)
Sidle, Henry: warrant, 2/20/1841 (Cumb. S658)
Sidle, Henry: survey, 5/14/1841 (C-205-234)
Seidel, Henry: patent, 8/5/1844 (H-45-236)
additional names:
Ege, Michael, other land of: 4/12/1796 to 12/2/1788
   (from C-51-209, C-35-294)
Duncan, John: 2/20/1809 (from A-26-230)
Sidle, Henry: 5/13/1841(from D-22-51)

89c.) (overlap of 88.)
109 acres, 156 perches
(Note: This tract appears to overlap no.88. See tract 88 for more possible names.)
Carl, George F.: warrant, 2/20/1841 (Cumb. C540)
Carl, George F.: survey, 5/13/1841 (D-22-51)
Patent not found.
additional names:
Vacant: 10/21/1794 (from A-26-230)
Ege, Michael, other land of: 4/12/1796 (from C-51-209)
Duncan, John: 2/20/1809 (from A-26-230)
Carl, George F.: 2/20/1841 (from C-205-234)

90.) ed. 1/12/1791
329 acres, 137 perches
Ege, Michael: warrant, 1/12/1791 (York E109)

Ege, Michael: survey, 4/12/1796 (C-51-209)
Ege, Michael, Jr.: patent, 6/17/1819 (H-17-51)
additional names:
Vacant barrens: 12/2/1788 (from C-51-209)
Carothers, John: 8/21/1794 (from A-26-229)
Ege, Michael: 5/17/1827 (from D-13-81)

91.) ed. 6/9/1792
35 acres, 86 perches
Ege, Michael: warrant, 7/19/1810 (Cumb. E130)
Ege, Michael: survey, 11/7/1811 (A-8-288)
Patent not found.
additional names:
Vacant: 11/10/1761 (from C-155-281)
Dickey, Robert: 6/9/1792 to 4/23/1811
   (from C-26-170, 161 & 173)
Beetem, William & Co.: 5/10/1860 (from D-21-193)

92.) ed. 3/15/1793
428 acres, 44 perches
Ege, Michael: warrant, 3/15/1793 (Cumb. E104)
Ege, Michael: survey, 10/21/1794 (C-60-180)
Ege, Michael: patent, 8/2/1813 (H-9-435)
additional names:
Ege, Michael: 6/20/1814 to 6/16/1815
   (from C-15-150, C-131-2)

93.) ed. 8/21/1794
10 acres
Donley, Barney: warrant. 5/7/1818 (Cumb. D317)
Donley, Barney: survey, 5/26/1818 (C-43-141)
Donley, Barney: patent, 4/1/1819 (H-16-574)
additional names:
By the foot of South Mountain: 12/27/1785
   (C-233-64 & 65)
Diviny, Hugh, improvement of: 8/21/1794
   (from A-26-229)

94.) ed. 10/18/1794
13 acres, 20 perches

Henry, Margaret (aka. "IndianPeg?"): warrant. 4/24/1816 (Cumb. H466)
Henry, Margaret: survey, 5/22/1816 (C-91-193)
Lutz, John: patent, 10/6/1843 (H-44-451)
additional names:
South Mountain: 4/27/1773 to as late as 4/15/1774 (from C-5-248, C-183-143)
Allen, Robert: 10/18/1794 (from A-28-225)
Bricker, Jacob?: 10/21/1794 (from A-26-229)
Family in residence: "There was a family actually residing on above described land at the time of making survey." 5/22/1816 (from note on survey C-91-193)

95.) ed. 4/12/1796
406 acres, 93 perches
(Note: This tract appears to overlap no.88. See tract 88 for more possible names.)
Bricker, Peter: warrant, 6/7/1814 (Cumb. B598)
Bricker, Peter: survey, 6/20/1814 (C-15-150)
Bricker, Peter: patent, 9/18/1816 (H-13-282)
additional names:
Vacant hills: 10/21/1794 (from C-60-180)
Ege, Michael, other land of: 4/12/1796 (from C-51-209)
Bricker, Peter: 6/16/1815 to 5/13/1841 (from C-131-2, D-22-51)

Ann Maria Bricker: d. September 1, 1832; Age 10 m, 15 d

APPENDIX C

The Old Graveyard at Mount Zion

There are approximately 177 people buried in our Old Graveyard. That information comes from four lists made by Clara and Ralph Frederick Goodyear, Jeremiah Zeamer, John Henry Cocklin, and Lenora Flower. These lists all have names that are not on the other lists. In 2005, the Anniversary Committee, under the direction of Shirley McGill Busch, compiled a master list and created the bronze plaques currently on the monument. Unfortunately, the missing pages of the Goodyear list were not discovered until after the plaques were ordered. That resulted in nine names from the Goodyear list that were not on the other lists being missing on the plaques.

The Zeamer list was done in 1901. Mr. Zeamer visited and recorded all the information on every tombstone in Cumberland County. Some stones could have been missing, and some graves may never have had stones. Lenora Flower described the cemetery as being in deplorable condition, with stones broken. The cemetery is reported to have been leveled, and the stones were buried in 1901.

Our neighbors, Michele and Dick Baublitz, several years ago found a tombstone buried on their property. They have given it to Mt. Zion in honor of our 225th anniversary. It appears to be the grave marker for Ann Maria Bricker, who died on September 1, 1832, at the age of 10 months and 15 days. We will find an appropriate place for Ann Maria's grave marker, possibly in the Old Graveyard, now our Peace Garden. As you read the list of names. You will notice most of those buried in our Old Graveyard are children.

The monument was erected in the early 20th century (1900–1910). The style of the monument and the type of lettering are consistent with that period. So is the Quincy granite, which came from Quincy, MA, and was quarried between 1870 and 1930. Quincy granite was popular at the beginning of the 20th century.

The inscription on the monument in the old graveyard is on the Boiling Springs Road side of the monument. It reads: *In Memory of the Dead Interred Here, 1st Body 1788, Last Body 1870.*

The names on the monument are listed on three bronze panels, beginning with the panel to the right of the inscription. Below are those names with birth and death dates and ages, as indicated in the 2005 book about the graveyard.

First Panel:
Sarah Aleson: d. June 11, 1824; Age 1 y, 6 m, 25 d
George Beltzhoover: b. February 12. 1766, d. April 27, 1846 (drowned in Yellow Breeches)

Mary Beltzhoover: d. March 16, 1857; Age 70 y, 11 m, 14 d
Daniel Beltzhoover: d. April 23, 1847; Age 17 y, 2 m, 12 d
Angeline Beltzhoover: b. November 25, 1837, d. June 20, 1838
Amanda Beltzhoover: b. February 26, 1829, d. March 3, 1829
Rebecca Beltzhoover: d. February 24, 1829; Age 27 y, 9 m, 22 d
Mary Beltzhoover: d. August 14, 1832; Age 29 y, 10 m, 17 d
Regina Beltzhoover: b. November 5, 1788, d. June 12, 1825
Sara Beltzhoover: b. July 9, 1805, d. May 28, 1856
Son of David and Rachel Bender: d. December 7, 1834; Age 15 d
Betty Ann Bender: b. June 22, 1838, d. August 4, 1853
Jacob Bender: b. July 31, 1839, d. August 22, 1839; Age 22 d
Margaretta Bitner: d. August 30, 1838; Age 10 y
Frederick Brechbill: b. September 11, 1774, d. June 1, 1846; Age 72 y
Anna Brechbull: b. March 23, 1776, d. March 23, 1841; Age 67 y
Sarah Breneise: d. October 2, 1823; Age 11 m, 12 d
John Breneise: d. July 24, 1825; Age 10 m, 10 d
Michael Breneizer: d. July 7, 1836; Age 34 y, 1 m, 7 d
Christiana Bentzel: b. June 15, 1798, d. July 22, 1798
George Bentsel: d. October 3, 1804; Age 48 y
Hannah Berlin: d. January 21, 1846; Age 42 y, 11 m, 29 d
Jacob Bricker: b. August 18, 1744, d. October 26, 1813
Margaret Bricker: b. 1739, d. August 26, 1805; Age 66 y, 3 m, 6 d
Jacob Bricker, Jr.: b. November 28, 1772, d. February 6, 1818
Ann Bricker: d. July 8, 1825; Age 4 y, 4 m, 2 d
Ann Maria Bricker: d. September 1, 1832; Age 10 m, 15 d
Clarissa Bricker: d. March 5, 1834; Age 5 y, 1 m, 7 d
Elizabeth Ann Bricker: d. March 26, 1835; Age 3 y, 1 m, 10 d
Elizabeth Bricker: b. June 4, 1806, d. February 4, 1810
David Boughter: d. August 24, 1817; Age 4 y, 7 m, 23 d
John Boughter: d. September 29, 1821; Age 16 y, 9 m, 27 d
Eva Carl: b. December 19, 1794, d. January 18, 1822
Twins of Joseph Carl
Evir Carle: b. December 10, 1783, d. January 18. 1862; Age 79 y
Ellen Cunningham: d. February 1, 1826; Age 54 y
Benjamin Diller: d. June 10, 1851; Age 72 y
Catherine Diller: b. November 26, 1783, d. March 9, 1852
Joseph Diller: b. March 3, 1837, d. July 19, 1837; Age 4 m
Julia Ann Diller Elberti: d. October 18, 1849
Martin Diller: b. October 8, 1760, d. March 1843; Age 83 y
Casper Diller: b. February 28, 1768, d. September 16, 1825; Age 57 y

Christiana Diller: b. April 11, 1772, d. April 27, 1834;m Age 62 y
Jolancia Diller: d. 1830; Age 43 y, 11 m
Sarah Diller: d. July 22, 1837; Age 10 m, 11 d
Ruben Diller: d. 1831; Age 2 y, 1 m, 2 d
Ermina Diller: d. 1823; Age 7 y, 3 m, 23 d
Anna May Diller: d. May 17, 1845
Barbara Diller: b. January 10, 1839, d. May 28, 1845; Age 6 y
John Diller: b. December 18, 1843, d. May 14, 1845 Age 2 y
Ignatius Ernst: b. April 2, 1749 d. November 19, 1835
Sophia Ernst: d. March 24, 1827; Age 85
Jacob Ewing: d. ? 25, 1825; Age 1 m, 25 d
Susan Fenicle: d. April 1, 1833; Age 4 y, 9 m, 5 d
Sarah Gardner: b. May 31, 1834, d. April 20, 1835
Regina Goodyear: b. March 15, 1756, d. January 5, 1839
Ludwick Goodyear: b. October 20, 1757, d. September 16, 1804
Philip Gros: b. July 10, 1817, d. October 17, 1822

Second Panel:
Sylvester Frederick Gruber: b. April 5, 1759, d. September 16, 1816
Susannah Gutshall: d. October 19, 1839; Age 28 y, 5 m, 17 d
Sabina Gutshall: d. October 10, 1837; Age 72 y, 11 m, 19 d
Samuel Gutriah: b. July 30, 1815, d. August 15, 1815; Age 2 w, 3 d
Ann E. Hockley: d. December 19, 1838
Lydia Hopple: d. May 2, 1840; Age 34 y, 6 m, 12 d
George Hopple: b. April 4, 1767, d. November 27, 1838
Esther Hopple: b. December 26, 1768, d. April 1849
Infant Hopple: d. 1830; Age 8 m, 10 d
John Hopple: d. August 8, 1837; Age 28 y, 4 m, 21 d
Elizabeth Hyer: b. June 9, 1783, d. November 1, 1852
Adam Kenower: b. May 7, 1800, d. January 27, 1842
Davis Kenower: d. November 24, 1825; Age 5 y, 2 m, 11, d
Maiya Magthalona Kenower: b. April 24, 1767, d. December 15, 1827
Jacob Kenower: b. September 1762, d. November 20, 1833
Mary Keesaman: d. July 4, 1843; Age 27 y, 7 m, 3 d
Helen Keeseman: b. December 8, 1848, d. December 15, 1850
Sarah Keeseman: b. July 21, 1841, d. September 2, 1842
Katharena Kessler: d. May 8, 1813; Age 64 y, 11m, 14 d
Rev. David Kessler: d. April 4, 1824; Age 77 y. 4 m, 25 d
Unknown Kessler
Jacob Kreisher: b. October 28, 1737, d. December 1, 1815

Barbara Kreisher: d. March 24, 1827; Age 85 y
John Kreysher: d. July 21, 1828; Age 8 y, 6 m, 1 d
Rachel Launa: b. January 9, 1832, d. January 11, 1833; Age 1 y, 1d
Catharine Leidy: d. December 26, 1857; Age 55 y, 1 m
Jacob Leidigh: d. August 13, 1833; Age 43 y, 10 m, 28 d
George Leidich: d. November 22, 1820; Age 25 y, 11m, 2 d
Adam Leidig: b. October 6, 1758, d. July 16, 1828
Magdalena Leidig: b. August 7, 1761, d. February 15, 1816
George Leidig: d. March 26, 1822; Age 36 y, 7 m, 8 d
David Leidig: d. May 7, 1842; Age 48 y, 9 m, 10 d
John Leib: b. January 28, 1782, d. August 13. 1829
Mary Leib: b. August 2, 1787, d. April 13, 1850
Johannes Leidig: d. September 5, 1826; Age 29 y, 4 d
Maria Oallo Werbt Line: b. July 29, 1802, d. March 30, 1818
Catherine Linis: b. June 15, ?, d. December 8, 1823
Anna Westhafer Martin: b. October 9, 1819, d. September 17, 1842
David Messinger: d. February 18, 1839; Age 6 y, 3 m
Johannes Messinger: d. June 15, 1834; Age 40 y, 6 m, 14 d
George Miller: d. July 17, 1825; Age 8 m, 15 d
Sarah Mill: d. July 18, 1825; Age 1 y, 11m, 11d
Adam Miller: d. August 26, 1830; Age 57 y, 9 m, 29 d
Conrad Moret: b. March 10, 1760, d. July 17, 1834; Age 74 y
Catharine Young Morrett: b. August 5, 1791, d. April 28, 1847
Michael Morrett: b. June 23, 1788, d. July 30, 1840
Gertraut Morrett: b, March 10, 1768, d. July 17, 1836
Hartman Morrett: d. November 13, 1822; Age 78 y, 5 m
Ellen Warfield Murphy: Age; 1 y, 2 m, 19 d
Daniel McNeal: d. January 16, 1828; Age 34 y, 4 m
Isabella B. Cunningham McClure: d. January 27, 1843; Age 27 y
Abraham Paul: d. September 20, 1836; Age 46 y, 7 m, 2 d
Eliza Plank: d. June 2, 1833; Age 12 y, 10 m, 2 d

Third Panel:
Barbara Peters: d. May 4, 1847: Age 59 y
Rachel Richwine: d. September 5, 1825; Age 3 y, 1 m, 10 d
Samuel Richwine: d. November 4, 1827; Age 11 m, 19 d
Annah Ritner: b. January 11, 1799, d. January 11, 1837; Age 38 y
Margaret Ritner: Age 13 y, 10 d
(The Ritners listed above are members of Governor Jacob Ritner's extended family, as noted on the Goodyear List.)

Linden Shaeffer: b. May 7, 1830, d. December 26, 1833; Age 3 y
Elvina Shaffer: d. January 7, ? (child)
Margretta Shaffer: d. July 14, 1838 (child)
Elizabeth Schneider: b. September 30, 1800, d. September 6, 1824
Mary Catherine Singiser: b. April 19, 1848, d. May 6, 1848
Elizabeth Schoff: d. February 10, 1843; Age 85 y, 10 m, 10 d
Jacob Schoff: b. April 9, 1765, d. May 6, 1848
Ann Strock: d. February 20, 1817; Age 7 y, 5 m, 17 d
Angelina Strock: d. April 21, 1835; Age 5 y, 4 m, 20 d
Urbanus Strock: d. September 12, 1837; Age 3 y, 2 m, 18 d
Reuben Vanasdal: d. August 14, 1837; Age 1 y, 11 m, 2 d
Rachael Ann Vanasdal: d. May 1, 1833; Age 1 y, 11 m, 2 d
George Vanasdlen: d. May 1, 1833; Age 4 y, 0 m, 18 d
Sarah Beltzhoover Vanasdlen: d. May 28, 1856; Age 51 y, 3 m, 12 d
Peter Vanasdlen: d. July 10, 1856; Age 47 y, 10 m, 20 d
John Welsh: d. October 4, 1837; Age 10 m, 25 d
William Westheffer: d. July 30, 1854; Age 3 m, 6 d
Maria Magdalena Westheffer: b. October 21, 1765, d. March 3, 1854
Ann Weise: d. January 24, 1828; Age 73 y, 8 m, 27 d
Jacob Weise: b. September 21, 1750, d. July 24, 1817
Barbara Ann Wise: b. May 22, 1831, d. June 1, 1831
Clarissa Wise: b. August 21, 1846, d. September 20, 1851
Ann Mary Wise: d. January 24, 1828; Age 73 y, 8 m, 27 d
John Jacob Wise: b. April 18, 1771, d. August 14, 1853
Jacob Wise, Sr.: b. February 9, 1745, d. 1830
Barbara Wonderlich Williams: b. June 13, 1802, d. January 15, 1854
David Williams: d. October 16, 1856; Age 60 y, 5 m, 2 d
Henry Williams: d. July 3, 1848; Age 26 y, 6 m, 17 d
Jacob Williams: b. February 11, 1799, d. March 15, 1830
Lucetta Whitcomb: d. October 18, 1832; Age 1 y, 2 m, 18 d
Han Jacob Wolf: b. December 21, 1766, d. December 23, 1825
Magdalena Wolf: d. December 11, 1838; Age 70 y
David Wolf: d. December 21, 1836; Age 44 y, 6 m, 6 d
Lydia Ann Wolf: d. July 31, 1837; Age 1 y, 1m, 23 d
Adam Wolf: d. March 31, 1835; Age 1 y, 11m, 19 d
Heinrich Wolf: b. April 6, 1781, d. August 5, 1816
Elizabeth Wolf: b. September 19, 1819. d. December 22, 1841
Margaret Wonderly; d. July 1839
John Wonderly: d, September 24, 1854; Age 61 y, 5 m, 23 d
John Wonderly: d. September 26, 1853; Age 84 y, 10 m, 12 d

Elizabeth Wonderly: b. February 1, 1780, d. March 14, 1848
Catherine Wunderlich: b. February 2, 1768; Age 52 y, 7 m
Elizabeth Wunderlich: b. 1805, d. 1806
Maria Gertrude Geyer Young: b. March 3, 1765, d. November 18, 1843
Matthias Young: b. September 2, 1757, d. January 5, 1839
Lidia Yung: d. June 17, 1826; Age 24 y, 10 m, 29
Rudolph Yung: b. April 29, 1763, d. December 4, 1825
Elizabeth Yung: b. July 17, 1789, d. September 30, 1832
Christina Buson Yung: d. February 10, 1830; Age 75 y, 9 m, 10 d
Peter Yung: b. October 16, 1744, d. March 10 1803
Peter Yung: b. July 5, 1806, d. July 14, 1806; Age 1 w, 2 d
Catharine Zeigler: d. September 3, 1856

Those buried here but not listed on the panels:
Joseph Bricker: b. June 16, 1794, d. August 29, 1828
Peter Diller: b. March 7, 1828, d. August 2, 1828; Age 5 m
John Ernist: b. September 18, 1818, d. May 12, 1819; Age 9 m
J. M. Ernist: b. April 12, 1825, d. March 19, 1849
Mary M. Fisher: b. October 6, 1822, d. July 1844: Age 22 y
Jacob Reif: b. March 21, 1750, d. July 24, 1817; Age 67 y
Emma Rife: b. August 5, 1755, d. January 24, 1828; Age 73 y
John Wonderly: b. April 1, 1781, d. September 23, 1831; Age 50 y
Catherine Young: b. September 3, 1756. d. May 17, 1788

www.ingramcontent.com/pod-product-compliance
Lightning Source LLC
Chambersburg PA
CBHW080837230426
43665CB00021B/2865